Concrete Architecture

This book is dedicated to Matilda, for setting an inescapable final deadline, and to Stuart, without whose love and support it would never have been met.

Published in 2004 by Laurence King Publishing Ltd
71 Great Russell Street
London WC1B 3BP
United Kingdom
Tel: + 44 (0)20 7430 8850
Fax: + 44 (0)20 7430 8880
e-mail: enquiries@laurenceking.co.uk
www.laurenceking.co.uk

Text © 2004 Catherine Croft
Design © Laurence King Publishing

All rights reserved. No part of this publication may be reproduced or transmitted in any form or by any means, electronic or mechanical, including photocopy, recording or any infomation storage and retrieval system, without prior permission in writing from the publisher.

A catalogue record for this book is available from the British Library

ISBN 1 85669 364 3

Designed by SEA

Printed in China

Happy Building
love Zoe.

Concrete Architecture

Catherine Croft

Laurence King Publishing

8 Preface

10 Introduction
The Challenge of Concrete

24 Chapter 1
Home

26 **Family Home**
Flasch, Switzerland, 2001
Bearth and Deplazes

30 **De Blas House**
Sevilla la Nueva, Spain, 2000
Estudio Alberto Campo Baeza

36 **Tokiwadai House**
Itabashi-ku, Tokyo, Japan
2000
Naoko Hirakura Architect and Associates

38 **Möbius House**
Het Gooi, Netherlands, 1998
UN Studio

42 **Space Blocks**
Kamishinjo, Osaka, Japan, 2001
Kazuhiro Kojima

46 **Loft**
Sandweiler, Luxemburg, 2000
Georges Servais

50 **C-House**
Brisbane, Australia, 1998
Donovan Hill Architects

54 **Bacon Street House**
London, UK, 2003
William Russell

58 **Visiting Artists' Studio**
Geyserville, California, USA, 2002
Jim Jennings

62 **Tilt-Up Slab House**
Venice, California, USA, 2001
Syndesis, Inc.

66 **House in Berlin**
Berlin, Germany, 2001
OIKOS

70 Chapter 2
Work

72 **Haslach School**
Au, Switzerland, 2000
Beat Consoni

78 **Federal Chancellery**
Berlin, Germany, 2001
Axel Schultes Architekten,
Frank Schultes Witt

82 **Canary Wharf Underground Station**
London, UK, 2000
Foster and Partners

86 **Ehime Prefectural Museum of General Science**
Niihama City, Japan, 1994
Kisho Kurokawa

90 **Diamond Ranch High School**
Diamond Bar, California, USA, 1999
Morphosis

96 **School of Arts, Córdoba University**
Córdoba, Argentina, 2002
Miguel Angel Roca

100 **Zenith Concert Hall and Exhibition Centre**
Rouen, France, 2001
Bernard Tschumi

104 **Kemeter Paint Warehouse**
Eichstätt, Germany, 1994
Hild und K Architekten

112 **The Laban Centre**
London, UK, 2003
Herzog & de Meuron

116 **Mathematics, Statistics and Computer Science Building**
University of Canterbury, Christchurch, New Zealand, 1998
Architectus (with Cook Hitchcock Sargisson and Royal Associates)

120 **LOOK UP Office Headquarters**
Gelsenkirchen, Germany, 1998
Anin Jeromin Fitilidis & Partner

124 **Lecture Hall 3, University of Alicante**
Alicante, Spain, 2001
Javier Garcia-Solera

128 **Haus der Architektur**
Munich, Germany, 2002
Drescher + Kubina

132 **Armani Headquarters and Theatre**
Milan, Italy, 2002
Tadao Ando Architect and Associates

138 Chapter 3
Play

140 **Tussols-Basil Bathing Pavilion**
Olot, Girona, Spain, 1998
RCR Arquitectes

144 **Ruffi Gymnasium**
Marseilles, France, 2001
Rémy Marciano

148 **Fishing Museum**
Karmøy, Norway, 1998
Snøhetta

154 **Museum of Scottish Country Life**
East Kilbride, Scotland, 2001
Page and Park

158 **Innside Hotel**
Düsseldorf, Germany, 2001
Schneider + Schumacher

162 **Oskar Reinhart Collection 'Am Römerholz'**
Winterthur, Switzerland, 1998
Gigon/Guyer

166 **La Coruña Swimming Pool**
La Coruña, Spain, 1999
Estudio Cano Lasso

170 **American Folk Art Museum**
New York, USA, 2001
Todd Williams Billie Tsien & Associates

174 **Pulitzer Foundation for the Arts**
St Louis, Missouri, USA, 2001
Tadao Ando Architect & Associates

178 **Kunstmuseum**
Vaduz, Liechtenstein, 2000
Morger Degelo Kerez

182 Chapter 4
Landscape

184 **Chapel and Residential Buildings**
Valleacerón, Ciudad Real, Spain, 2001
Estudio Sancho-Madridejos

188 **Barcelona Botanic Garden**
Barcelona, Spain, 1999
Carlos Ferrater, Bet Figueras and José Luís Canosa

192 **Sculptural Overlook, Maryhill Museum of Art**
Goldendale, Washington, USA, 1999
Allied Works Architecture

200 **Municipal Mortuary**
León, Spain, 2001
BAAS

206 **La Granja Stairways**
Toledo, Spain, 2000
José Antonio Martínez Lapeña & Elías Torres Tur Arquitectos

210 **Thames Barrier Park**
London, UK, 2000
Patel Taylor/Groupe Signes

214 **Cemetery**
Borghetto Santo Spirito, Italy, 2002
Marco Ciarlo

218 **Tulach a' tSolais**
Oulart Hill, Wexford, Ireland, 1998
Scott Tallon Walker

224 **Cathedral of Our Lady of the Angels**
Los Angeles, California, USA, 2002
Rafael Moneo

228 Notes
230 Project credits
232 Index
238 Picture Credits
239 Acknowledgements

Preface

This book is a celebration of concrete. The material has made it into the glossy magazines, with concrete worktops and even concrete fruit bowls and jewellery featured on the style pages. But is concrete's rehabilitation permanent? I remember going, as a child, to Denys Lasdun's National Theatre (1967–70) in London in the 1970s, and running my fingers lovingly over the rough texture of the board-marked concrete. No wallpaper, no skirting boards, but a high, concrete-coffered ceiling and the same balustrade details for both inside and the wide, outdoor balconies that look across the River Thames. I can't have been the only child for whom such visits marked the start of an increasing obsession with architecture and, less consciously, with concrete. Lasdun once said to his son, 'You know, James, there's something aphrodisiacal about the smell of wet concrete.'[1] The concrete may have been set by the time I arrived, but the magic was still apparent – and is equally potent at Le Corbusier's Notre-Dame-du-Haut at Ronchamp, France, where the great east door is a pivoting wedge of thick concrete, with cockle shells embedded in it, like a slab of smooth seashore.

Many of my most memorable architectural encounters have been with beautiful and resonant concrete structures. However, I was also aware that concrete had a less attractive side – not only in the form of inner-city housing estates and car parks – and, indeed, had many detractors. Reading Ian McEwan's morbidly fascinating novel *The Cement Garden* (1978) (which should have been titled *The Concrete Garden*, as the 'stiff grey sludge' in which the children prepare to encase their mother's body is a mix of sand, cement and water), the idea that the world of 'concrete boots', of concrete as an agent of oblivion that could invade domestic life, entered my imagination. There has always been something sinister about concrete, beyond the straightforward negative associations and prejudice, which recent architects using the material have successfully challenged. This is a great triumph.

The case studies in this book have been chosen to reflect the diversity of ways in which concrete can be used, and to show how different the surface texture of concrete can be – how what goes into the mix, what makes the mould or how the surface is finished can have an enormous impact on the end result. There is cheap concrete and very expensive concrete; white concrete, grey concrete and pigmented concrete; smooth, homogeneous concrete; and richly textured concrete. Construction techniques and available materials vary from country to country: this affects the material's use. As does climate, landscape and culture. There are many projects that could have fitted into more than one of the categories presented, but this need not be problematic. In grouping the projects as they have been, rather than, say, chronologically, geographically or by technique, it becomes clear that concrete is being used today in all sorts of environments – it is no longer seen as intrinsically tough or sterile, butch or institutional. Nor is it any longer perceived as depressing or monotonous. Concrete works well in isolation, or contrasted with steel, glass or wood. It looks good in urban locations or landscape settings, and is successful not just for factories and multi-storey parking garages, but also for public buildings, offices and even homes.

Before examining the historical development of concrete, the following introduction offers a brief technical discussion of the material – its differing types, various manufacturing processes and different uses – which readers who are less familiar with it in the context of construction should find particularly helpful.

What is Concrete?

Concrete is a strong material. It can combine the tensile strength of steel with the compressive strength of stone. It has been used – particularly in its reinforced form – for most types of engineering project, but is especially valued where span constructions are needed. Approximately 70 per cent of all bridges built in Britain since 1945 have been made of concrete.

Its strength, and the use to which it is put, is determined by its constituent parts – cement, water and aggregates. The cement – a chemical mix of calcium, silica, alumina, iron and gypsum – is the basic building material. The proportion of water added to the mix establishes its permeability, its resistance to weather and wear, and how it is used in construction. About three-quarters (by volume) of concrete consists of a combination of fine and coarse aggregates – sand, gravel and crushed rock. As well as making up the 'bulk' of the concrete, it can be, like the other elements, a critical determinant of the concrete's use. As Sarah Gaventa has said[2]:

The versatility of concrete seems to defy all our preconceptions of the material. Simply by changing the type of aggregate used, concrete can be made so light that it can float on water, or made so heavy that it is almost twice its usual density. Concrete can be made totally impermeable to moisture for use in the construction of gigantic dams, or porous enough to be used in the making of filter-beds at sewage treatment plants, where water needs to percolate freely through as part of its whole cleansing and purification process.

Reinforced and Pre-stressed Concrete in the 20th century

The history of concrete's development as a significant building material is, in part, the search for ways of combining concrete with steel to

Preceding pages
National Theatre, London,
Denys Lasdun, 1967–70.

Following page
Assembly Building, Dacca,
Bangladesh, Louis Kahn, 1962–74.

create a material which is both flexible and strong – reinforced concrete. Like stone, unreinforced mass concrete is strong in compression, but weak in tension. This means that if a concrete beam spans between two supports and a load is applied to it (for instance if a concrete lintel over a doorway is carrying the weight of the wall above it), it will most likely fail on the underside, in effect tearing apart. Any beam will deflect under this type of load, that is, it will bend into a curve (if a visually imperceptible one), with the upper surface shortening and the lower one stretching. With a steel beam, stretching is not a problem, as steel is strong in tension, yet it is more likely to fail by snapping or buckling when compressed.

By contrast, concrete can be squashed or compressed without failing. Unreinforced concrete works well (like stone) in load-bearing block structures and arches, but for wide spans and large openings, the sorts of structures that epitomize concrete construction, only reinforced concrete is appropriate. It has steel rods (or sometimes mesh), or occasionally some other material that is strong in tension, cast into it where tension forces will occur. In a straightforward beam, this is near the lower side, but in a more complex structure, where the distribution of loads will be more complicated, designing the amount of steel reinforcement necessary and positioning it is a job for a skilled engineer.

Pre-stressed concrete is a further refinement. This is a form of concrete that has a longer span than reinforced concrete, which allows the building of longer and more elegant designs. Pre-stressing can reduce the size of a beam required to perform a specific task. Before a beam is put into place, a load is applied to the steel reinforcement within it. There are two forms of pre-stressed concrete – pre- and post-tensioned. A pre-tensioned beam is cast around steel, which is already held in tension in the mould. To make a post-tensioned beam, the concrete is cast with a hole running through it. When it is set, a bar, rod or cable can be threaded through the hole, anchored at each end and then tightened. The amounts of steel needed can be minimized by carefully positioning the sheath, so that the steel will sit where the tension will be greatest. A profiled steel section can also reduce the amount of steel required, and hence both its weight and cost – maximum thickness will be needed at the centre and the steel can be thinner towards each end.

In both pre- and post-tensioned pre-stressed concrete, the two ends of the reinforcement are pulled away from each other and held tight, like a taut rubber band. The effect of this is that the beam is, in essence, effectively bent upwards at each end – the upper surface becomes shorter, and this means that the concrete is put into compression. Extra load can then be applied, as the initial loading will only return the beam to its original state, and it will take a greater applied load before the concrete is in danger of being in tension, which is what leads to failure. The disadvantages of pre-tensioned structures are that they are more complex, require greater design and construction precision, and can be problematic if a building is subsequently demolished or altered. Cutting through a pre-tensioned beam is a dangerous proposition; in the same way that a stretched elastic band 'pings' when snipped, a pre-tensioned beam can behave unpredictably and with considerable violence when approached without a thorough knowledge of this type of engineering.

The development of concrete as a building material from the 1920s to the 1970s included new types of concrete, new structural and casting techniques, and new kinds of concrete components – all of which are closely interrelated. Concrete building blocks came into common usage after 1945, and the output of Portland Cement in Britain trebled between 1945 and 1970. The manually-operated concrete mixer was invented by Louis Cézanne in 1857, and the first transit-mixer, mounted on a lorry, was used in the United States in 1926. The pre-stressing and pre-casting of concrete panels – the British Pre-Cast Concrete Federation was formed in 1918 – ensured higher standards only attainable under factory conditions.[3]

Introduction
The Challenge of Concrete

Concrete is now a favoured material, not just of architects but of designers, style magazines, and, increasingly, the general public. A material once associated with urban brutalism and Modernist rigor (and hence seen as challenging to appreciate) is now equally at home in chic restaurants, couture houses, churches and even country houses. What has been responsible for this wholehearted enthusiasm? Certainly concrete is versatile. Architects are able to achieve forms and structures that were previously unthinkable. Concrete can also take on any number of finishes, colours and textures and can be cheaply mass-produced or expensively crafted to individual specifications. Given all of these advantages, it is almost hard to believe that the use of concrete was a source of such debate throughout the last century. Concrete has had more admirers among architects, of course, but even they have been divided over its merits. Some practitioners have made their reputations through buildings that make extensive and very successful use of concrete – but even some of these have been reluctant to be identified as concrete specialists or enthusiasts. For instance, when it was put to Paul Rudolph (architect of the Yale University Arts and Architecture Building (1962–63), and many other seminal concrete projects) that textured concrete surfaces were his 'signature', he responded defensively: 'Every material has its own intrinsic values and uses. And I'm interested in every material, not just one. It's wrong to think that I'm only interested in concrete …. So please don't think of me as just a concrete architect.'[1] It is hard to imagine an architect responding so emphatically to being associated with any other material. There are architects who acknowledge concrete's visual shortcomings, but also praise its flexibility, versatility and good value as a building material. Many still consider it to be a good material, provided it is not visually exposed. Others seem not to like it on principle, preferring more traditional construction materials, for both their constructional and aesthetic properties. To understand concrete's role, it is necessary to explore the image of concrete, and to trace its history – to see how the two interact in the changing environments of the past two centuries.

Concrete has had to contend with a number of obstacles in achieving any degree of popularity with architects, engineers, builders and, above all, the public. On the whole, architects were impressed by the potential value of concrete and the enormous possibilities it seemed to offer from very early on in its development as a mass construction material. As early as the 1850s, concrete was identified as the ideal material – cheap and easily produced – to meet the building needs of Paris. First of all, there have been issues surrounding its safety and reliability as a building material. The second issue was whether or not concrete was a suitable building material for prestigious buildings, or whether, regardless of its advantages, it would always be inferior to traditional materials. This was hotly debated on an almost philosophical level in the late nineteenth century.

The suitability of concrete to be seen, as in exposed, was the third, and most controversial, issue. At the International Congress of Architects, held in London in 1906, Spaniard Joaquin Bassegoda expressed a popularly held view that bare concrete was unacceptable: 'if reinforced concrete must enter into the category of architectonic constructions … it must be clothed in materials, which, by their appearance and richness, make us forget the poverty of that concretion.'[2] Given the fact that 'truth to materials' is an absolutely central tenet of the Arts and Crafts movement, it is perhaps surprising to hear this view also expounded by W R Lethaby: 'it had a poor surface and colour, but its worst disability, and one which until it was got rid of would practically make it impossible for many uses, was its unfortunate habit of cracking.'[3] In 1913, he advised, 'in a highly civilized building it would be well to veneer the surface with thin plates of marble, or gold mosaic, or paint' (for which he claimed Roman precedents).[4]

From these issues sprang others. How suitable was concrete for northern European and American climates? How durable was it? Was it easy to use in an elegant way? Early discussions about concrete spring, however, not just from rational, practical concerns, but also from a realization of the enormous potential it had to challenge the architectural status quo and revolutionize architectural design and practice. A tension between function and image runs throughout the story of concrete, but the bad press that concrete has often received, based on some aesthetic assessment of it, disguises the real issue – that concrete is the material of modern and contemporary challenges to the

Top
Pantheon, Rome, c.126AD.

Centre
William E Ward House, Port Chester, 1873.

Above
Wilkinson Cottage, Newcastle-upon-Tyne, c. 1865.

architectural establishment and has frequently been implicated in wider social, technological and economic changes. It is not just the quintessential material of post-war social architecture, but of new roads, power stations and the structures of war-time defence and Cold War vigilance.

Early History

The word 'concrete' has been in use in English since at least the fifteenth century, but its meaning has evolved, so that it now has several different meanings in different contexts. The underpinning idea is, however, one of the coalescing of particles to form a solid.

The use of mortar mixed with small stones to produce a hard, monolithic mass was described by Roman architect and engineer Vitruvius in his writing, and repeated by Renaissance (and later) writers, including Alberti, Palladio and Philibert de l'Orme. The Romans are often credited with the 'invention' of concrete, and they did indeed use naturally occurring cements to create the material used to build the dome of the Pantheon over eighteen hundred years ago. But this was not concrete in the modern sense of the word. The material was not mixed before laying, and there was no attempt to use calculated proportions of lime or cement, sand and aggregate. And even if some of the principles or possibilities of concrete manufacturing were understood by the Romans – the idea of moulding form with shuttering, for instance – they were not developed until the second half of the eighteenth century.

Why such a gap? Peter Collins – still the most authoritative historian of concrete – says that the cause of this failure to explore the potential of a material that promised to be both so cheap and so versatile was 'partly due to the inadequacy of ordinary lime mortar as a bonding material, but mainly to an ingrained conviction that ashlar was the only respectable material for better class building'[5]. This attitude was beginning to break down in the eighteenth century, owing in part to the cost of building in stone, but also to the fashionable desirability of stucco. Collins locates the start of the revival of interest in concrete as a construction material in late-eighteenth-century France. François Cointeraux, for example, published a number of pamphlets about the potential of concrete and built a 'fireproof house' at Amiens in 1787. Concrete's practical values were beginning to be recognized.

Experimentation continued on both sides of the English Channel in the first half of the nineteenth century. The industrialist François Coignet built a new chemical factory at Saint-Denis, near Paris, entirely out of concrete (1852–3). In the process of doing so, he experimented with aggregates (although, in the end, he followed convention and used light-coloured sand, rather than the cinders or bulkier aggregates he had considered) and also investigated the impact of varying the proportion of water in the mix. He soon understood that the strength of his concrete was related chemically to the precise amount of water added. Excessive amounts of water led to weakness, but too dry a mix was difficult to pour and might not coat the aggregate tightly enough, and thus leave gaps in the mould. In 1853, he built a concrete house at Saint-Denis, opposite his new factory. This was notable for being the first attempt to construct sophisticated façades entirely out of monolithic concrete, with mouldings, string courses, entablatures and a balustrade all in concrete. The material was, however, being made to replicate stone, rather than evolve its own aesthetic. Unfortunately, Coignet's business failed, and, although he can rightly be regarded as the man who first introduced mass concrete construction to the modern world, no one followed up his work in France, so the initiative for the next developments in the concrete story passed to England and the USA. In 1836, the first Gold Medal ever awarded by the Royal Institute of British Architects was given to George Godwin for an essay entitled 'The Nature and Properties of Concrete and its Applications to Construction Up to the Present Period'. Godwin believed 'concrete' to be a modern word – or at least to have acquired its modern meaning only 15 or 20 years earlier – even though it is clear that Godwin's definition of the material was one in which it was not essential to mix the constituents together before laying it. By the 1850s, concrete was accepted as a term to describe the material we know today – cement, aggregate and water, thoroughly mixed together before being poured into position – albeit one which was used, generally, only for foundations.

The widespread exploitation of concrete as a practical building material was closely tied to the development of cement. It was considered vital to have a mortar that would give a predictable and reliable set every time. The first commercial use of the name Portland Cement was by Joseph Aspdin, who started to manufacture Aspdin's Portland Cement in Gateshead and Wakefield, in the north of England, in 1824. The significant thing about this product was that it was an artificial cement, a compound of separate materials, rather than a naturally occurring deposit that just happened to have the right properties, but which might often be in short supply, or easily contaminated. In 1845, I C Johnson (at his works in Swanscombe, Kent) used higher temperatures and finer grinding, and it is his product that is generally recognized as the first true Portland Cement. With good concrete now possible, the next challenge was to strengthen it by combining concrete with iron. Without reinforcement, concrete is strong in compression but weak in tension, and can only be laid in a similar way to stone. With reinforcement, longer spans and more innovative structures would become possible.

The acknowledged pioneer of reinforced concrete was the Englishman William Boutland Wilkinson. His 1854 patent for reinforced concrete beams was based on an awareness of the technical problems involved in constructing large, open-plan spaces for factories. Wilkinson's fireproof floor beams were reinforced with lengths of old, wire colliery ropes, flayed out at the ends, in order to bond thoroughly with the concrete, and carefully positioned within the beam to provide maximum strength. Wilkinson's concrete was very coarse. The only evidence of its use was on a small scale – a cottage he built in Newcastle-upon-Tyne, probably in 1865. This cottage, the earliest reinforced-concrete house in the world, was pulled down in 1954, leaving the distinction of oldest surviving reinforced-concrete house to that built by William E Ward at Port Chester, New York (1873).

It was not until the 1880s, however, that sufficiently strong and reliable cements were commercially available and reinforced concrete construction became generally practical. Between 1880 and 1900, a number of able and enthusiastic research engineers and architects, mostly in Germany and France, succeeded in establishing the characteristics of reinforced concrete and in working out calculations for structures using this material, albeit mainly industrial or agricultural ones. One of the most important of these figures was François Hennebique, who discovered the nature of shearing stress in concrete, in 1880, and how to counteract it by introducing vertical J-shaped bars, called stirrups, into the ends of the beam to bond the upper and lower layers together. But his true significance in the development of a concrete-architectural industry was that, once he had secured his patents in Belgium and France in 1892, he established himself as a consultant engineer and affiliated to his organization a number of established building contractors whom he could trust. Between them, they could guarantee clients a consistently high quality in design and construction. Throughout the 1890s and into the new century, Hennebique produced a number of outstanding buildings, wrote books and articles, and generally publicized the virtues of concrete as a building material. Although his patents did not expire until 1907, Hennebique's own efforts had ensured that his methods became public property long before then. Concrete had arrived as a reputable building material.[6]

By 1900, the scene was set for the widespread use of concrete. How far the material had been accepted by the general public is difficult to tell, but many engineers and architects were keen to experiment. Concrete was an exciting new material for the new century. Few had any reason to question its aesthetic value, and its future seemed bright.

Putting Concrete to Use: 1900–1940
Concrete was seen as the quintessential twentieth-century building material. Many of the world's most innovative architects chose to design in reinforced concrete because it allowed them an exceptional degree of freedom

Top
Royal Liver Building, Liverpool,
Thomas and Mouchel, 1909.

Above
Tavanasa Bridge, Grisons, Robert
Maillart, 1905.

Top
Airship hangars, Orly Airport, Eugène Freyssinet, 1916–24.

Centre
Notre-Dame, Le Raincy, Auguste Perret, 1922.

Bottom
Underside of spiral ramp at Fiat Factory, Turin, Giacomo Matté Trocco, 1915.

to solve design problems in satisfying and uncompromising ways. Others followed suit, and concrete became at times almost ubiquitous, both for structural elements and for the visible surface of buildings.

There was a strong feeling at the beginning of the 1900s that concrete might only really be suitable for industrial buildings or engineering works, such as bridges and roads. It did achieve some popularity in those parts of the British Empire where stone was scarce and the labour force generally unskilled in the manufacture of the material. Leonard Stokes built the Georgetown Roman Catholic Cathedral in concrete in 1914, and new concrete government offices were built in Kingston, Jamaica, following an earthquake in 1907. Generally, however, the view was that concrete was best used, but not seen. At the start of the twentieth century, most concrete buildings tended to hide their use of the material. Yet the concrete-frame structure was, in fact, far more popular than might now be imagined; many buildings that appear to be traditionally constructed are hiding a concrete frame beneath an outer cladding. In Britain, these include Stoke Town Hall (1910), designed by Wallis and Bowden and built by the American firm Julius Kahn, which had started in Detroit in 1903, opening an office in London in 1906, and would go on to build in the USSR; and the iconic Royal Liver Building on the banks of the River Mersey in Liverpool (see page 13, top), by Aubrey Thomas and L G Mouchel, which had the highest concrete frame in Europe (8 storeys plus two attics) when it was completed in 1909, but which was covered entirely with flamboyant Renaissance detail, carved in Scottish and Norwegian granite. In London, right opposite Westminster Abbey, the Kahn organization also built the Wesleyan Hall, by Lancaster and Rickards, but that too was plastered internally and clad outside in traditional materials.

Was the situation any different in the USA? One might think so, for, in 1909, a town called Concrete was established in Washington State. Early settlers arrived at the Baker river in 1871, calling the original settlement on the west bank Minnehaha. In 1890, a post office was established and the settlement was renamed Baker. On the east bank of the river, the community that sprang up around the Washington Portland Cement Company plant (constructed in 1905) was called Cement City. After the Superior Portland Cement Company plant was built in Baker (1908), it was decided to merge the two towns, and, in 1909, after much discussion, the newly expanded community settled on the name of Concrete. Prior to 1921, several fires destroyed most of the original wooden buildings that had lined Main Street. Thereafter, since concrete was in ample supply, it was decided that subsequent buildings would be made from this nonflammable material. The town has a number of interesting early concrete structures. The Henry Thompson Bridge (1916–18) was the longest single-span cement bridge when built, and the Lower Baker Dam (1925–27) was the largest hydroelectric dam in the world at the time of its construction. Early concrete public buildings included the Town Hall and Library (1908), the Old Concrete School Buildings (1910, 1923 and 1938) and the Concrete Theater (1923).

It used to be the case in the town of Concrete that prospective builders could only buy a lot on condition that they built a concrete house on it. Concrete was seen as having great scope for small-scale construction, even self-build projects. Yet on a larger scale, it was generally less favoured than in Britain. Why was this? In part, it is an accident of history. Until comparatively recently, Portland Cement was an expensive import to the USA, while steel was produced domestically – so the skyscraper phenomenon was mainly a steel-frame boom.

Engineering Developments

Before the full potential of reinforced concrete as a building material could be realized, much practical development work needed to be done. Robert Maillart (1872–1940), a Swiss engineer and architect who had worked for François Hennibique, was one of the most important of the material's pioneers. In 1901, he built his first three-hinged, reinforced-concrete bridge, and went on to build a series of graceful and structurally efficient bridges in dramatic mountain locations – for example, the Tavanasa

Bridge of 1905 crossing the Rhine in Grisons, Switzerland (see page 13, bottom) – which helped to lend them a certain impact when photographs of the projects were included in influential publications. He also introduced mushroom-slab construction (up to this point, slabs had been treated as sets of beams lying side by side – the big step forward was to consider reinforcing the concrete in a crosswise manner, so that multi-directional stress forces could be taken), the first example being a warehouse in Zurich in 1910.

With the advent of mushroom-slab construction, reinforced concrete was able to solve the problem of large-span roofs. Early examples of this include Max Berg's Centenary Hall in Breslau (1912–13) and Eugène Freyssinet's two airship hangars at Orly Airport (1916–24). These are barrel vaults, constructed of a thin skin of concrete that has been pleated to give the necessary rigidity. The most outstanding early architect in reinforced concrete, however, was Auguste Perret, whose highly rational and generally trabeated buildings articulate the structural role of each separate part, so that beams and columns are clearly expressed and are shaped to reflect the loads they carry and to counter optical distortions. He designed a garage for Renault (1905), the Théâtre des Champs-Elysées in Paris (1911), industrial and technical buildings (such as the Esders Clothing Factory, Paris (1919)), and public buildings, including the Musée des Travaux Publics (1938). He also built a number of concrete churches, including the early Notre-Dame at Le Raincy (1922)[7] where costs were kept to a minimum by the use of pierced, precast concrete panels and an exposed-concrete barrel roof. Perret was still building churches in concrete 30 years later, and his atelier became the alternative training ground offering more traditional options for many leading modernists. The most famous of his pupils was Le Corbusier, who said of his teacher: 'I wonder today if anyone realizes what a heroic part Perret played in those years…. Perret had the temerity to build in exposed reinforced concrete, and he insisted that his new structural method was destined to revolutionize our architecture.'[8]

Concrete and New Thinking in Architecture

What was particularly important about Auguste Perret, some of his contemporaries and certainly his pupils was that they were excited by the possibilities of the 'new material' and linked it with thinking about new styles of architecture – concrete was not just to be a substitute for stone. After the First World War, concrete became associated with radical and innovative developments in architecture. A prime example of this is engineer Giacomo Matté-Trucco's factory for Fiat in Lingotto, Turin (1915), a giant, reinforced-concrete structure, where fully assembled cars rolled off the production line onto the factory roof, which had been designed as a test track. Once tested, the vehicles were sent down to the ground via a spiral ramp. Even the Arts and Crafts architects, who one might have expected to continue championing traditional construction, began showing an interest. In 1919, C F A Voysey acknowledged, with reference to the opportunities concrete offered, that 'precedent and ancient fashions will not help, and new modes must be evolved for new materials'. James Salmon (of Salmon, Son & Gillespie of Glasgow) had been the architect of Lawyers Chambers on the corner of Hope Street and Bath Lane. (L G Mouchel was the engineer.) This had an exposed concrete frame, flush with cement-coated infill panels. In a lecture to the Glasgow Institute of Architects in 1908, he told his audience that 'the Scottish style, I mean especially that of the old rough-cast castle, is eminently adaptable to a development suited to reinforced concrete construction…the freedom to do anything you like…this new material, reinforced concrete, could induce us to drop all the ridiculous accretion of absurdities which we plaster onto stone.'[9]

Other experimental buildings are much more part of the established canon of Modernism. For instance, Antoni Gaudí used concrete for two houses in Barcelona between 1905 and 1910. Eric Mendelsohn built the Schocken Department Store in Stuttgart, Germany (1926), with a concrete frame, and would have liked the curved forms of the Einstein Tower in Potsdam to have been realized in concrete, but it proved too expensive and too much of an unknown quantity

Right
Stockholm Library, Erik Gunnar Asplund (1918–27).

Below
Ingalls Building, Cincinnati, Elzner & Anderson, 1902–03.

15 The Challenge of Concrete

Left
Lovell Beach House, Newport Beach, Rudolf Schindler, 1922–6.

Centre
Unity Temple, Oak Park, Frank Lloyd Wright, 1906.

Bottom
Fallingwater, Bear Run, Frank Lloyd Wright, 1934.

for the contractor and client to be convinced. In Austria, Otto Wagner built the Post Office Savings Bank in Vienna (1904–12) using concrete. In the 1920s, landmark buildings in concrete were to be found all across mainland Europe. In Scandinavia, Erik Gunnar Asplund built the Stockholm Library (1918–27; see page 15, top), and Alvar Aalto, most often associated with wood and glass, developed concrete-frame industrial buildings, such as the stepped housing at Kauttua.[10]

Across the Atlantic, there was a similar flowering of new and innovative concrete buildings, by both modernists and others. From 1902 to 1903, the first concrete skyscraper – the Ingalls Building in Cincinnati, Ohio (see page 16, bottom) – was erected by Elzner & Anderson.[11] Another early exponent of concrete was Albert Kahn, responsible for the Burroughs Company building in Plymouth, Michigan (1904). Also of note are some highly personal and eccentric creations, including Henry Mercer's house/museum and tileworks in Doylestown, Pennsylvania (1914), and Julia Morgan's flamboyant stage set for European architectural salvage and historical fantasy – the San Simeon villa estate for William Randolph Hearst, begun in 1922. Rudolf Schindler's pioneering Lovell Beach House at Newport Beach, California, (1922–6) uses five parallel concrete frames, which allow the beach to extend underneath it as an exterior room. Frank Lloyd Wright made a very disparaging assessment of concrete in 1928, saying, 'aesthetically it has neither song nor story. Nor is it easy to see in this conglomerate a high aesthetic property, because it is an amalgam…cement, the binding medium, is characterless in itself. The net result is, usually, an artificial stone at best, or a petrified sand heap at worst.'[12] This statement came after his pioneering use of concrete at the Unity Temple, Oak Park, Illinois (1906). It also post-dates his textile block houses in and around Los Angeles, such as the Ennis House (1923), which was constructed with specially cast, decorative concrete blocks, reinforced with steel rods. It is interesting to note that he went on to comment that although 'it will faithfully hang as a slab, stand delicately perforated like a Persian faience screen', it has 'the misfortune to project as beams' and 'unluckily it will stand up and take the form (and texture too) of wooden posts and planks. It is supine, and it sets as the fool, whose matrix it receives, wills.'[13] He maintained that he preferred terracotta, although he admitted that concrete's plasticity had great potential. Describing the material as an 'insensate brute', he suggested that 'concrete would be better named "conglomerate" as concrete is a noble word which this mixture fails to live up to.'[14] Wright is not the only famous twentieth-century architect to make a reputation largely based on his exploitation of the material, but to deny its virtues. Fallingwater (1934), perhaps his greatest house, is dependent on concrete for its dramatic cantilevers that hang out over the cascades of Bear Run, Pennsylvania.

All of the issues raised in Europe in the early years of reinforced concrete being used as a building material reappeared in the USA in the 1920s and 1930s, when its architectural and aesthetic virtues were hotly debated by practitioners. In early 1920s California, Rudolf Schindler designed for client W L Lloyd – a San Diego dentist – Pueblo Ribera, an apartment complex with a traditional southwestern flavour. Schindler was adamant that the walls should be of concrete, not wood-frame, but lenders would not advance money to the development project because they felt concrete would be more expensive and that 'the low esteem in which concrete was held (good for basements and utilitarian structures, but not the walls of houses) would make the units difficult to rent.'[15] Furthermore, there was no proof it would be structurally sound. Sadly, the concrete cracked and water leaked into the apartments, in part because salt from the sand, which had not been properly rinsed, contaminated the mix.

While concrete began to be used for all styles of building, and was especially well suited to Art Deco, it became associated primarily with the development of the International Style. Although Le Corbusier's *Towards a New Architecture* included American concrete grain silos as sources for global inspiration[16], because of their fitness for purpose and sculptural boldness, others were making more fancifully symbolic claims for concrete's universal appropriateness. 'The Ferro-Concrete building with its millions of pebbles and sand specks moulded into a monolith is a symbol of united humanity,' wrote Francis S Onderdonk in his 1928 publication *The Ferro-Concrete Style*. It is interesting to note, however, that he was perceptive enough to realize that some variations in technique and application would be necessary, and predicted that 'climatic difference and historic backgrounds will prevent monotony'.[17]

The impact of the flight of refugee architects westwards from Fascist Europe on the stylistic development of Modernism has been studied extensively. Equally important, however, and inextricably linked, was the spread of knowledge about the technical possibilities of concrete, and a desire to push these further. The architectural critic Alan Colquhoun writes that 'the modern architecture of the 1920s was born under the sign of reinforced concrete'[18], citing Le Corbusier's Maison Dom-ino of 1914 (a prefabricated system of concrete wall plates and columns) as a significant precursor. Berthold Lubetkin, for example, had studied reinforced concrete in Berlin, and, like Le Corbusier, had attended Perret's enormously influential atelier in Paris. While working on his first project at London Zoo – the Gorilla House – he was introduced to Ove Arup, the chief London-based designer of engineering contractors Christiani & Nielson. (Arup went on to set himself up as a consulting engineer in 1946, and to have a key role in the development of concrete construction in the UK and worldwide – notably realizing fellow Dane Jørn Utzon's iconic concrete shells at Sydney Opera House. The competition was won on the basis of a sketch scheme, which, at the time, Utzon had no idea how to construct.) Lubetkin followed the Gorilla House with the even more innovative Penguin Pool (1936), a structure comprising two interlocking spiral ramps and a trapezoidal section, which captured the public imagination.

It is easy to generalize about the homogeneity of interwar concrete construction. Crisp black-and-white photography suggests a consistent vocabulary of smooth, flat planes, perfectly sharp corners and white surfaces, with no joints anywhere – the essence of the machine age. Concrete becomes a hard, impervious skin, wrapping a form that may also have been achieved using the structural possibilities of a concrete structural frame. In fact, many buildings were painted, many used render over brick or block-work, rather than concrete, as contractors remained conservative, and many mixed concrete with other materials and textures, while using colour to emphasize or regress certain parts of their composition. For example Greenside, in Surrey, England, by Connell, Ward & Lucas (1936), was painted brown, cream and green.[19] The imaginative use of paints and renders in conjunction with concrete was both part of the material's appeal to those architects who liked it and part of its saving grace for those who were not so keen.

Some of the problems with concrete's image in the 1920s and 1930s might be ascribed to poor construction techniques and a general ignorance about how best to use it. John Faber, grandson of Oscar Faber, whose *Reinforced Concrete Simply Explained* was a pioneering work in 1922, states that, at this time, concrete was 'shrouded in some mystery', as there had been 'no helpful literature' on it.[20] Others also felt that the architectural use of concrete was still at an experimental stage. Ludwig Mies van der Rohe wrote in 1923 on the subject of concrete:

…there have been repeated attempts to introduce ferro-concrete as a building material for apartment building construction. Mostly, however, ineptly. The advantages of this material have not been exploited, nor its disadvantages avoided. One believes one has acknowledged the material sufficiently if one rounds off the corners of he house and of the individual rooms. The round corners are totally irrelevant for concrete and not even all that easy to execute. It will not do to translate a brick house into ferro-concrete. I see the main advantage of ferro-concrete in the possibility of considerable savings in material…the disadvantage of ferro-concrete, as I see it, lies in its low insulating properties and its poor sound absorption.

Top
Penguin Pool, London Zoo, Berthold Lubetkin, 1936.

Centre
High-rise public housing estate, Sheffield, England, 1960s.

Bottom
Unité d'Habitation, Marseilles, Le Corbusier, 1947–52.

Top
Yale Art Gallery, New Haven,
Louis Kahn, 1953.

Above
Salk Institute, La Jolla, Louis Kahn,
1959–66.

Mies also observed that it 'demands most precise planning before its execution'.[21]

Some architects have linked concrete's poor image to the fact that buildings using the material did not generally follow traditional forms, which created doubts about its suitability, although younger practitioners might be more excited than deterred by this. By 1927, Bennett and Yerbury could conclude that concrete has a 'strange appeal which leaves the spectator divided between admiration of its skill and originality and anger for its disdainful abandonment of all recognized forms. It lacks repose, yet it is an extraordinary fascinating structure.'[22] We can see here a challenge to the assumption that concrete was aesthetically unappealing. Some architects were prepared to concede that concrete buildings could be both innovative in function and visually exciting, but this view was only slowly adopted. In 1926, an editorial in the Architectural Journal said bluntly, 'perhaps it will presently be realized that as far as street architecture is concerted the concrete age should be a stucco age', and 'because a material can do certain things this is not an adequate reason why it should do them.'[23]

While the debate about the aesthetic properties of exposed concrete continued, suggestions came forward as to ways in which it could be masked, because of its reputation of weathering poorly. Many had felt from the beginning that exposed concrete would only be a material suitable for industrial and similar buildings, and had assumed that if it were used for domestic or more prestigious buildings, then it would have to be clad in a more pleasing and durable material. Yet the issue later became one of whether this was practically necessary or visually desirable. The debate moved from 'Can exposed concrete buildings be tolerated in the landscape?' to 'Are they positively adding visual value?' In 1932, the Architectural Review reported that 'the public has been encouraged to have a holy horror of concrete unless its shameful identity is cloaked by a veneer' of traditional materials[24], and a 1946 guide to the use of concrete was very negative about its possibilities, stating that 'the natural grey of Portland cement is cold and depressing', as well as unpleasantly 'patchy'. It also expressed popular concerns about the suitability of concrete for northern climates and doubts about its ability to age gracefully: 'time and weather, which give mellowness to brick and stone, make untreated concrete more and more dirty, dark and untidy, and rapidly lower its initially low power of reflecting light.'[25]

By 1939, exposed concrete appeared to be losing the battle to win over the hearts of the architectural profession. Le Corbusier and the émigré architects had had some impact, but their buildings were mostly one-offs, and concrete had not yet become a material for mass housing. The Second World War did little to convince the general public. Concrete was widely employed for beach defences, tank traps, pill boxes, airfield runways and hangars, and air-raid shelters. Yet, after the war, the need – real and perceived – to reconstruct rapidly and to renew cities all across Europe created a new opportunity for concrete to prove its worth as a mass-building material for a new era.

Concrete and the Post-War World

The accepted story about post-war concrete's popularity is that there was a huge need for rapid reconstruction, a shortage of steel and insufficient skilled labour. These conditions opened the way for concrete to become more widely used and accepted. At the same time, there was an enthusiasm for 'modernization' and a desire to make a visual and social break with the past – again something that favoured concrete construction. While many post-war architects, in many parts of the world, carried on using concrete in innovative and imaginative ways, in the development of system-built public housing pragmatism and profit gained the upper hand, to the detriment of the material.[26] In the 1940s, the only significant British experiment with prefabricated concrete for housing was for two-storey apartment blocks in Glasgow. Most prefabricated systems at this stage (for housing, as well as for innovative schools projects) used metal, asbestos and timber. The majority of multi-storey housing in the immediate post-war period was architect-designed, but technological and cost imperatives were to change this. In the late

1940s, the development of the 10- to 15-storey Grindelberg apartments in Berlin switched from steel to concrete construction, saving 20 per cent of overall costs. Prestressed beams were used increasingly for floor construction, cutting the complexity and time of on-site building, while wall heights and room dimensions became more and more standardized, meaning that standardized shuttering could be used. Box-frame and cross-wall construction also became widespread, allowing standard layouts and simple stacking to be introduced.

The famous Alton Estate (1952–60) in Roehampton, London, is useful in charting the next stage of concrete's history. Built by two different teams of architects working for the London County Council, the first phase is Swedish-inspired and has a concrete frame, clad in diverse materials, including white brick and tile. The later phase uses storey-high concrete cladding (something that could not be achieved until tower cranes were available to lift such elements into place). While the group of architects responsible for the latter part of the project – Howell, Killick, Partridge and Amis – went into private practice and became specialists in highly geometric, deeply articulated, precast concrete façades for clients with generous budgets (for instance, the Wolfson and Rayne Buildings at St Anne's College, Oxford), the use of precast concrete cladding of a less refined nature was to dominate public housing.

The first major prefab 'systems' were introduced to the UK in the early 1960s. There was the French Camus system and the Danish Larsen Nielsen version. Other systems were to follow, including one by a company called Concrete Ltd, and before long it was these versions that dominated the market in public housing. By the mid-1960s, there were over 200 of these prefab systems in Britain alone (for example, see image of Sheffield housing estate on page 17, centre). Rumours of corruption between local politicians and contractors were numerous, and, undoubtedly, huge amounts of money were spent with minimal scrutiny. It is interesting to note that when an exceptionally strong-minded public-sector architect, Ted Hollamby, of the London Borough of Lambeth, got involved in a project, the resulting blocks were far more craggy, vigorously profiled and exciting – but the contractor, Wates, lost money on it. On the whole, these system-built blocks were poorly detailed, suffered from condensation and heat-loss problems, were inadequately landscaped and serviced, and did concrete a great disservice. Meanwhile, the attitude to in situ concrete was about to be transformed.

Le Corbusier and the Unité Experience
Whereas in the pre-war period, the ideal had been to create perfectly smooth and unblemished concrete surfaces, Le Corbusier's construction of the Unité d'Habitation (1947–52; see page 17, bottom) in Marseilles was to radically transform concrete's aesthetic standards, as well as impact on urban planning and wider design issues. He wrote polemically about what he had seen and learnt:

The realization of the Unité at Marseilles has shown the splendor which is possible by the use of reinforced concrete as a natural material…worthy of being exposed in its natural state…. [It] was constructed during five difficult years and was constantly upset by a variety of circumstances; coordination was lacking and indifferent workmen, even within the trade, were maladjusted to one another. For instance the concreters and the carpenters, who made the shuttering, did the work under the impression that their defects (as usual) would be made good with the trowel, plastered or painted over when the shuttering was struck. The defects shout at one from all parts of the structure!…but these are magnificent to look at, they are interesting to observe, to those who have a little imagination they add certain richness…. Faults are human; they are ourselves, our daily lives. What matters is to go further, to live, to be intense, to aim high, and to be loyal.[27]

Le Corbusier called his concrete 'beton brut' and the critic Reyner Banham pointed out that the Unité was 'designed to recognize that concrete starts life as a messy soup of suspended dusts, grits and slumpy aggregate, mixed and poured under conditions subject to the vagaries of

Top
Watergate Complex, Washington DC, Luigi Moretti, 1960–1963.

Above
St Mary's Cathedral, Tokyo, Kenzo Tange, 1963.

Left
Sydney Opera House, Jørn Utzon, 1957–73.

Centre
Concrete beams, Sydney Opera House concourse.

Bottom
Concrete end-fixing for shell plinth, Sydney Opera House.

weather, and human fallibility, and left to harden in formwork whose carpentry rarely (in France) attained the level of precision required in the construction of a garden fence.' Banham also noted that 'Le Corbusier conjured concrete almost as a new material, exploiting its crudities and those of the wooden formwork to produce an architectural surface of a rugged grandeur.' Like a well-weathered Greek temple, 'the concrete work at Marseilles started as a magnificent ruin even before the building was completed.' Banham concluded that 'the crucial innovation of the Unité was not its heroic scale. Nor its originalities in sectional organization, nor its sociological pretensions – it was, more than anything else, the fact that Corbusier had abandoned the pre-war fiction that reinforced concrete was a precise "machine-age" material.'[28] The work of Le Corbusier – particularly the Unité – had an enormous philosophical and symbolic influence on architecture in the second half of the twentieth century, and established concrete as the dominant material for decades to come.

Concrete and New Brutalism

Although there is now a common assumption that Brutalist architecture is concrete architecture, and 'Brutalist' is frequently used pejoratively to dismiss large-scale 1960s concrete buildings as inhuman, when the term was initially coined it referred to a new tendency in architecture to use any material in a directly expressed way – the examples included Peter and Alison Smithson's steel-framed Hunstanton School, Norfolk, England, as well as Le Corbusier's Unité d'Habitation. Reyner Banham's influential book *The New Brutalism* (published in 1966 and subtitled *Ethic or Aesthetic?*) was developed from a brief article of the same title in the *Architectural Design* of January 1955. This single-page manifesto was introduced by Theo Crosby and supplemented with an edited statement by the Smithsons. Both emphasized the importance of Japanese traditions, praising 'a sort of reverence for the natural world and from that, for the materials of the built world'.[29] This, then, is the context in which the post-war emphasis on the rough surface of concrete, on the enjoyment of using different forms of shuttering to create different textures and patterns, evolved, and to which many contemporary architects using concrete acknowledge a direct debt. Louis Kahn, speaking in 1955 about the Yale Art Gallery (see page 18, top), articulated the increasingly popular argument that concrete did have aesthetic qualities, in spite of the way it is created:

…the formwork was made from floor to floor, and this line was accented in the design; because what we tried to do in the expression of the building was to show in every way how it was built. This formwork was made of small floorboards, and the little holes that you see there indicated the tie thoughts in the formwork. These were left as holes in the concrete so that in every way, how it was made is apparent. We accentuated the struggle of building…. When you take the forms off, something always happens in an ugly soupy way…if you actually know that [and you put in a joint] so you can really see it, then it sets up its own pattern. And I believe that these joints are the beginning of ornament.[30]

Kahn later put this argument into practice at the Salk Institute (1959–66; see page 18, bottom), La Jolla, California, in which he specified that the walls be set using teak shutters, and that the joints be left visible, both as a record of the casting process, and as a form of ornament. At the National Assembly Building in Dacca, Bangladesh (1962–74; see page 10), Kahn further elevated the status of the material by marking the joints between the concrete pours with thin strips of marble.

Organic Form

Concrete attracted some of the best and most innovative international architects of the post-war period. In Brazil, Oscar Niemeyer was appointed Chief Architect for the new capital, Brasilia, and during the 1950s and 1960s pushed back technical boundaries in concrete construction to create sculptural forms on a large scale. Le Corbusier had visited Niemeyer in Brazil in 1929 and 1936, and told him 'you know how to give full freedom to the discoveries of modern architecture.'[31] It was the lack of steel production in Brazil that led to the development of concrete architecture there.[32] In the USA, the Italian architect Luigi Moretti used concrete to achieve the curvilinear forms of the Watergate Complex in Washington, DC (1960–63; see page 19, top). While the flowing lines echo the adjacent Potomac, Moretti also sought to create a city within a city, linked by a unified terraced landscape with saucer-like concrete fountains.

Concrete became a major building material in Japan after the war, where leading exponent Kenzo Tange built the Hiroshima Peace Center (1949–56), followed by the Nichinan Cultural Center and St Mary's Cathedral, Tokyo (see page 19, bottom), both completed in 1963. In Australia, Jørn Utzon started work on the Sydney Opera House in 1957, which was completed in 1973. Concrete was instrumental in meeting the exacting standards needed to achieve the perfectly spherical shells. The concrete end-fixings for the post-tensioning cables of the shell plinths are a sculptural work of art in their own right.

Concrete Adapts

Concrete buildings were, in the 1960s, still rarely praised for their aesthetic properties, although, from time to time, concrete was seen as an appropriate material for a building, which was at least, in part, contextual. A new branch of Lloyds Bank, in the historic and predominantly half-timbered market town of Shrewsbury, England, designed by Cardiff-based modernists Sir Percy Thomas and Partners, won a Civic Trust Award in 1968. Described by the award's assessors as 'uncompromisingly of today', it still strikingly terminates a major High Street vista, where it replaced a Victorian neo-Tudor building. One assessor has noted that despite being 'the essence of modern architecture', it nevertheless manages 'a skilful bridging of the centuries',[33] for it reinterprets traditional Tudor elements – pitched roof, cantilevered, jettied floors, an oriel window and black-and-white materials – with black aluminium window frames and white precast concrete panels on an in situ concrete frame.

Indeed, in the mid-1960s, there emerged a real focus on the effects of weathering on concrete. *Concrete Quarterly* pointed to Tempest Anderson Hall in York, England, a 1912 classical-structural, concrete lecture hall. It noted that, 'It has weathered – all those who worry about concrete growing old gracefully, please note – with distinction and even vitality.'[34] A symposium entitled 'The Weathering of Concrete' was held at the Royal Institute of British Architects in London on 7 January, 1971. Here, it was suggested that 'the real test of weathering must be whether it adds to or detracts from the original design, and if it detracts (as it usually must to some extent) whether it detracts disastrously or whether it can be termed a mellowing.' Its colour was a disadvantage. 'The small scale pattern of brickwork joints and the darker colours cover up streaking and staining much better', and the 'design of concrete demands more than aiming at a good, lasting surface finish. It demands that the material be moulded in such a way that the innate aesthetic qualities of concrete are retained. If the detailing [for weathering purposes] does not serve this purpose or becomes obtrusive then the whole point has been lost.'[35]

The reputation of concrete had already suffered as a result of the effects of weathering and time on some well-known International Style buildings of the 1920s and 1930s. For example Le Corbusier's workers' housing at Pessac, France, now shows much surface erosion and staining because the owners were unable (and possibly not inclined) to maintain the building's original pristine conditions.

However, many recent architects have turned the effects of weathering to their advantage. At the Oskar Reinhart Collection extension (see page 162) in Winterthur, Switzerland, Gigon/Guyer designed the concrete exterior with future weathering in mind. Rainwater from the copper roof has left a streaky, green patina on the walls, a sympathetic nod to the copper roof of the early twentieth-century adjacent villa.

Concrete's Contemporary Image

Gigon/Guyer's approach exemplifies architects' current attitude to concrete. Architectural assessments – even lay ones – focus more and more on form and fitness for purpose rather

Below
Workers' housing at Pessac, Le Corbusier, 1925.

Centre
Oskar Reinhart Collection, Winterthur, Gigon/Guyer, 1998.

Bottom
Eberswalde Technical School, Herzog and de Meuron, 1997–9.

Top
House at Bordeaux, Rem Koolhaas/OMA, 1998.

Middle
Minnaert Building, Utrecht, Neutelings Riedijk, 1997.

Bottom
Swissbau Pavilion, Basel, Santiago Calatrava, 1989.

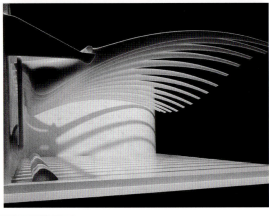

than fretting obsessively about staining and the psychological damage to those who come into contact with the material. When Hugh Pearman, architectural critic of the *Sunday Times*, can write sarcastically that 'the concrete aesthetic is a cliché', and that concrete is a 'material rehabilitated recently as ultra chic by the modernism-loving urbanites who use the word "brutalist" as a compliment', one somehow knows that the corner has been turned and the old negative image has become a positive one.

Rehabilitation is indeed happening everywhere. Despite criticism in the 1980s, projects such as London's South Bank still survive and are fast gaining friends. In 2003, a new glass foyer to the South Bank's Hayward Gallery opened, designed by architects Howarth Tompkins, in collaboration with artist Dan Graham. This is a scheme that recognizes the strength of the original building and tweaks it, rather than obliterating its character. Is this symptomatic of a wider softening of attitudes towards concrete architecture? Are we starting to recognize the merits of historic concrete architecture, as well as build with it anew?

Recent Concrete

Many of the architects working in concrete today have been inspired by Japanese and Swiss projects – it is in these countries, in particular, that a refined and highly crafted exploration has been most widespread. The Swiss architects Jacques Herzog and Pierre de Meuron set up their partnership in 1978. Their Tone House (1985–8) in Tavole, Italy, uses natural stone to infill the precise grid of an exposed concrete frame, contrasting the two textures in a flush plane, while the Eberswalde Technical School (1997–9; see page 21, bottom) in Germany uses a serilith process to transfer photographs onto its concrete surface. As images are also silk-screened onto flush glass panels, the entire skin of the building is a seamless, textile-like, tightly stretched surface.

Peter Zumthor set up his practice in the Swiss canton of Graubunden in 1979, and for over 15 years his main works were confined to the region. In 1997, however, he completed the Art Museum in Bregenz, Austria, then won the 1998 Carlsberg Prize for Architecture, and, in the same year, published a series of his lectures under the title *Thinking Architecture*. Zumthor believes that 'a good building must be capable of absorbing traces of human life, of taking on a specific richness…I think of the patina of age on materials, of innumerable small scratches on surfaces.' At Bregenz, the interior walls are of "velvety grey" concrete, cast against smooth shuttering, with all evidence of daywork suppressed.'[36] In the Netherlands, there has been a similar emergence of home talent on the international stage. UN Studio's stunning Mobius House is looked at in detail on page 38. In the same year, Rem Koolhaas and the Office for Metropolitan Architecture completed the House at Bordeaux. Most noted for its room that moves up and down through the building like an elevator (the client was disabled), it also uses concrete internally and externally – a stone-clad plinth contrasts with an over-sailing concrete bar, perforated with circular windows (a form that would be hard to construct in another material), and, inside, the kitchen has a freestanding concrete work surface. Concrete was also crucial to the form of many of OMA's larger projects – the ramped cross-sections of the Kunsthal in Rotterdam (1992) and the Educatorium at Utrecht University (1997) are both buildings where concrete ramps provide innovative circulation and blur the boundary between internal and external space. At MVRDV's Villa VPRO (offices for a broadcasting company) in Hilversum (1997) the snaking folds of concrete floors are clearly expressed on elevations – exposed concrete contrasts with a baroque chandelier. In the Minnaert Building at Utrecht (also 1997), architects Neutelings Riedijk sprayed red concrete onto the surface of the building, so that it has the appearance of a rough, rippling hide.

Spanish-born architect-engineer Santiago Calatrava has been a prolific designer of virtuoso bridges and other structures, which, rather than suggesting stability and balance, express the stresses within them and the potential for movement and dynamism. (In fact, some actually do move.) He first became known for the Stadelhofen Railway Station in Zurich (1988–90), which, like many of his projects, combines different materials. Concrete is most evident in the underground passage way, which has been referred to as a 'dinosaur tail' – a curving enclosure, formed from repeated concrete supports, like multifaceted, curved vertebrae, and punctured by deeply scooped, egg-shaped openings, which allow light to penetrate through glass blocks. A temporary structure for the Swissbau Pavilion at Basel in 1989 used zoomorphic concrete forms, precast to give high tolerances. Fourteen vast, curved and tapering ribs are supported at one end only on rods, which rotate on discs. Thus, the ribs move slowly in a smooth, undulating manner, reminiscent of both flight and wave motion, creating spectacular shadows. Calatrava's bridge in Seville for Expo '92 used a single-angled concrete pylon for the steel cables supporting the bridgeway, and it this element that has greatest sculptural presence. More recently, the City of Science at Valencia (2000) incorporates concrete to achieve exuberantly Gaudiesque forms. 'Concrete offers amazing sculptural possibilities…concrete, left unfinished after having been removed from its moulds, is the material of structural expression par excellence.'[37]

The Japanese architect Tadao Ando has been described as the 'concrete poet'. Born in Osaka in 1941, he is a self-taught practitioner, who has fused the best of Western Modernism with traditional Japanese architecture and Eastern philosophy. Ando's trademark concrete walls are constructed on a block-like grid, each block having six exposed holes, the result of the moulding-board screws used during construction.[38] His key early work – perhaps the most influential and defining – was the Koshino House (1979–84), which combines concrete and glazed walls to create a beguiling interplay of light and texture. Indeed, it is the wall, enlivened and transformed seasonally by light, that is the essential part of his architecture. Ando's walls are made from exquisitely smooth poured concrete. His secret lies not in any special concrete mix, but in close supervision and the manual skills of his workmen. The smoothness nevertheless often reveals the traces of successive pours, but this is not a problem for Ando. Immaculately crafted and generally lacquered with a protective coating, the luminous sheen of the concrete walls has a strangely ethereal delicacy, which contradicts their robustness. When animated by changing light, the material assumes the sublime potency of mass altered by nature.[39] As Ando poetically describes it, 'The way I employ concrete, it lacks sculpturesque solidity and weight. It serves to produce light, homogeneous surfaces. I treat concrete as a cool, inorganic material with a concealed background of strength. My intent is not to express the nature of the material itself, but to employ it to establish the single intent of the space.'[40]

Where are we now?

As a result of the innovations and creative explorations described here, concrete has won its place in contemporary architecture. Despite the popularity of steel, glass and wood, concrete is still strong and getting stronger as a material of choice for imaginative architects and clients. The projects illustrated in the following pages serve to highlight the exciting technological and stylistic advances that are happening in the world of concrete building.

Right
Koshino House, Tadao Ando, 1979–84.

Bottom
City of Science, Valencia, Santiago Calatrava, 2000.

Chapter 1
Home

Perhaps the last place one would have expected to find exposed concrete making a strong resurgence is in the private home. Yet, as these examples of recent houses show, concrete has done just this. Just how and why has concrete made it to this most intimate of spheres? Does it work? Is it comfortable to live with, or have owners been seduced by a fashion for an aesthetic best kept to the public realm?

When Daniel Libeskind (architect of the Jewish Museum in Berlin and New York's Ground Zero redevelopment plans) completed Studio Weil in Mallorca, his first concrete house, in 2003, critic Jonathan Glancey described how 'from the outside, and from certain angles it has the look of an unnatural and all-but-unattainable cliff … [an] impenetrable geological outcrop or a wholly unexpected museum. What it does not seem to be is homely.' Glancey referred to its 'threatening concrete walls', its 'church-like, even sepulchral' interior, and reported that the 'echoing bare concrete was otherworldly'. Studio Weil has been specifically designed as a house for an artist, and, as such, it is part studio, part gallery and part meditative space for inspiration, but it is also somewhere to eat, sleep and relax – it is certainly not cosy, but seems to work for its client.

Less dramatically, I admire the way in which Jim Cadbury Brown, architect of London's Brutalist Royal College of Art (1963), allows a little bit of concrete into his own domestic life. In the single-story house he and his wife built for themselves at Aldeburgh, on the Suffolk coast (1964), he used the cubes that were poured to test the strength of the concrete as plinths for display in his living room – the dates when they were cast are scrawled onto them. Here, tightly prescribed concrete with a personal history sits happily with a wealth of other materials through 40 years of changing image and reputation – but again it is perhaps the direct association of concrete with artworks which has made it acceptable.

A pivotal point, in Britain at least, came in 1993, with the construction of Rachel Whiteread's *House* – a work that soon gained an international reputation. The artist located a typical East London town house and pumped it full of concrete. The concept was to use the wall and floors of the building as shuttering. This was then cut away and all that was left standing were the spaces where people had once lived, rendered solid and three-dimensional in concrete and scarred with the detritus of everyday life. Remembrances of where hands must once have touched surfaces were made visible – the hollow form of electrical switches, balustrades and so on. This very solid ghost house captured the public imagination, and when time came to demolish it to make way for a public park there was widespread opposition. This was just the sort of house that in, the 1950s and 1960s, would have been swept away and replaced with a very different form of concrete – the concrete slabs and towers of post-war public housing. But whereas these housing estates have come to epitomize social alienation, Whiteread's project let concrete be a medium of humane scrutiny.

In the examples that follow, some of the architects use concrete for reasons of economy and practicality – for instance the owners of the Tilt-Up Slab house love the way they can swill out the sand their children have tracked in from the nearby beach (see page 62). Speed of construction can also be an attraction – Syndesis Inc.'s tilt-slab construction method develops a technique used previously by Rudolf Schindler for his own house in Los Angeles in 1921. Many of the houses featured here, however, have a very high specification, requiring complex and precise formwork and were far from cheap to build, proving that, among architects and their clients, concrete is as equally valued as wood, glass or marble.

Family Home

Flasch, Switzerland, 2001
Bearth and Deplazes

The thickness and solidity of the walls is further emphasized by setting the windows back, so that they are flush with the inside walls.

This trapezoidal tower is a family house on the edge of a village, overlooking some vineyards. Its plan form is a pentagon that follows the irregular shape of the site. The walls are 500 millimetres (20 inches) thick and made of a specially developed concrete without the normal aggregate component. The mix consists purely of cement and foamed glass, and is therefore lightweight and highly insulated. While concrete surfaces are generally expected to radiate coldness, to give off a chill, this product is 'totally different', according to Andrea Deplazes. As professor of architecture and construction at the Federal Institute of Technology, Zurich, he is still refining the mix, which, in his words, 'feels like warm velvet'.

Steel shuttering was used inside the house, but this was replaced by rough timber boarding externally because the steel trapped surface water extruded from the setting concrete – and also because the architect wanted to achieve a less pristine surface finish, given the village context.

Since the windows are set flush to the inner face of the walls, they are deeply recessed on all external elevations. The building looks as if it has been bashed roughly into shape, like a wedged lump of clay that has been hollowed out. The windows give the impression of having been randomly placed, not indicating floor levels, and the entrance door is no more elaborate than the smallest windows.

The structure is a tough, stocky fortress, with its monopitch roof forms suggesting an industrial or agricultural building. On casual inspection, it looks almost derelict, perhaps awaiting conversion and subsequent elaboration or refinement.

Above
An ornate chandelier in the entrance hall softens the minimalist interior. Seeking to avoid either an ultra-modern or a rustic vernacular extreme, Deplazes has added what he calls 'a touch of baroque dialogue'.

Left
The built-in shelving and daybed on the top floor recall a traditional settle, though the elements themselves are modern.

Far left
Long section. There is a basement followed by three levels. The kitchen is on the first level, the bedrooms on the second, and the large, open studio is at the top.

The main living and studio space is located on the top floor to take full advantage of the views over the surrounding vineyards. There is also a kitchen and dining area on the ground floor, with doors onto the small, south-facing garden. The client was keen that someone entering the house should immediately be able to see right through it, and this has been achieved.

The bedrooms and a linear bathroom are on the first floor, and the staircase is arranged to link the floors above and below with minimum impact on privacy. The timber used for the floors on the first-floor level is deliberately rough – to avoid 'a yuppie atmosphere', as Deplazes puts it.

The house's built-in furniture recalls traditional pieces, especially the shelf and the daybed screen, resembling an enveloping settle, which faces the fireplace on the top floor. Deplazes says that he has no interest in traditional forms, nor any desire to create 'a rustic atmosphere', but he is fascinated by 'traditional qualities of behaviour' – the idea of inhabiting a cosy zone that is not closed away.

Just inside the front door, the ornate light fitting is another very deliberate choice and a rejection of both overtly 'modernistic design' and 'rustic games'. 'It's a baroque dialogue,' says Deplazes, with evident amusement, but serious intent. It is a counterpoint that underscores the richness of this seemingly simple composition.

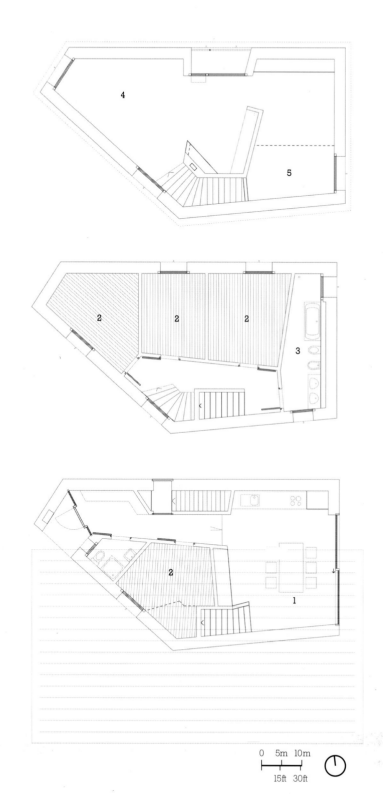

28 Home

Above and top right
Sliding doors on the east façade (above) open out onto the garden, while the south façade (top right) presents a more private face to the street.

Right
At night, light from the deep-set windows creates a warm glow and makes a pattern of coloured squares that enlivens otherwise austere walls.

Opposite
From bottom: plans of the first, second and third levels.
1. kitchen/dining area,
2. bedroooms, 3. bathroom,
4. living area, 5. studio

29 Home

De Blas House

Sevilla la Nueva, Spain, 2000
Estudio Alberto Campo Baeza

Opposite
The building has been positioned to make the most of the mountainous views to the north (out of sight to the right). Someone standing under the canopy sees the mountains framed by the glass box and flooded by a light from the south that makes them seem to advance towards the observer.

Below
South–north section, showing the cave-like situation of the concrete podium.

Bottom
Consisting of a concrete box, a glass cube and a light steel canopy, the apparently insubstantial house blends subtly with its environment, domesticating an inhospitable landscape.

This house stands on rugged terrain, with views north to the distant Sierra de Gredos mountains. It is a hostile environment, with little vegetation. Rather than try to tame the setting, Campo Baeza has produced an elemental solution, emphasizing the barren beauty of the place and hinting at the innovation and excitement of a basic homestead, a pioneering venture in a newly found land.

But this is no primitive shack. A platform makes the steep site traversable and provides a magnificent viewpoint, as well as somewhere to sit on or shelter under. A glazed structure on top gives protection from wind, and a carved-out space beneath serves as a refuge from winter cold and summer heat.

'I needed to express the stereotonic character of the basement piece,' explains Campo Baeza. 'The podium should declare its continuity with the earth, like a cave.' He decided that concrete was the best aesthetic solution, as well as being the cheapest and structurally the most straightforward. He likes concrete because 'it gives great unity. It is strong. It is silent.' He compares working with concrete to 'creating the earth'. Horizontal timber boarding, used as framework, provides the exterior of the box with a rich texture, but phenolic panels were used in the interior to give a smoother finish.

All the regular rooms in the house are located in this cave-like space, with bedrooms and living rooms looking out towards the mountains and with service rooms at the rear. The two bedrooms are at opposite ends of the building, and the central part is an open-plan living/dining room, with a steel-framed, cast-concrete central door to the outside. Tucked behind the dramatically enclosed single flight of stairs leading up to the platform is a linear kitchen; there is no separate central circulation space. The superstructure is referred to as 'the hut', but also as an 'urn' or a 'coffin', suggesting a fairytale glass coffin, an otherworldly place suspended in time. Campo Baeza describes how a 'very good metal worker' welded from standard industrial profiles the equivalent of a large rectangular table with eight legs, which was then painted white. The roof is made of precast concrete panels, simply dropped into the frame of the steelwork.

The concrete box is 9 x 27 metres (30 x 89 feet). The steelwork is 6 x 15 metres (20 x 49 feet) and the glazed enclosure 4.5 x 9 metres (15 x 30 feet). The steel is off-centre on the concrete, but the glazed box is central within it, yet pushed forward within the frame. This positioning strategy is key to the composition. The superstructure has no specific function other than simply to be 'a space from which to contemplate nature' and it is essential that it is pristine – the glazed walls do not engage with the steelwork, but sit within it, with no mullions at the between panels or at the corners.

There is no upstand or visible threshold to the enclosure, and within it the glass stair balustrade is effectively invisible. The stairwell and the pool read as precisely positioned, primary cut-out forms – one reflective by day, the other radiant by night, a glowing entrance to the world beneath.

Achieving more with less has remained Campo Baeza's constant aim. His primary geometric forms are devoid of all decoration.

The difference between the quality of light on the two levels is important to Campo Baeza. He explains how the spectator in the shade of the upper level sees the view 'underlined in such a way that it comes towards him and the architecture, making him feel more part of the landscape'. In contrast, the views framed by the relatively small, deeply carved windows on the lower level seem to 'escape' from the spectator, adding to the sense of being safe and protected.

Born in 1946, Campo Baeza studied at ETSAM, the architectural school in Madrid, where he became professor of design in 1982. He has also taught in Zurich, Dublin, Naples, Copenhagen and the USA. His works include schools and offices, as well as private houses. His highly acclaimed bank, the Caja General de Ahorros in Granada (2001), and the Centre for Innovative Technologies in Majorca (1998) also make extensive use of concrete.

At one point categorized as a minimalist, Campo Baeza has sought to detach himself from Silvestrin, Ando and Pawson, calling himself an 'elementalist' and stressing his debt to Mediterranean vernacular architecture, as well as to Loos and Mies van der Rohe. While 'less is more' for Mies, Baeza subscribes to 'more with less', where he identifies 'idea, light and space' as the three essential components of a meaningful architecture 'capable of touching people'.

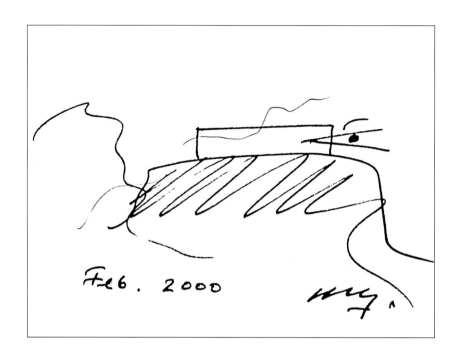

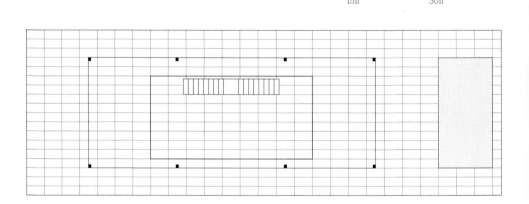

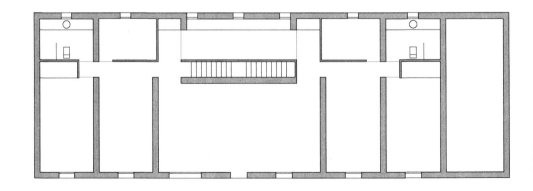

The heavy concrete base anchors the building to its rugged surroundings.

Opposite top
Architect's sketch showing the glass box and concrete volume perched atop the hillside.

Opposite
From bottom: plans of the concrete basement podium and the top level with the glass box in the centre and the pool on the right.

A steel-framed, cast-concrete central door links the open-plan living/dining room with the exterior.

Tokiwadai House

Itabashi-ku, Tokyo, Japan, 2000
Naoko Hirakura Architect and Associates

Constructed in a suburb of Tokyo that resembles a 1930s garden city, this house for a professor and his family was designed to fit into a mature landscape. In fact, the site retains part of the pre-existing house, with its hedge and garden, and is built at the original level, slightly above the street. The part of the old house that survives is now guest accommodation, while the newly built part provides living space and a library, together with a study for the professor's wife and a room for his daughter. The eastern façade incorporates a wall of the old house, in order, explains Hirakura, 'to pass the family's history on to the next generation'.

Described by the architect as 'a tube-like space', the house is conceptually a rectangular extrusion, aligned north–south. The eastern and western sides are, for the most part, closed up, while the northern and southern ends of the 'tube' are kept as open as possible. The walls of the tube are made of thin reinforced concrete, eliminating the need for an expressed structural frame, which would visually subdivide the house into bays. The tube is cut into three sections, which are spaced apart to allow light and breeze to penetrate the house. The first in-between space incorporates a ventilation shaft and a glass floor, which links the basement library to the upper floors. The second incorporates the staircase and a private terrace.

Hirakura describes how this strategy 'allows the space to be created in the simplest and most minimal way', and feels that the house's success is a result of keeping the proportions of the concrete 'thin and planar, and harmonized with the other materials and elements'.

Hirakura's previous projects have included a house designed to accommodate a man with Parkinson's disease, and a mountain lodge for an actor, which features a large, semi-outdoor porch that can serve as a performance or rehearsal area. In contrast with the Tokiwadai House, this rural building has pitched roofs and lapped larch boarding.

Below
As illustrated in this axonometric diagram, the architect refers to the profile of the house as a 'tube', which she has cut and pulled into three distinct elements, the spaces in between allowing light and air into the building.

Below right
By minimizing the use of structure, the architect has translated a traditional Japanese building practice into a modern vernacular. Spaces are clearly demarcated, yet are allowed to flow together.

Top right
A wall of the original house has been retained and parts of it can be seen in the east façade.

Right
View into the large living space from the courtyard at night. By keeping the concrete thin (30 centimetres/11¾ inches), a delicate balance has been maintained between it and the other materials used.

Möbius House

Het Gooi, Netherlands, 1998
UN Studio

Opposite
Concrete and glass act as sculptural elements, while also defining and revealing space.

Below
The clients, who both work from home, wanted an environment in which they could remain separate, but which shared a communal meeting area, seen here at night from the garden. A concrete conference table juts out from a dividing partition.

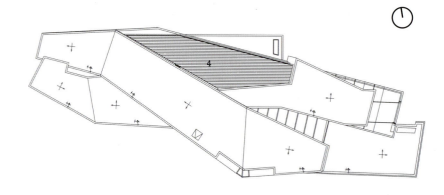

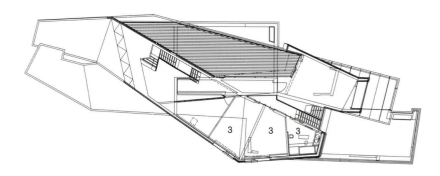

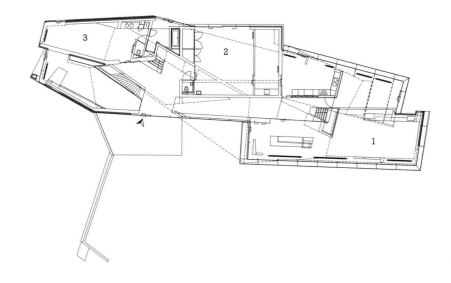

Top
The main dining and living areas are located on the lower ground floor. Fractured and fragmented, concrete blocks appear to float in mid-air.

Above
A studio space and the main bedroom are housed in a glazed runway, which cantilevers out over a guest apartment at ground level.

Right
From bottom: first-, second- and top-level plans.
1. living area, 2. garage,
3. bedroom, 4. roof garden

The glass and concrete spaces flow into one another, linked by ramps or steps, as seen in the distance in this image.

Architect Ben van Berkel of UN Studio explains that the Möbius House, just outside Amsterdam, 'is about how two people spend their day together'. The owners, a husband and wife, both work from home; during the day, they want complete privacy, but they also want to be able to make immediate contact with one another. UN Studio's solution is a relatively small and compact house, but one with multiple routes. Moving through it is like a game of snakes and ladders, where a gentle looping progression can be cut short by surprisingly direct links.

The design creates a sense of calm, suffused with latent dynamism. It was inspired by a mathematical model called a Möbius strip – a flat strip that has been twisted once and then had its ends joined to make a loop. Topologically, it has only one surface and any point on it can be reached from any other. The Möbius house is not a literal application of the model to an architectural programme, but, rather, generates a sense of wonder that something so apparently simple can be so unfathomable.

The fluid use of concrete and glass throughout has made a series of spaces that flow into one another and are linked by ramps and steps. The contractor has likened the process of building the formwork to 'making fitted wardrobes' – such was the need for precision and attention to detail. While most of the concrete is standard in situ construction, there are some areas that consist of concrete that has been sprayed onto insulation with a mesh support. This technique was used for the roof-edge panel and upper south-wall facia to reduce loading. The bathrooms are lined with precast-concrete panels 100 millimetres (4 inches) thick and up to 4 metres (13 feet) in length and 3 metres (10 feet) in width; they have a dark, polished terrazzo finish. Other interior walls and floors are finished with a light cement wash to unify the surface, and the primary structure is differentiated from other elements by the filling in of shuttering boltholes on the former. The crystalline angular forms of the house reach out into the wooded setting – so much so that, when standing in a room, it is hard to determine whether adjacent spaces are internal circulation or penetrating fingers of exterior space. This is also, in part, because of the extensive use of top lighting and the deployment of exposed concrete for both internal and external wall surfaces.

Concrete is used for furniture and fittings, which emerge from walls and floors, but which are detailed to suggest that they are floating in space – like the impression given by the house itself. Its precast-concrete cill detail lifts the structure clear of the ground, even as the concrete weathers and blends with the landscape. The diving-board-like table and the projections of one volume into another are beautifully finished inset concrete forms that can be seen from the exterior, as well as dominating the interior. Conversely, there is an unexpected feeling of intimacy and enclosure throughout the house.

The husband's studio/office is on the lower floor, next to the main entrance, which is at basement level and reached by passing right under the house. A deliberately vertiginous and twisting stair leads up to it, with a deep gully on each side of the treads – like a flight of steps cut into rock at the seashore. The studio/office can also be reached via the garage and kitchen entrance. The second office is on the upper level, along with a children's bedroom and a generous roof terrace. There are sizeable storage rooms at both levels – essential to prevent the build-up of clutter.

Space Blocks

Kamishinjo, Osaka, Japan, 2001
Kazuhiro Kojima

Non-loadbearing walls can be removed and spaces rearranged to extend living areas, and to incorporate neighbouring ones if desired.

Basic building blocks have been linked in linear sequences, sometimes vertically and sometimes horizontally, to form a variety of mixed-use spaces.

Cubes cantilever out of walls and add to the disjointed profile of the building, which integrates so well with its irregularly shaped site.

Right
Long section. The commercial spaces are on the ground level, with apartments on the floors above.

Space Blocks is a group of one-room apartments and shops near the centre of Osaka, Japan's second largest city. Although Kamishinjo is an area of relatively low-rise buildings, the population density is very high. There are lots of bars, small shops, factories and warehouses, as well as cheap apartments. Kamishinjo is not a luxurious or smart part of the city. Even by Japanese standards, the module chosen for the Space Blocks project (a 2.4 metre/8 foot cube) is small, but the way the concrete blocks are stacked allows great variety of form – the individual units comprise between three and six of these connected cubes, in a range of spatial and functional combinations.

The project concept is one of 'sampling' existing urban spaces and then abstracting these spaces into clusters of cubes, or 'basic space blocks'. The cubes are then combined in one of many possible configurations, with special care being given to the composition of both internal and external spaces. The scheme has been compared to a three-dimensional version of the computer game Tetris. It is as if the architect has searched for a variety of ways in which the cubes could be interlocked.

Some of the third-floor and fourth-floor apartments extend over two levels, with double-height spaces. The fourth-floor units have especially large roof terraces. Units can be one, two or, occasionally, three modules wide. Non-loadbearing walls between apartments are constructed of concrete blocks, so that two or more units can be joined together, if desired. The emphasis throughout is on flexibility and a controlled balance between continuity and separation.

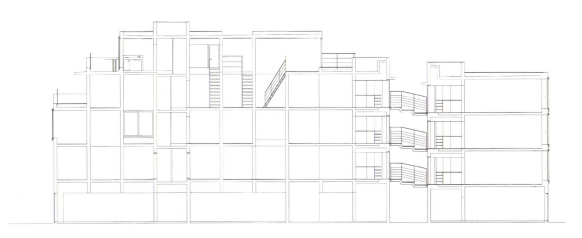

External surfaces are coated with a translucent, water-repellent sealant, and inside the apartments some walls are painted with white emulsion, while others are left uncoated.

The plan is that the Space Blocks concept could be applied to any size or shape of site, as Kojima's students at Tokyo University demonstrated in 1999, when they developed a version for Hanoi, Vietnam, the construction costs of which were subsidized by the Japanese government. There, the traditional Vietnamese patio was expanded into a sequence of three-dimensional spaces – there is a 50:50 ratio of patio to solid construction.

Kojima's other projects that make significant use of concrete include the Black/White Himuro House in Osaka (2002), where cantilevered concrete plates support columns that act as buttresses to realize a long tube-like space, and the Hakuou High School, Miyagi Prefecture (2001), where he mixed precast and in situ concrete. He cites Kiasma, the contemporary art museum in Helsinki by Steven Holl, as an inspirational project, admiring the way its roughly finished atrium has a unique texture which responds well to the northern light.

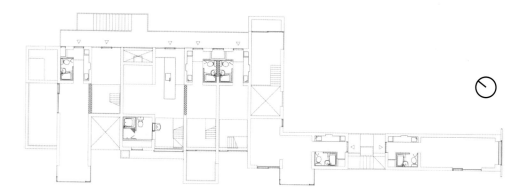

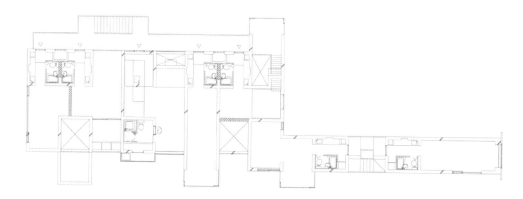

From bottom: plans of the third and fourth floors, where the double-height apartments are located.

Since Japan is plagued by earthquakes, it is a big risk to build a concrete-wall structure there. However, by using a series of 2.4 metre (8 foot) cubes, there is no individual structure that carries through from the ground to top floor.

Loft

Sandweiler, Luxemburg, 2000
Georges Servais

The main screen (foreground) separates the kitchen area (left) from the bathroom. The screen's formwork is constructed from finely sawed wood planks, which give the concrete surface a smooth, yet animated, texture.

The fireplace in the living area. The mezzanine-level studio is above the fireplace, accessed via a flight of stairs on the other side of the cement screen to the left.

Georges Servais had not had the chance to use concrete extensively in his work until he came to build his own house. He attributes this, in part, to the 'very bad reputation' that concrete has in Luxemburg. Acting as his own client meant he had far more freedom and could experiment with a material he admired. 'I very much like the depth of concrete,' he explains. Indeed, his praise for concrete is almost romantic; it stirs his imagination through its unpredictability and he enjoys the idiosyncrasies of a crafted finish: 'In opposition to any surface-treated material, concrete has a very lively surface, which lets you discover multiple layers of colours, nuances, clouds.' He admires the work of Kahn and Ando more than 'the polished perfection' of some concrete buildings, such as I M Pei's work at the Louvre in Paris.

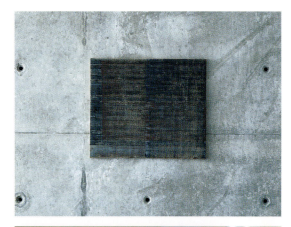

The architect was attracted to concrete because of its 'unpredictablility... idiosyncrasies of a crafted finish'. At first glance, the plastered walls of the original building blend with the new extension. Closer observation reveals the more refined nature of the concrete's surface.

The bathroom is located on the other side of the main cement screen in the entrance hall. The design of this space reflects the open, simple aesthetic of the rest of the loft.

At Sandweiler, Servais's plan was 'to combine the rawness of the existing hull' of a small building that he had acquired with 'the apparent "brutality" of concrete'. He wanted to play up the contrast. The original building was not special. Built at the start of the twentieth century, it had been a village community centre until the mid-1960s, when it became a store for fire-fighting equipment. It was an unpretentious and utilitarian structure, with a gable roof and roughly plastered walls.

What appealed to Servais was the way in which he could manipulate viewers' expectations and make them do a double-take. At first glance, the original walls and the grey concrete screens seem 'to be of the same nature, belong to the same family', as he puts it, but on closer examination it is clear how different they are. The use of finely sawn wooden planks for all the formwork resulted in a surface texture that is quite smooth, but also very animated. Servais delights in the fact that it is 'sensible to the slightest changes of light'. Indeed, it is far more sophisticated than it at first appears.

The spatial concept was to leave the original volume of the building as open as possible, but to use concrete screens to provide some definition, and to incorporate some service functions. The biggest screen separates the living space from the bathroom and other rooms, but allows light to penetrate from the west façade. (Neither the east nor the north façade has any windows.) Servais wanted to use concrete to define the garden as well, but the planners ruled this out on the grounds that concrete was 'too ugly a material' to inflict on the neighbours. A wooden fence was built instead.

There is nothing technologically innovative or complex about the construction of Servais's house, and the contractor had no specialist knowledge. The screens are not load-bearing, but strong Portland 50 Cement was used, mainly because it was the only dark-grey cement available at the time. The standard product in Luxemburg is B35 cement, consisting of yellow sand from the River Mosel, but Servais wanted a dark surface.

The first attempt at erecting the longest screen was unsuccessful, and it had to be taken down and redone. The concrete had been too viscous when it was poured – a problem exacerbated by the fact the screens were only 20 centimetres (8 inches) thick. A resin was added, and the final result was much better. Servais is pleased that the sealant he applied to reduce concrete dust has not altered the material's appearance, although it contained a solvent that made it unpleasant to use.

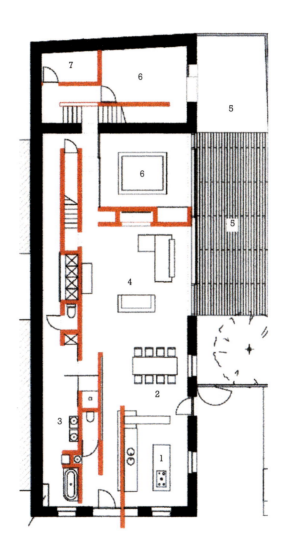
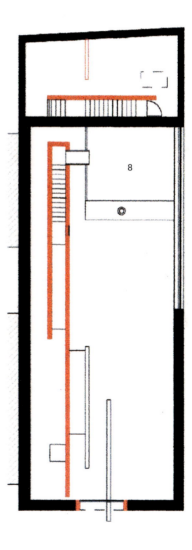

From left: plans of the main living space and the mezzanine-level studio. 1. kitchen, 2. dining area, 3. bathroom, 4. living area, 5. garden/terrace, 6. bedroom, 7. storage, 8. studio

C-House

Brisbane, Australia, 1998
Donovan Hill Architects

The double-height, centrally placed outdoor room is a reference to Islamic architecture. All the living quarters in the house open onto this space.

Donovan Hill Architects have built numerous houses in the subtropical Brisbane suburbs, and are well aware of the extent to which changing circumstances mean that owners want to carry out substantial alterations, often quite soon after completion. The C-House anticipates change and can function as a family house, a shared house, a multi-residence or a home-office, without expensive modification – especially given that, in this instance, the client works for a construction company.

The client's involvement in civil engineering also informed the choice of concrete. Timothy Hill enjoys the sense of homogeneity and weight that it gives the building. 'When working with concrete, you can fashion the landscape, the wall, the roof, the floor, the structure, the openings, the edge, the finish,' he says. Moreover, since it can be used both internally and externally, concrete can function as a means of connecting inside and outside.

Whereas most suburban developments have rows of compact buildings set in the middle of their plots, the C-House has a large garden to the front but otherwise pushes elements of the building towards the perimeter of the plot, creating a large 'outdoor room'. There is a similarity here with Islamic houses, where a central garden often provides open-air privacy. It is a strategy that Donovan Hill have used in a number of projects, which they identify as part of their desire to see more public spaces in suburban settings.

Section showing the complex multi-level arrangement of rooms and spaces.

The second-floor-level pool commands wonderful views of the Brisbane skyline.

Many textures and finishes have been used throughout the building, including the wood-grain shuttering shown in this detail.

The large front garden is overlooked by the kitchen (right), the pool (left), and the bower-like *iwan* (an Arabic term meaning external terrace or colonnade).

The C-House has been identified by architectural critics as one of the most significant houses of the twentieth century; Palladio, Le Corbusier, Wright, Scarpa and modern Japanese architecture have been citied as influences. Hill agrees that all of these may have informed the design process, but also mentions Aalto, Lewerentz, Lutyens and vernacular buildings. 'Looking at it now, I can see some of those influences very vividly,' he says. 'I think that it came about because as practitioners we were so young, and continuing the natural momentum of our education.'

Donovan and Hill also studied Islamic houses with growing interest, not only because they were built for hot climates, but also because the design of many of them had remained unchanged – they appeared to have worked well. The architects use the Arabic term *iwan* for the C-House's timber lookout at the front corner; the separation of the kitchen from the rest of the house, found here, is common in Arab architecture.

Brian Donovan and Timothy Hill established their practice in 1992. Both studied at the University of Queensland, but met later, while working for Brit Anderson and Peter O'Gorman, who both taught at the university. They enjoy working in Brisbane, a city that Hill believes has 'a branding problem' but is an architecturally exciting environment. 'There's no overheated competition or style wars. If you look at the work that gets done, there is more range around here than in almost any other city.'

Both partners reject interpretations of their work in terms of craftsmanship. 'A lot of what is written about our buildings goes up the blind alley of talking about craftsmanship, and that's not what's interesting about them,' says Hill. 'The reason they are carefully built comes from our idea about how we want to keep certain cultural traditions alive. It's not about craftsmanship for its own sake.' Asked to define what they are seeking to do, he suggests that they are attempting to discover 'the poetic potential of the pragmatic determinates'.

Below
The outdoor room forms the centre of the house, with the long, narrow pool at the far left and the front garden at the bottom left of the site plan.

Below right
Built-in concrete elements in the outdoor room include a fireplace and seating.

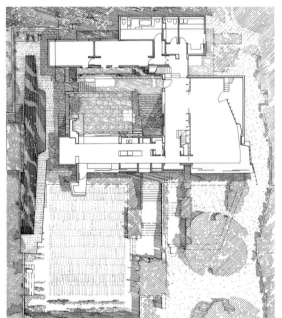

Bacon Street House

London, UK, 2003
William Russell

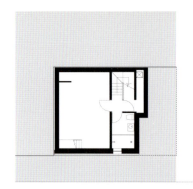
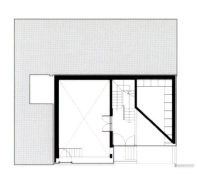

'My house was an experiment in contemporary design, as well as a home for me and my family,' says William Russell. It is built on a small corner site just off Brick Lane, famous for its Bangladeshi restaurants and cafés. This is a vibrant, fast-changing part of east London – but one still referred to as 'grittily urban', which demanded a robust architectural response.

Russell says that one of his self-imposed restrictions for the project was to use a minimum number of materials. It became apparent that he would need to sink concrete pile foundations 10 metres (33 feet) deep, so concrete seemed the clear choice for the superstructure, too – but very little concrete is visible from the outside. Long fascinated by Le Corbusier's prototype Domino House project (1914–15), Russell wanted the structure of his house to be seen and understood both externally and internally. During the day, it is not obvious that this is a concrete-framed house, but at dusk, when the building is internally lit, the shadows of the concrete structure are revealed.

Inside the house, the concrete is obvious. Walls, floors and ceilings are all made of concrete cast in situ, as are the built-in work surfaces. Standard ready-mixed structural concrete was delivered to site, and no particular attention was paid to the design of the phenolic-faced plywood shuttering. As Russell explains, 'Although I admire "beautiful" Ando finishes, I do not think they are practically achievable or appropriate in Europe.' While not wanting to be 'over-prescriptive' by predetermining exactly where shuttering joints should occur, he did push the contractor to achieve as precise and well-finished a surface as possible on areas of maximum visibility, and in places where people would have direct physical contact with the concrete, such as the staircase. He says that he likes 'the crudeness of finish contrasted with the clarity of form' and the way that concrete 'reflects its process of construction'.

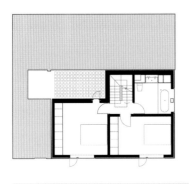
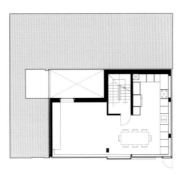
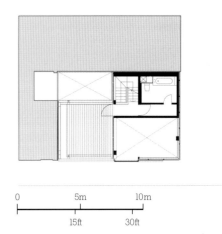

From left to right: plans for the basement, ground, first, second and third floors.

Opposite
The double-height kitchen/dining area is overlooked by a roof terrace, beneath which is the single-storey main living space.

For the moment, the building is divided in two. The basement and ground floor will initially be let out, but will eventually be reincorporated as a double-height studio space. The first floor, behind the central bands of steel cladding, is the bedroom level, with a terrace to the main bedroom, which uses pavement lights to provide extra illumination to the floor below. The lantern-like top two floors contain the main living spaces. At second-floor level is an L-shaped kitchen/living/dining room, and the dining area is double-height, making the large table the focal point of family life. The top floor is mainly given over to a roof terrace, which can be opened up to the living area by folding back a full wall of glazing, so that, in effect, the terrace is an outdoor balcony to the living space.

Externally, it is the cladding that dominates. The steel panels are a version of a standard product called Cryoform – previously used for fireproof sheds and industrial buildings, rather than for houses. Made of a layer of insulation, sandwiched between two layers of galvanized sheet steel, this wraps the upper part of the ground floor, the whole of the first floor and up to dado level on the second floor. The full-height first-floor windows (one in each bedroom) do not open, but adjacent Cryoform split-height panels are hinged to give ventilation. The glazing above is mainly translucent to the street perimeter, and the double-height sliding window weighs 750 kilograms (1,650 pounds) and is fixed with large bolts. The cill line of this sets a dado level to the main room and gives it a sense of scale and proportion. The entrance door and internal doors are clad with galvanized stainless steel, and the back wall of the building is faced with the same rubber as the roof. Russell sees the plywood fitted furniture as having a 'softening' effect on the other materials, but acknowledges that the style is not overtly domestic. 'I suppose it's a reaction against the traditional domestic space,' he reflects, 'an attempt to create the kind of house I would have liked to grow up in.'

The design was drawn up in ink on tracing paper, without the use of a computer, and work started while Russell was in partnership with David Adjaye. He now runs a small independent practice and, as well as houses, is designing shops for fashion guru Alexander McQueen. Projects in Tokyo, New York and London have already been completed. They use fibrous plaster walls and columns, and terrazzo floors to create organic, almost Saarinen-like curved spaces, which feel as if they may have been carved out of a solid block – a quite distinct aesthetic and approach to materials.

Opposite
The galvanized-steel and glass façade is wrapped around a concrete frame. From the exterior, it is not obvious that concrete has been used, but at night the shadowy superstructure can be seen through the large windows and transparent walls.

Far left
The entrance looking towards the stairs.

Left
The concrete surface on the stairs was diamond-ground to expose the rough texture of the aggregate, and then matt-sealed for practicality.

The glazed doors to the roof terrace open concertina-style, allowing light and air to flood into the house.

Visiting Artists' Studio

Geyserville, California, USA, 2002
Jim Jennings

Fellow architect Steven Holl admires Jim Jennings's work, and compares it to that of artists Agnes Martin and Giorgio Morandi. According to Holl, he, like them, 'focuses on the small, and records the known in sensitive sparseness'. This building, consisting of a pair of small houses, designed for visitors to a client's ranch outside San Francisco, is one of the crispest and simplest of Jennings's projects, yet it has a sophistication and rigour that is not immediately apparent. It is also an excellent example of collaboration between architect and artist, where the latter, David Rabinowitch, was introduced to a new medium – concrete.

The client was Steve Oliver, a building contractor, who is on the board of San Francisco's Museum of Modern Art. Oliver has a collection of specially commissioned sculptures by artists including Richard Serra, Robert Stackhouse and Bruce Nauman. It is easy to see Jennings's contribution as just another large sculpture, but it manages to combine a strong form with a sensitive concern for residential requirements, and, at the same time, establishes a close relationship with the landscape.

Two concrete walls, cast in situ, slice though a hillside. At first, they seem to be parallel, prizing open an elemental living space, like a cave or a crevasse in a rock. In fact, the walls are at an angle to each other; their convergence draws the eye to a Stackhouse sculpture some distance away. The contrived perspective makes the building a perceptual telescope – the sculpture appears larger, while the apparent distance to a small lake in the opposite direction is decreased. The walls' inner faces are inscribed with great curving lines. This is a site-specific work by David Rabinowitch that fits perfectly with the architecture. Jennings's project had a ten-year gestation period, with only minor changes once Rabinowitch had been commissioned. The walls, measuring 63 and 64 metres (207 and 209 feet) in length, offered him a perfect canvas, linking interior and exterior space. The architect used a fine aggregate and added 10 centimetres (4 inches) to the depth of the concrete, making the walls, which are partly, of course, retaining walls, 26 centimetres (14 inches) deep overall – to allow Rabinowitch to carve into the surface without encountering reinforcement.

Jennings also added skylights and fibre-optic lighting to focus attention on the wall surfaces. The artist, who had previously made similar pieces in plaster, appreciated the challenge of working in concrete, and said it had never been his intention to ornament Jennings's building, but to add to 'a totality'. Simple rugs add colour and softness.

Each house can be entered in one of two ways – either from a central excavated courtyard, down one of a pair of concrete steps, designed as mirror images of each other, or, more informally, from its terrace. In either case, it is the bedroom that looks outwards, which gives direct access to the terrace. The walls lend shelter and privacy to this area. Both living areas are situated alongside the central terrace, an arrangement that encourages visitors (mainly artists installing work) to meet. The maple floors and wood-slat ceilings seem almost to float between the concrete walls – an impression heightened by the continuous band of skylights along each edge. In each house, a small kitchen and bathroom area is enclosed in aluminium, providing a contrast to the feeling of heavy massing and permanence of the perimeter.

The bedroom area of one of the studios. The thickness of the concrete walls was increased so that the artist David Rabinowitch could incise his designs deeply without encountering any structural reinforcements.

Opposite
At first glance, the two concrete fins which cut into the landscape appear to be parallel, but the plan (below) reveals that they have been cleverly tapered to create strong perspective lines.
1. courtyard, 2. bedroom, 3. bathroom, 4. kitchen, 5. living room, 6. central courtyard, 7. utility

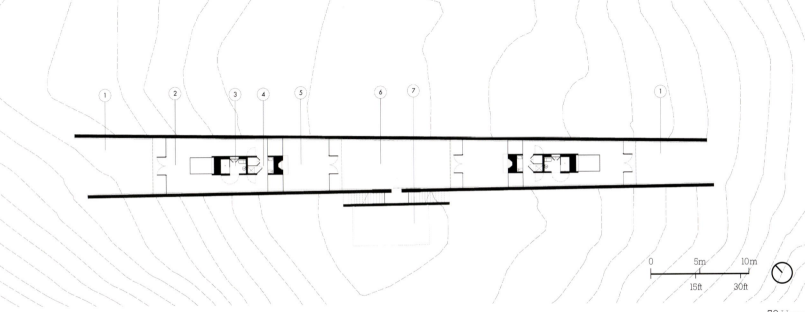

59 Home

Left
The guest houses can be reached either by two mirror-imaged staircases, which lead into a central courtyard, or from the terrace. The patterns on the walls continue into the interiors, linking inside and outside spaces.

Below
At night the interiors shine like a beacon, allowing a view from one end of this architectural 'crevasse' to the other.

From top: long section and south elevation, showing how the two walls slice through the hillside.

Jennings has used concrete in other projects, notably his offices for Group One T, a conversion where, by contrasting the existing concrete ceiling and mushroom columns with sandblasted-glass office walls, he made deliberate reference to the ephemeral nature of his client's work. His Howard Street House, with its Cor-ten steel front, pierced with holes that project, like a camera obscura, blurred images of passers-by onto the glass wall behind, also incorporated pre-existing concrete in a positive way. It rests on the foundations of a small industrial building and retains some of its concrete perimeter walls, which Jennings describes as 'ragged and gritty in an attractively hip way'. The walls at the Visiting Artists' House are conceived almost as a found element, and their inscription by Rabinowitch reinforces this.

Jim Jennings was born in Santa Barbara in 1940, so his first memories of Los Angeles are essentially, as he puts it, 'pre-freeway' – of a time when there were more orange groves than concrete in the city. He cites as early influences the Bradbury Building in downtown Los Angeles, the Hollywood Bowl, Frank Lloyd Wright houses and Schindler's Lovell House at Newport Beach. Most importantly, he explains, 'Growing up when and where I did gave me the opportunity to see so much being built. As a kid, I was always prowling around building sites.' He initially studied engineering, and after switching to architecture remained inspired by engineers such as Auguste Perret, Pier Luigi Nervi and Felix Candela. It is this combination of skills and experience that has been brought to bear on the Visiting Artists' House.

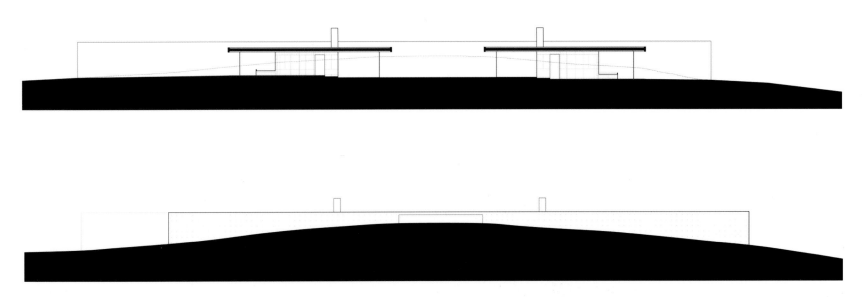

Tilt-Up Slab House

Venice, California, USA, 2001
Syndesis, Inc.

The front elevation. The concrete panels were individually designed to allow for window openings and to articulate the different elements of the façade.

On the Syndesis, Inc. website, principal David Hertz records the building of the Tilt-Up Slab House in a 'construction timeline' – a series of photographs showing what happened not over weeks or months, but in a single day from seven o'clock in the morning onwards. The exterior walls of the house are formed of 14 white concrete panels, each 15 centimetres (6 inches) thick, lined up and facing each other along the longitudinal edges of the site. Eleven of these were poured off-site and winched in, but the tight surroundings of the Venice Beach corner lot meant that it was easier for three of them to be cast in situ, each using a different perimeter framework on the same ground-slab casting surface. They were then raised into a vertical position and were all in place by five o'clock that afternoon.

The tilt-up process is popular in industrial building in the USA because it requires little formwork or skill and minimal handling of large components. It is also inexpensive. The panels of this house, however, are not just rudimentary rectangles, but vary in width from 3.5 to 4.5 metres (12 to 15 feet) and are individually designed to incorporate window openings that articulate the façade and emphasize the panel construction. One of the building's elevations is extremely visible since it stands right on the boundary of the 10 x 24 metre (32 x 80 foot) lot. Although the house is not a kit, its elements read as a crisp horizontal jigsaw, or a row of individual letters, which have been brought together to form a single word, but which equally might be reordered to say something else.

The concrete is left exposed on both the exterior and the interior, but the latter is burnished. White cement was used to create a light colour, and the surface of the concrete casting slab was steel-trowelled to provide a smooth surface. Some cracks later developed in the casting surface, and, although these were filled, they remained visible on the finished panels. Each panel is suspended from a steel moment frame, designed to take lateral loads. Two shorter panels seem to float over the courtyard and garage entrances without lintels. All doors and windows are custom-made; aluminium storefront sections and the doors pivot. There are no internal doors between the ground-floor rooms, and full-height openings create a sequence of spaces that are loosely articulated, like the panels. Apart from the clearly expressed chimney stack, the end wall is almost completely glazed. First-floor balconies are placed off the master bedroom and the staircase.

The accommodation brief was complex since the clients were a professional couple living with their two teenaged children and a permanent guest, a grandparent. As well as a home, the couple wanted separate studies; their budget was only $270,000. The solution was to create two structures: a rear garage building with two bedrooms and a study above it, separated by a 4.5 metre (15 foot) internal courtyard from a larger block, housing a kitchen, a living/dining room and a study on the ground floor, and two more bedrooms, including the master bedroom, on the first floor. A bridge across the courtyard connects the two parts.

Light from a large skylight and an atrium floods both floors of the front block, so that the need for openings directly onto the adjacent alleyway is minimized. Apart from a tiny slot that brings light into the kitchen, there are no ground-floor windows on the alleyway elevation. The ground-floor study has its own door onto the courtyard, but also borrows light though a translucent panel from the skylight.

Right
Natural light and ventilation are allowed to enter the house through the almost entirely glazed front façade.

Far right
Detail of the garage entrance on the east elevation.

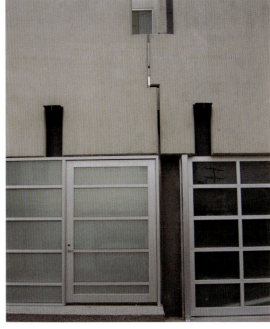

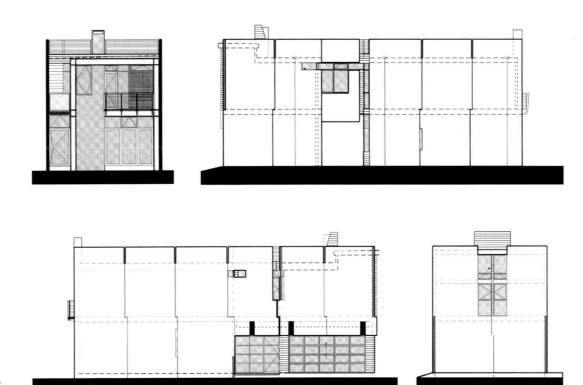

Clockwise from top left: south, west, east and north elevations.

63 Home

All but three of the 15 centimetre (6 inch) thick tilt-up white concrete panels were cast off site, and all were erected in a day. The images show the floor being lowered into place in the morning (left) and one of the short walls being positioned (right) at midday.

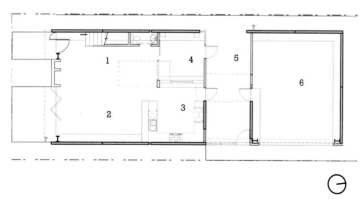 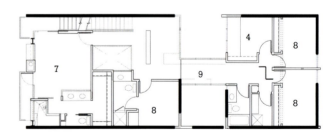

From left: ground- and first-floor plans. 1. living area, 2. dining area, 3. kitchen, 4. study, 5. courtyard, 6. garage, 7. master bedroom, 8. bedroom, 9. bridge

David Hertz worked for John Lautner and Frank Gehry before starting his own practice. He is a passionate advocate of concrete, saying, 'I find concrete an amazing material, unlimited in colour, texture and shape.' He set up the separate firm, Syndesis, Inc., to market a material that he himself invented, called Syndecrete, and his own house is a testament to his conviction, with all worktops, basins, tubs, showers and fireplaces made out of the material. Robust concrete finishes were added so that 'the kids can come in off the beach and skateboard', while concrete floors were cast on a slight slope so 'we can hose it out'.

In the Tilt-Up Slab House, Hertz feels he has created an 'impure' structure by mixing concrete and steel. He speculates that 'the hybrid condition produced creates an interesting possibility … which moves forward from the modernist idea of identity of structure with space. It is perhaps closer to the way traditional buildings mixed technology and materials.'

The concrete walls of the interiors are hand-sanded, sealed and waxed, and the floors are burnished. The sound-proofing and thermal properties of the concrete were an added bonus to the clients, who both work from home.

The skylight and atrium below it allow light to penetrate both floors of the front block.

House in Berlin

Berlin, Germany, 2001
OIKOS

The main living areas are contained in the larch-clad block (left), while the smaller concrete block (right) houses services and a study.

The upper level is reached by a cantilevered concrete plank stair in the central glazed link.

Peter Herrle and Werner Stoll, founder and partner, respectively, of the Berlin firm OIKOS, have designed this house, on a corner site in suburban Berlin, with a clear diagrammatic form. It consists of two long, narrow boxes, side by side, joined by a glazed link. The basic conceit is manipulated to provide a home with a logical sense of space that allows light to penetrate into the core of the volume.

The narrow concrete block to the north houses the entrance area and service spaces, including a large kitchen and a first-floor study. The ceilings are made of exposed concrete, as is the interior wall to the link, while the exterior wall is insulated and plastered. There is also a huge storage room. The short ends of this block are set back within a concrete frame and filled with the same horizontal larch cladding used on the other block. This creates the impression that, while the southern pitched-roof element is a solid geometric form, the concrete one is, by contrast, an extrusion, a slice of something larger, cut down to size and dropped into position.

The very small, deeply set square windows that punctuate the façade and the clearly visible lines of the separated, horizontal lifts of the concrete emphasize the structure's machine-like role – it is a generator or a workhouse clipped to its essentially 'house-shaped' wooden big brother. It is, in fact, only the storage room and toilets. While they rely on the tiny windows, kitchen, bathroom and study gain extra light from windows in the timber ends. These windows are expressed as hatches with shutters that can be closed to hide them seamlessly away.

The glazed link between the two blocks is the main circulation space. It contains a cantilevered concrete plank stair, behind which is a garden door. At the street end of the ground floor, the link connects the bathroom and kitchen of a small self-contained apartment with its own living room/bedroom. This unit is reached by a private door at this end of the link. The use of glass balustrades for the two first-floor bridges across the link emphasizes the separation of the two elements, which is underlined by the visibility of the external materials of each block from within the other. Someone climbing the stair or crossing between the blocks is brought up close to the concrete and the timber cladding. (Where they have been cut back, the circular timber posts suggest a crude timber frame beneath.) This means that the contrast of materials is a constant aid to orientation.

Left
The tiny windows and visible joins in the concrete lifts emphasize the smaller block's machine-like role.

Opposite
The glazed link allows light to penetrate into the core of the building. The open upper-level circulation gallery in the main part of the house is to the right.

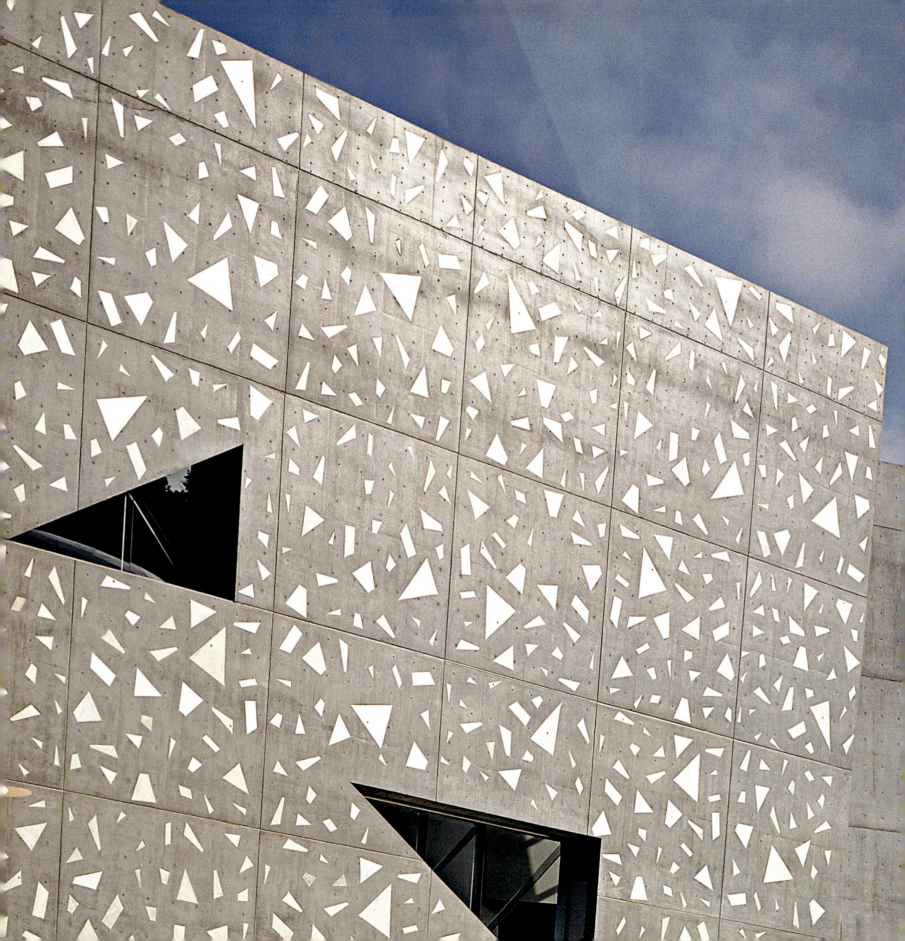

Chapter 2
Work

Many of the major innovations in the development of concrete construction arose out of the requirements of industry. The need for large-span spaces and for fireproof construction, for warehouses as well as for factories, provided the impetus for both practical engineering and for visionary thinking. The Futurist Antonio Sant'Elia's designs of 1913 and 1914 for industrial buildings were not realized, but inspired future generations. His influence can be seen in structures such as Alvar Aalto's wood chip container at the Toppila Pulp Mill at Oulu, Finland (1930–33). British engineer Owen Williams influenced industrial building in both the US and UK, and worked in close collaboration with many architects. Williams began working for the American Indented Bar and Concrete Engineering Company in 1911, went on to set up the London office of the Trussed Concrete Company, and was responsible for the most influential British factories of the interwar period. His factories for the pharmaceutical company Boots, at Beeston in Nottinghamshire, were revolutionary, especially the so-called 'Wets' building (1930–32) – designed for the packing of toothpaste and lotions – which has a concrete frame and a glass curtain wall.

The influence of photographs of industrial and engineer-designed structures such as grain silos on the broader development of architecture (through inclusion in works such as Le Corbusier's *Vers Une Architecture*) has been noted in the main introduction. This subject was more deeply explored from the 1960s onwards in the photographic work of Bernd and Hilla Becher. Their series of 'portraits' cataloguing the typologies of a variety of industrial structures – including concrete water towers – celebrates the sculptural impressiveness of previously unnoticed or stigmatized objects. Through their work the Bechers have given an aesthetic legitimacy to industrial structures, not least those in concrete.

Not only the preserve of exteriors, concrete was, in the first half of the twentieth century, also becoming a material that could be expressed internally. The Fiat Lingotto factory in Turin, designed by company engineer Giacomo Matté Trucco in 1915, is famous for its interior ramp and cambered rooftop test track (see page 14). This explicitly functional building draws a diagram of what happens at the factory, in a similar way to which the transparency and exposed stair of the LOOK UP office building (see page 120) gives an immediate graphic image of the company's activities. The central space of Frank Lloyd Wright's administration building for Johnson Wax at Racine, Wisconsin (1936–9), features 54 white, hollow concrete columns reinforced with metal mesh. At its top each column mushrooms out from a 23 centimetre (9 inch) diameter base to form the roof. It is a spectacular space to which – in its scale, sense of efficiency and dynamism – Canary Wharf Underground Station (see page 82) owes a debt.

Today the office block, disassociated with any site of manufacture, is as much the totemic work building as the factory, and for an early prototype one can look to Mies van der Rohe's Concrete Office Building Project of 1922. Explored through a series of long charcoal drawings, this was a prototype for a seven-storey high trapezoidal solid, each floor stepping out over the one below, with ribbon windows and deep horizontal parapet walls. The project was never built, but it was published and explained purely as a result of structural calculation.

The examples in this chapter also include schools, universities and a dance centre. These use concrete in a variety of ways, but all draw on a distinguished history of concrete put to good use in this area. The post-war period saw a great expansion in the university sector and some of the best new buildings at existing universities – as well as entirely new campuses – were built in concrete. Pre-eminent among these is Denys Lasdun's University of East Anglia (1963) at Norwich, England, where the concrete ziggurat-form accommodation blocks are just part of a complex plan built along a raised spinal walkway. The London firm of Howell Killick Partridge and Amis (HKPA) – great exponents of precast concrete – built extensively at the universities of Birmingham, Oxford and Cambridge. The very high quality of the buildings' concrete panels meant that they were accepted in highly sensitive historic locations, where previously even the most modern interventions had been faced with smooth limestone so as to be in keeping with their surroundings.

It is safe to say that the once separate aesthetics for industrial, public and educational architecture have truly merged. While some residential and exhibition spaces featured in these pages exhibit a distinctly rough, industrial feel, some projects in this chapter achieve the opposite. The Armani Headquarters and Theatre in Milan (see page 132) are based in a converted industrial building, but rather than follow through with this type of aesthetic the architect, Tadao Ando, has used beautifully finished concrete to achieve the look of a smooth, modern gallery, blurring the boundaries between art and industry.

Haslach School

Au, Switzerland, 2000
Beat Consoni

Solid concrete was chosen for the exterior because of its exposed setting overlooking the Rhine Valley.

The corridors have built-in furniture so that the classrooms can, if necessary, expand into them. The staircase and elevator hall are lit by a skylight.

This austere, rectilinear building was the surprising winner of a competition to build a new primary school near a church in an attractive Swiss village. Its restrained and abstract form could be seen as unsympathetic to its environs and unwelcoming to very young children, but, in fact, its design provides easily comprehended, bright spaces. The plain interior walls look great when covered with the young pupils' pictures. Because of its extremely exposed location, solid concrete was used for the external walls, and the shuttering was left in place for four days, to ensure a full set.

The school is aligned east–west along the gradient of a hillside, and makes good use of the slope. The front of the building looks south across the Rhine Valley and the land rises steeply behind. The basement workshop has its own separate outdoor area, so that activities can take place outside in good weather. There is also a large, well-lit bicycle shed, but the lack of glazing on the face of the building at this level means that all the openings read as dark, cave-like voids, making the structure seem more firmly anchored.

The main entrance is one floor up, but, because of the sloping site, is still at ground level. The glass door is elegantly sheltered by the projection of the two storeys above. At the entrance level, the circulation corridor runs the length of the front of the building, past the staff room, to a multi-purpose hall with a stage, and is lit by full-height glazing all the way. On the next two levels, the arrangement changes – there are classrooms at the front of the building and a corridor at the back.

This difference is reinscribed in other forms of glazing on the front elevation – and in different types of blinds at night. At the far end of the building, the stair and lift hall is top-lit by a generous skylight. The precast open treads of the staircase allow light to filter down to basement level, and the walls here are made of fair-faced concrete.

Concrete has also been used to landscape the site. The main playground, to the south, is shaded by plane trees. To the north, there is a multi-purpose hard court for sports, with graduated terracing that provides concrete bench seating. Back inside, the upper-level corridors have narrow bands of windows at two levels, so, from the back, the building reads initially as if it had far more than three storeys. The upper band is effectively a clerestory, while the lower provides direct views out for those sitting at the built-in, lift-up desks, which, together with the row of cupboards above, create the sense of a much thicker protective wall to the mountain side.

Consoni has previously used concrete to good effect in domestic projects. In 1993, at the Gnadinger House, St Gallen, the architect contrasted a robust new garage/workshop building in concrete, glass and steel, and set into a grass slope with an in situ grass roof, with the renovated pitched-roof form of the house itself, painted blue and covered in a translucent polycarbonate cladding.

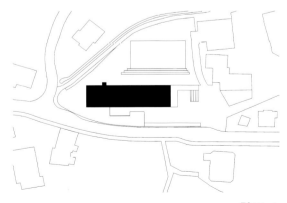

Shallow bands of windows in two sizes run the full length of the north elevation, giving the impression that the building is higher than two storeys and adding a clever articulation to its otherwise austere rectilinearity.

Top left
The austere concrete school building makes a striking addition to the picturesque Swiss village.

Left
At first sight, the massive barren walls might appear intimidating to children, but they are intended to be covered by colourful artwork.

Opposite top
The short section and long section show the way in which the building sits on the sloping site.

Opposite bottom
From bottom: ground-, first- and second-floor plans.

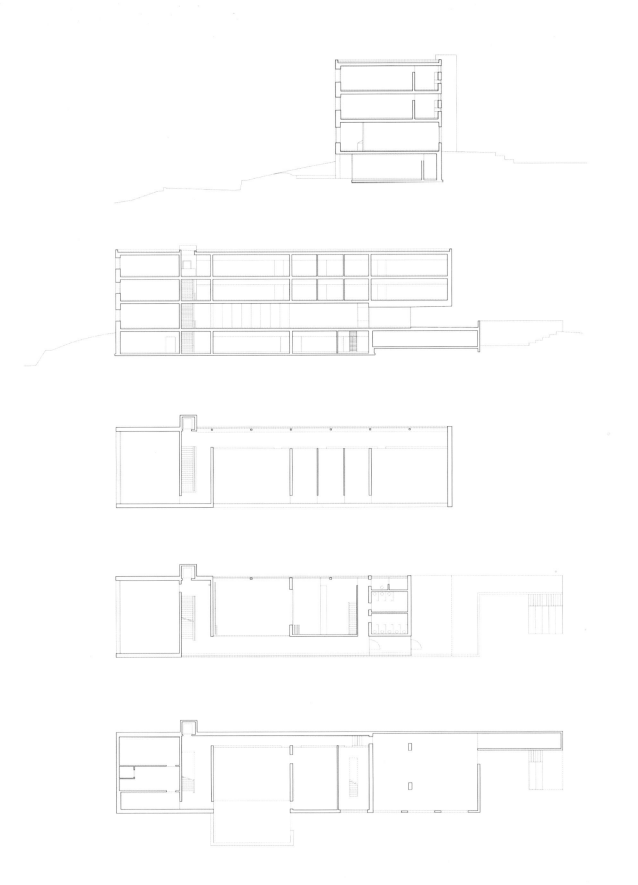

Federal Chancellery

Berlin, Germany, 2001
Axel Schultes Architekten, Frank Schultes Witt

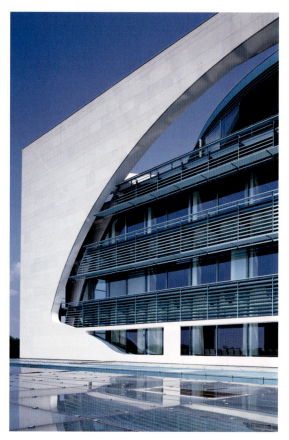

Schultes's design was influenced by the monumental architecture of the past. Huge side windows flood the interior with daylight.

Commissioned by Chancellor Helmut Kohl for the newly reunited Germany, the Federal Chancellery building has proved controversial. 'Is it too grandiose and formal?' asked the *Architectural Review*, suggesting that its large courtyard, with flanking blocks of government workers' offices, subservient to the central building that houses the politicians, might be inappropriate for a modern, pluralist democracy. While Kohl's successor, Gerhard Schröder, has let it be known that he would have favoured something 'more Bauhaus' (*Architectural Review*, August 2001), and locals have dubbed it 'the Federal Washing Machine', this building is clearly a sophisticated composition, with high-quality concrete construction.

At the opening ceremony, architect Frank Schultes explained that, while today we have retained 'an idea about the magic and timelessness of spaces' and 'a yearning for suggestive spatial quality', what we have lost is an ability to implement this simultaneously with the enjoyment of 'luxury materials'. For this reason, Schultes wanted to build not with expensive stone, but with 'simple materials'. In his words, concrete allows him the freedom to sidestep materials that are 'mere surrogates for money' and enables him to concentrate on creating 'contrasts in dimension, mood and atmosphere'.

Before receiving this commission, Schultes's practice had already been given responsibility for the master-planning of this part of Berlin. They envisaged the Chancellery as one element on a 'ribbon of government buildings' ('Band des Bundes'). This would stretch across the looping line of the River Spree no less than three times, and symbolically knit together east and west.

The Chancellery's composition reflects Schultes's interest in the monumental architecture of past civilizations, in particular Hagia Sophia and the temples of the Nile Valley, but the architect also had in mind these words of Nietzsche: 'All good things have a lightness of touch to them, reclining like cows in the meadow.' There is certainly a relaxed aspect to the disposition of the elements – curved forms complement the basic Euclidian geometry of the formal blocks with their circular cut-outs.

Massive concrete planters are used to lift up pear trees to the ballroom level, and similar structures house air-conditioning equipment. These form a backdrop to the Court of Honour to the east, which looks towards the Reichstag and is designed for the reception of state visitors – they are a softer option than the initial suggestion of corrugated, concreted doors 12 metres (40 feet) high. In the central block, large outdoor staircases lead up to the main conference room. While the north and south façades are faced with stone, the east elevation reveals the concrete structure, and the curved white concrete roof form is emphasized by the tensile fabric canopy below; in front of this stands Eduardo Chillida's Cor-ten steel sculpture entitled *Berlin*. The comb form of the offices, with a solid back to the site perimeter and a series of winter gardens on the courtyard side, offer well-lit accommodation for government employees, and behind the main block the Chancellor's garden leads down to the River Spree.

Irregularly spaced columns, resembling a natural planting of trees, pierce the roof, letting in circles of natural light. They recall those at the Treptow Cemetery, the architect's other major concrete building of recent years, which has the same sense of grandeur and formality as the Chancellery, and is similarly endowed with elements designed to have a softening effect. What is remarkable is that those elements are also constructed in concrete.

Left
The Court of Honour faces east towards the Reichstag. Its grand entrance is sheltered by a tensile fabric canopy – an accent added by Schultes to soften the imposing front façade. Eduardo Chillida's Cor-ten steel sculpture *Berlin* greets visitors on their way in.

Bottom left
Dubbed 'the Federal Washing Machine', the Chancellery is the highlight of Schultes's masterplan for a ribbon of government buildings running along the River Spree and uniting east and west Berlin.

Below
Criticism has been levelled at the undemocratic layout of the Chancellery, which houses the politicians in an impressive central block, while the civil servants' offices are sited in subservient positions on either side.

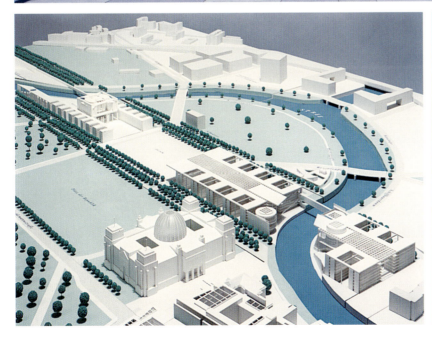

Below left
Irregularly placed concrete columns in the courtyards pierce the roof, admitting light and air to the lower levels. Circles of sunlight soften the starkness of the concrete floor below.

Below right
The geometrical appearance of the Court of Honour is overlaid by the curved and freer forms of massive planters and columns containing air-conditioning equipment.

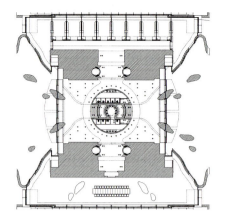
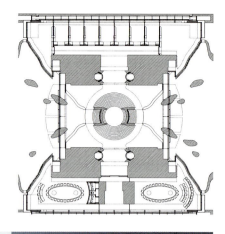

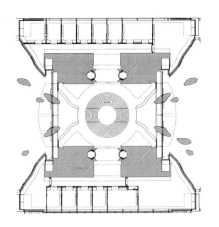
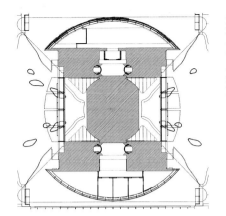

Left
From far left to right: fifth-, sixth-, seventh- and eighth-floor plans of the main building.

Below
From bottom: site plans of the ground and first-floor levels.

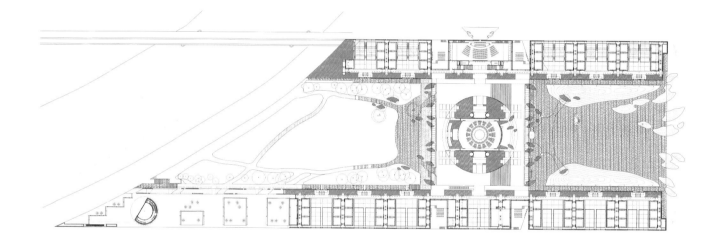
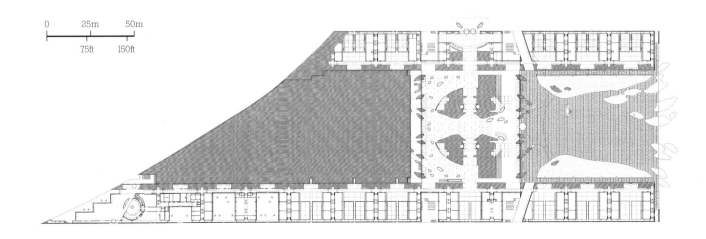

81 Work

Canary Wharf Underground Station
Jubilee Line Extension

London, UK, 2000
Foster and Partners

Foster's intention to minimize the need for signage by making passengers use daylight to navigate their way through the station means that the light has to filter down to platform level. Artificial lighting is kept below the normal level to emphasize natural light, and surfaces are as reflective as possible to aid circulation.

Canary Wharf is one of 11 new stations on a major extension of the Jubilee Line, part of London's rail network, which leads east from the centre of the city. The route was designed to serve the new office buildings that have replaced the disused docks, and to link the Millennium Dome with the rest of the city. While individual stations were designed by different architects, the whole project was masterminded for London Underground by chief architect Roland Paoletti, who drew a musical analogy when he suggested that 'The JLE is like a tune, like jazz. The whole piece has movement and integrity. But within the tune there are crescendos. Canary Wharf is one of those crescendos.'

The station is a cut-and-cover structure, built on the site of the old West India Dock, and it is as long as Cesar Pelli's glitzy postmodern tower (which stands beside it) is tall. Before work on the station could begin, wells were sunk into the underlying chalk to pump out ground water. The dock water was then parted by sinking cofferdams, allowing the creation of a box 24 metres (80 feet) deep by 280 (920 feet) long by 32 metres (105 feet) wide, supported by 148 T-shaped diaphragm walls. The base slab had to resist an uplift force of 220,000 tonnes (216,525 tons) and required 163 piles.

The engineers were Arup, and while the initial concept was that the project architects should just clad out a finished shell, Gerard Evenden, project director for Foster and Partners, credits Paoletti with enabling the practice to extend their brief. Foster and Partners became involved while major engineering decisions were still being made, thereby achieving a much more dramatic result. The best example of this is the distinctive elliptical form of the columns. Their unusual shape is an elegant response to the problem of fitting in the required facilities and creating sufficient space to allow up to 40,000 people per hour to pass through the station.

The project has been described as the 'cathedral' of the new line, with its creation of a huge linear public space and its ribbed-concrete vaulted roof. Like a cathedral, the station uses light to draw people through the space, and in this case raise them up and out of the building. It is a double-ended cathedral, however, with exits at each end, and its columns stride down its very centre, rather than being pushed to each side of a nave, giving it greater dynamism.

Since the architects aimed to minimize the need for signage by making passengers aware of daylight from the moment they step off a train (and then, logically, move towards the light), the lighting strategy was a crucial part of the scheme. Daylight was required to penetrate as far as platform level, and the architects needed to use a material with a surface that would be at least 50 per cent light-reflective in order for the vaults to reflect sufficient light downwards, acting like an artificial sky. Evenden was surprised to find that many concrete samples that he examined met this criterion. 'Concrete is lighter than you think,' he says, acknowledging that it is still assumed to be a dark, dreary material. The roof structure is made of glass-silicate concrete, chosen because it needed to be fully waterproof, particularly since

Canary Wharf Underground Station is used by up to 40,000 people an hour. The huge entrance extends down into what was once West India Dock. Durability and ease of maintenance – key factors in the design – are reflected in the use of fair-faced concrete, steel and glass.

it lies beneath the grass mound, seen from the outside. This initially cures to a blue tint, but then lightens. Elsewhere, the mix was standard London concrete. A variety of shuttering was used, and the experience led Evenden to revise his view that stainless steel always gives the most pristine result. A 36 metre (118 foot) long stainless-steel shutter was used for the roof, but steel sections were deemed too expensive for the complex geometry of the double-curved exit/entrance canopies. Instead, timber was deployed here. The skill of the boat-builders who worked on them, together with the thorough pre-planning (which involved a trial erection of one of the structures off site), ensured that an equally good result was achieved.

Extensive site supervision meant that the basic timber shuttering on areas such as the machine chambers was also of a high quality. Care was also taken to ensure that, as far as possible, the joints formed a perfect grid and that there were no small sections. At platform level, on the far side of the tracks, the rough surface of the diaphragm wall was left as it was struck, looking like a rock face.

Top
The monumentality of the design recalls religious architecture. The cathedral-like main hall has a series of columns running down the centre, dividing the 'nave' in two. The ribbed and vaulted roof is constructed in high-class silicate concrete, while the other surfaces are made of standard London concrete.

Left
As in a cathedral, light is used to direct, as well as to inspire. In this case, it is used to raise the 'faithful' up and out of the building.

Above
Boat builders advised on the building of the timber canopy, and the structure was trial-tested off site.

Below
From top: long section and plan.

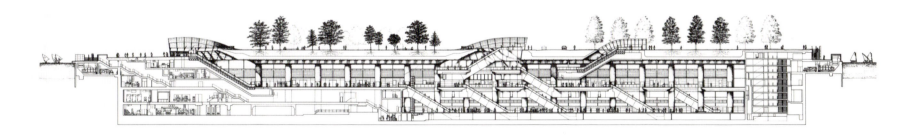

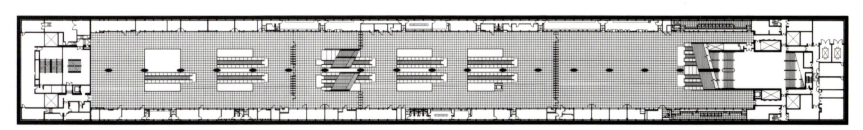

85 Work

Ehime Prefectural Museum of General Science

Niihama City, Japan, 1994
Kisho Kurokawa

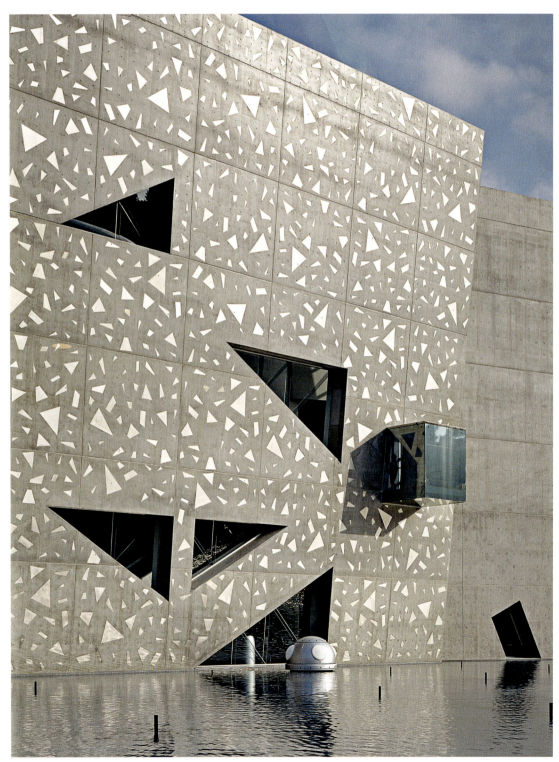

Above
The crescent-shaped restaurant block looks out onto the spherical planetarium, the largest of its kind in the world.

Left
Precast concrete forms a base for more precious materials – titanium, marble and granite – which were cut into trapezoid chips and laid in the base of the mould. In situ, they catch the sunlight and are reflected in the pool below.

Opposite
Site plan.

The Ehime Prefectural Museum of General Science consists of a group of separate structures – a crescent, a cube, a sphere, a triangle and a cone. Rather than create a monolithic institutional building, the architect Kisho Kurokawa has drawn together a variety of forms (to house a collection of exhibits and ideas) that recall the elemental shapes of a child's set of building blocks. The disposition of the elements refers to the free arrangement of stepping stones in a Japanese garden. It is a deliberate expression of the asymmetry of Japanese traditions, and yet the relationships between the parts of the overall composition are highly considered.

The rich surface pattern on the concrete walls is created by the inclusion of trapezoidal and triangular chips of titanium, marble and granite in the mix. While some of the structure was cast in situ, the chips were laid into the base of the precast panel moulds. Stainless-steel anchors on the back of each section of concrete allow secure fixing. The surface patternn also mirrors the sharply angular form of the triangular windows, which are also freely distributed, emphasizing the canting of the walls.

Niihama City stands at the foot of western Japan's tallest mountain. The museum often gets bright sunshine while the mountain is clouded, a contrast that adds to the drama of the structure's external appearance. The glazed cone, with a spiral ramp around its perimeter, forms the entrance building. The spherical form houses a planetarium and the crescent a restaurant, while the large triangle is a multi-storey car park. The display space is situated in the distorted cube form, which sits above a large reflecting pool, beneath which a passageway links the entrance to the planetarium. Following on from this project, Kurokawa designed an egg-shaped concrete building for the Fukui Prefectural Dinosaur Museum, Katsuyama (completed 2000).

Kurokawa describes his work as a response to 'the ambivalent, heterogeneous nature of man', and discusses his 'philosophy of symbiosis' in a series of books and articles, which he started to publish in the 1980s. Influenced by Buddhism, he has explored the interrelationships of man and technology, and time and space. The creation of a science museum was a perfect opportunity to give material form to his ideas.

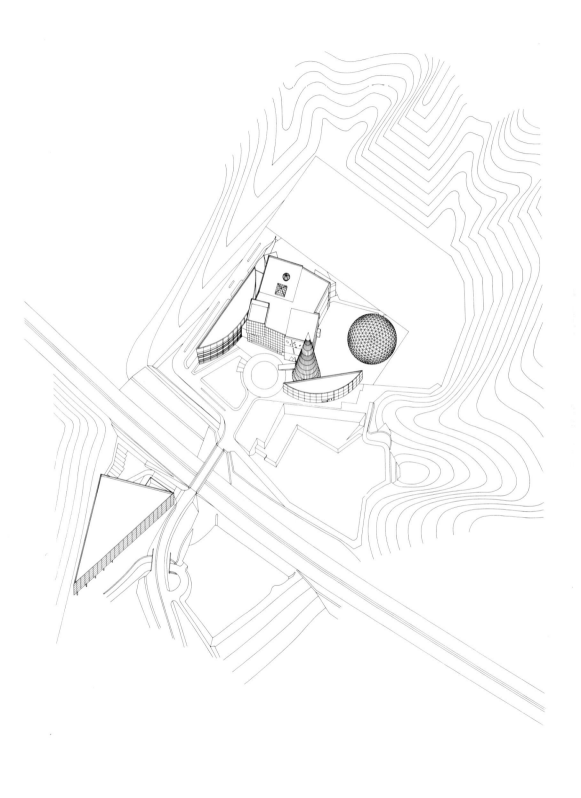

Exhibition areas are housed in a series of geometrically shaped buildings. The cone that forms the entrance symbolizes the workings of nature and the human pursuit of scientific knowledge.

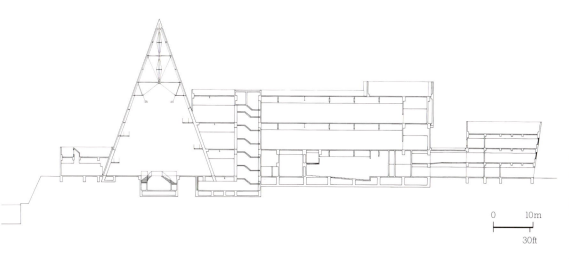

Above
Long section.

Far left
The museum stands at the foot of the highest mountain in western Japan, setting up a futuristic contrast with the traditional Japanese architecture that surrounds it.

Left
A close-up of the concrete matrix reveals a beautiful symbiosis of base and precious materials.

89 Work

Diamond Ranch High School

Diamond Bar, California, USA, 1999
Morphosis

Above
A row of buildings runs either side of a main 'street' in the vast campus, which accommodates 1,600 students, 50 teachers and 15 administrative staff. The rows are divided into clusters, each with its own classrooms and courtyard.

Left
The jagged shapes of the Los Angeles hills and the area's seismic instability inform the language of the buildings.

Diamond Ranch High School is constructed on an extremely steep site in eastern Los Angeles, about 130 kilometres (80 miles) from centre, at a point where (in the words of the architect) 'the city starts to break apart'. It is a large building, housing 1,600 students, 50 teachers and 15 administrative staff. In some places, the site gradient is 2:1, and, as well as 15,000 square metres (162,000 square feet) of building, the brief called for large playing fields and parking for 770 cars – a complex problem in both design and structural terms.

It was Morphosis's intent to create a building that is perceived as being 'at one with the site', rather than 'on top of the site'. Partner Thom Mayne suggests that the key was inherent in the brief: 'It was about two conflicting issues. One was the programme and taking care of children, and the other was the site not being the right site.' Mayne's initial appraisal was 'the site does not want a building on it', and that the ideal image would be that of a parent leaving a child in a beautiful park, a natural setting, rather than in a built structure.

Even in California, however, this turned out to be an impractical option, and the final assessment was that the slope was 'an advantage, in that it provided a receptive opportunity to continue our explorations into an architectural language that blurs the distinction between object and site.'

Morphosis has been influenced by the, mostly American, 1960s generation of land artists. By looking at works such as Michael Heizer's *Double Negative* (1969–70), they have learnt that 'You can make space as easily by subtraction as by addition,' and a body of the practice's work has drawn on Heizer's ideas, as well as projects by Richard Long, Robert Smithson and James Turrell. According to Mayne, 'All of this work that has to do with cutting and subtraction, carving and sculpting the land, draws from these artists. All of a sudden, the site becomes the focus and the object is all but consumed by it.'

The first step was to create a computer model of the site. (The project was designed just at the time when computers were being introduced to the office.) This was then manipulated into cuts and folds, producing a terracing effect down the slope – in other words, an abstracted version of the existing topography provided the basic form of the design. Key to the project was the construction of a very long, three-storey, buttressed concrete retaining wall, spanning the length of the building: 'This allowed us essentially to step the building down the hillside.' Further retaining walls were used to help achieve this stepping, and to allow the integration of landscape in the form of various courtyard areas throughout the campus.

The primary connecting route through the school is a 'pedestrian street', which also acts as the main social space, and which runs between the north and south parts of the school. This axis comes as quite a surprise at the end of the long entry drive, where it is reached up a narrow set of stairs. By this point, the impression gained from a distance of an ordered building has disintegrated. Instead, one faces a series of distorted, angled roofscapes that resemble shifted geological plates. The pedestrian street is deliberately urban in scale and feel, in contrast with the suburban surroundings. An important element is the main staircase, which, in the view of the architects, resembles the stair of the Metropolitan Museum of Art in New York.

A central corridor links the northern and southern parts of the school. This 'pedestrian street', an important social meeting place, is reached by a surprisingly narrow flight of stairs.

Opposite
Glass, steel and concrete are used to dramatic effect at the main entrance to the site.

Left
Concrete was chosen for its durability and resistance to graffiti. Its flexibility enabled the architect to create forms not limited by geometry. The concrete was cast in situ and reinforced in steel.

Below
From left to right: plans of the lower and upper levels.

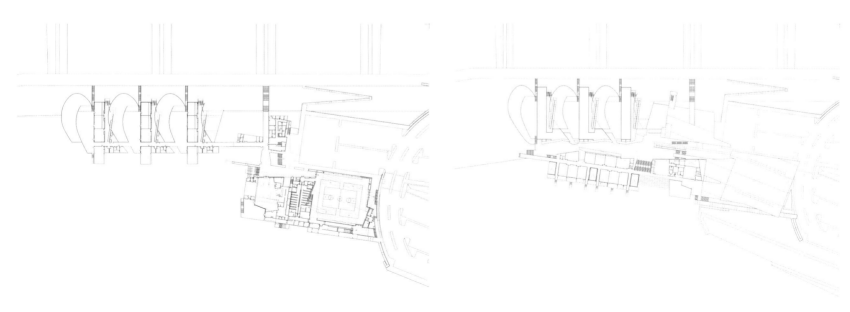

In this computer model, the topography of the site is abstracted and folded, as if it were a piece of origami, to form not only the school's roof, but also its main masses and voids.

Following traditional school design, classrooms for each age group are clustered together. The ninth- and tenth-grade pupils are housed to the north of the street, in buildings conceived as small 'schools within the school' – a cluster of six, two-storey structures, each with a teacher's workroom and guidance area, and its own outdoor meeting area. Most classrooms for grades 11 and 12 are south of the street, arranged around open courtyards; core-curriculum subjects are taught on the second level, and subjects such as business studies, home economics and industrial technology are taught on the first level, which has direct access to the street.

As well as using concrete for the retaining walls, the architects used the material for the lower parts of the building. 'The concrete at Diamond Ranch is considered formally as a base, from which the rest of the building emerges,' explains Brandon Welling, who was part of the design team. 'It manifests itself in retaining walls, stair towers, seating and walking surfaces.' The concrete on the stair towers and the faculty courtyard is highly textured. It was cast using 15 centimetre (6 inch) wide wood slats with a deep grain, set so that the concrete could ooze out slightly between them. The original aim was to use this method throughout, but cost constraints meant that in other areas 1.5 x 3 metre (4 x 8 foot) plywood sheets had to be used for the formwork. The architects liked the resulting contrast.

As well as the phenomenological influences of land art, Morphosis's partners credit 'Archigram vision and Gruen office ethic' with informing the development of their work. Mayne explains that, although he was not a student at UCLA – where Peter Cook, Ron Herron and Warren Chalk, the core of Archigram, were teaching in the mid-1960s – 'Even at an ultraconservative place like USC we were reading Ginsberg and experiencing the same forces.' He later worked for a redevelopment agency on urban-scale projects, before meeting his future partner, Jim Styfford, working at Gruen Associates (where Frank Gehry and Cesar Pelli had also worked). Morphosis's first project was the Sequoia Elementary School, which drew on classes taken at the Harvard Graduate School of Design, where Mathias Ungers, Colin Rowe and Jim Stirling had explored an interest in historical language. A trip to the Pompidou Centre 'showed radical neutrality was impossible', and a series of highly intellectualized hybrid structures followed.

'Diamond Ranch represents a radical shift for me because I actually had a singular strategy that went through the whole project,' says Mayne. Yet, curiously, although at Diamond Ranch he was 'consciously trying to maintain a level of coherence and singularity', he perceives the result as being characterized by 'greater differentiation' within the project. A limited budget meant that they had to dispense with the original idea for a special roof, which was to slide off the gymnasium and up into the landscape, providing the most literal link with the natural surroundings. The architects feel the building is only 75 per cent of what it was intended to be, but they still regard it as a triumph.

One of the three cantilevered classroom volumes.

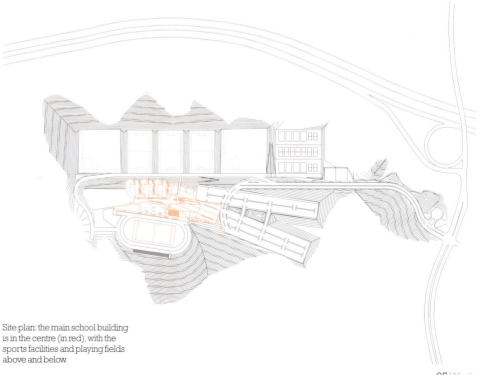

Site plan: the main school building is in the centre (in red), with the sports facilities and playing fields above and below.

School of Arts, Córdoba University

Córdoba, Argentina, 2002
Miguel Angel Roca

Each of the four departments housed in this faculty building has different requirements. They are accommodated in what Miguel Roca describes as 'four warehouse boxes that say nothing'. The boxes are mysterious; they intrigue both by their similarity and by their subtle differences, stirring curiosity about what is going on inside them.

The four three-storey units house the departments of drama, film, music and sculpture. They are arranged in a pinwheel formation around a central, single-storey hub. The sculpture building is skewed at an angle, adding to the dynamism of the group. Each block is constructed partly in rough in situ concrete and partly in black, oxidized steel panels, the balance between the two materials varying, and each contains a mix of double- and single-storey-height spaces. The drama and music departments contain large performance spaces; the former has an experimental horseshoe-shaped theatre and the latter a rectangular auditorium, with a small gallery and narrow horizontal slot windows to bring in natural light without creating distracting views. Between the two departments are shared toilets and dressing rooms.

The entrance is to the left of the music block, so approaching visitors can clearly see what appear to be four diagonally slanted, projecting light boxes clinging to its roof line. In fact, these are roof lights that cut laterally across the building and top-light the space. To the left of the entrance, the sculpture department has an exhibition space on the ground floor, and a library on the floor above. The T form of the main concrete wall marks the position of the most dramatic staircase in the complex. The library is well lit by a tower of glazing on each side.

The theatre and cinema require no natural light, and therefore appear from the outside as the most solid concrete columns. Both have recessed corners from the first floor upwards, giving them a ziggurat form. Inside, concrete surfaces are evident thoughout. The central circulation space and foyer is described by Roca as a covered piazza, but, rather than a glazed canopy, it has a square, honeycomb roof, with deep soffits. While the music auditorium is partially lined out in timber, the library walls are all concrete, offset only by a narrow steel and glass rail to the mezzanine.

According to Roca, concrete is a material that is 'utilitarian and modest, potent and poor'. He likes the fact that it 'shows traces of its origin' and enjoys working with 'an aesthetic of imperfection', pointing out that the stone-like concrete finishes achieved on his projects in Japan and Switzerland, but not replicable in Argentina, look more like natural stone or tense fabric.

The library. Roca likes concrete for its modest, utilitarian qualities. Having no form of its own, it adapts to its framework and forms striking, flat, 'imperfect' surfaces.

Above
Four apparently similar, two-storey, monolithic blocks, constructed in varying proportions of black oxidized steel and concrete, are in fact subtly different. To the left is the 'blind-box' film department and to the right is the sculpture school.

Right
Sketches of the street façade (bottom) showing the lecture hall and sculpture department, and the façade of the film school with the sculpture department to the left (top).

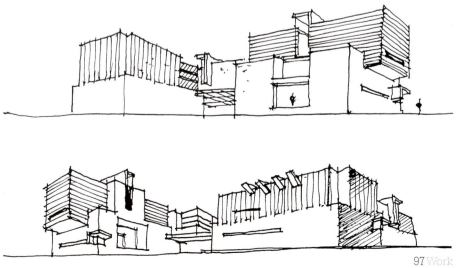

The entrance hall of the sculpture studio has panels of floor-to-ceiling glazing that allow light to flood into the space.

Street façade: the main music and drama auditorium on the right is distinguished by its four light boxes. The sculpture department is on the left.

Roca characterizes his work as being 'between a toned-down brutalism and minimalism'. He has completed many buildings for Córdoba University, which became the main educational, and artistic focus of Argentina in the seventeenth and eighteenth centuries. Founded in 1613, it is one of the oldest universities in Latin America.

Roca opened his own studio in 1970, and has taught in Argentina, the USA and Europe, as well as writing on Latin American architecture and producing a monograph on Louis Kahn, with whom he had studied at Pennsylvania University, before working for him for a year.

Roca has been called a one-man band, changing Córdoba on his own. From 1979 to 1998, he was Córdoba's secretary of public works, and his projects included the refurbishment of old markets, as well as several landscaping schemes, such as Plaza Italia, where three hillocks are topped by concrete cubes, each with another cube inside – somewhat similar to the concept for the School of Arts. He has also acted as town-planning architect and adviser to the governor of La Paz, Bolivia.

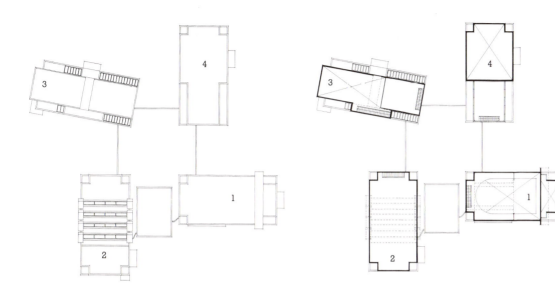
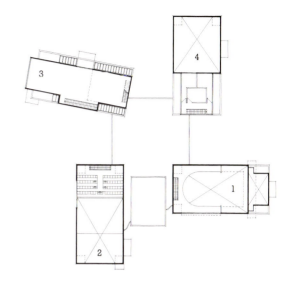

Above
From left: roof, first-floor and ground-floor plans.
1. drama department, 2. music department, 3. sculpture department, 4. film department.

To improve acoustics, a generous amount of timber was used in the experimental theatre (left) and the main auditorium (below).

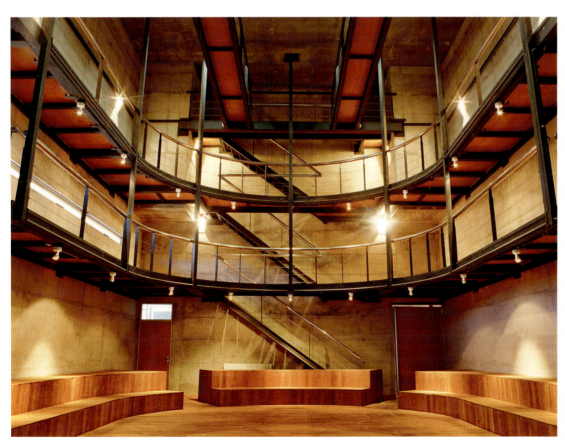

99 Work

Zenith Concert Hall and Exhibition Centre

Rouen, France, 2001
Bernard Tschumi

A contrast of materials is used to striking effect. The cavernous concrete lobby (below), with its open-riser stairs, is as impressive as the curved, corrugated-steel cladding of the exterior (left). The tilted masts hold the roof in place.

For most people, the initial view of Tschumi's edge-of-town concert hall is dominated by its curving corrugated-steel cladding, which is clearly visible from the nearby road to Paris. But the building's lobby is equally dramatic. The critic Suzanne Stephens has described this volume as combining 'the dynamic spaces of Piranesi with the tectonic concrete architecture of Auguste Perret', remarking on 'the consistency of vanilla pudding' achieved with the concrete (see *Architectural Record*, June 2001).

What makes the building so instantly impressive is the contrast between the outer skin – which seems almost to have sagged under its own weight, or to have been bent into a simple, embracing curve – and the solidity of the exposed structure within. There is no plinth to the building, and the walls are glazed to a height of 2.75 metres (9 feet) all round, an effect that is far more evident from inside than from out. Tschumi has concentrated on creating 'unprogrammed' spaces where, as he puts it, 'flows and vectors intersect'.

The contrasting materials are brought together straightforwardly, without any virtuosic detailing. 'There are no self-indulgent details à la Carlo Scarpa,' says Tschumi, and he explains that concrete was chosen because it is a good sound insulator (which is important, as there are houses nearby), and that a mixture of in situ and precast was used for reasons of structural economy.

The building is approached across a large-scale space, laid out with strips of concrete that are punctuated with points of light. The concrete inside the building is emphasized by uplighters. The rear façade is made entirely of exposed concrete, and is given an almost abstract treatment, with no attempt made to conceal the service ducts that sit above the band of glazing at the foot of the wall. Tschumi's declaration that 'everything is utilitarian' is something of an exaggeration, but, for all its geometric sophistication, the building has a direct and pragmatic spirit.

Rouen's Zenith Concert Hall and Exhibition Centre is one of a series of ten similar projects initially sponsored by the French Ministry of Culture in the 1980s to promote culture and commerce in deprived areas. (Located 110 kilometres (70 miles) from Paris, Rouen was once a thriving port, but is now economically depressed.) However, Tschumi's building is unusual in that its precursors were generally low-budget buildings on restricted inner-city sites, whereas his is a prestige building on a peripheral site. In fact, the 28.5 hectare (70 acre) site had been an airfield before the exhibition centre was constructed, and the project includes renovation of some of the industrial hangers, but also features a structure that would contribute to creating a new image for the city – it was important that it was finished in time for the local elections in March 2001.

The design is based on an earlier scheme that Tschumi devised in 1991 for a multi-use building in Chartres. The exisiting plan combined three elliptical walls of curved aluminium, with flat roofs suspended from masts. The concept has been simplified here to good effect. There are two, essentially concentric, envelopes, the outer one of steel and the inner of concrete. The outer skin is a broken torus – it is made up of two segments of hyperbolic form (not semicircular arcs, as might at first appear). They have slightly different radii, and one is tilted, which means that, rather than butting together, one segment overlaps the other at the point where they meet. This junction is used by Tschumi to create an elegant entrance, which is glazed to full height, with panels arranged like vertical paving slabs.

Within the lobby, it is the open-riser stairs and attenuated columns that dominate, and there are 15 separate entrances to the auditorium, which is an irregular fan shape. The auditorium can be divided into three and reconfigured for different sizes of audience. Able to seat up to 7,000 people, it is used for all sorts of events, including pop concerts and sporting fixtures. Transparent, acrylic foldable seating allows the concrete form to remain visible and the colour of the concrete to dominate the space. Cool air is delivered via the floor, and the whole front section of seating is removable. Commercial exhibitions are housed in the adjoining block, which runs to the south and is clad with glass and aluminium curtain walls; 215 metres (700 feet) long, it is a single, clear-span volume, slightly vaulted and 140 metres (459 feet) wide to allow maximum flexibility.

Tschumi won the commission for this project in an invited architectural competition. His practice has offices in New York and Paris, but, as a writer and Dean of Columbia University's graduate school for 15 years, he is known as a theorist, rather than a practitioner. His best-known built project, Parc de la Villette in Paris, has certainly strengthened this view, since the pavilions resemble large-scale theoretical models, and the project has become seminal in deconstructivist architecture. He is now building increasingly large projects, including the Le Fresnoy National Studio for Contemporary Arts at Tourcoing, France, which developed an even more dramatic 'in-between' space than the Rouen foyer – one sandwiched between the tiled roof of a pre-existing structure and a new steel envelope. He has also just finished an architecture school for Florida International University, Miami, where a wall of precast concrete panels is punctuated with regularly spaced punched windows, which contrasts with glazed elevations and brightly coloured, enamelled metal plates.

'I try not to rely on form over materials,' says Tschumi, who accepts that computer-generated designs can often ignore the importance of materials. In the Rouen project, he sees references to the work of Paul Nelson, to Oscar Nitzchke's cable-supported concrete Palace of Discovery project from 1938, and to the work of Expressionist Frederick Kiesler, but it has also been likened to a living form. One critic wrote that it has 'something of the movement of a living, breathing lung about it; its forms seem to ripple in and out.'

Above
The main entrance to the 7,000-seat auditorium is formed by two exaggerated and overlapping arcs of slightly different radii. The space between has been glazed from floor to ceiling, with panels arranged in a pavement pattern.

Left
Plan. 1. entrance, 2. auditorium, 3. backstage rooms

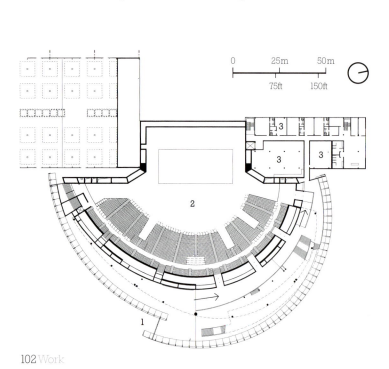

Above
The curvilinear walls seem to bulge outwards under their own great weight, but nevertheless 'float' on almost 3 metres (9 feet) of glazing. To the left is a glass and aluminium block, 213 metres (700 feet) long, which houses commercial exhibitions.

Below
Transverse section. 1. auditorium, 2. plenum, 3. suspended ceiling, 4. lightweight truss, 5. concrete enclosure, 6. lobby

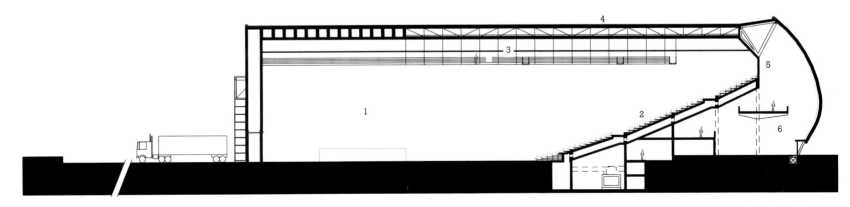

103 Work

Kemeter Paint Warehouse

Eichstätt, Germany, 1994
Hild und K Architekten

The warehouse glows at dusk when light pours through its irregularly shaped windows and from the exterior top-lighters, situated under the slightly protruding roof.

As foundations are difficult on a flood plain, the part-retail, part-wholesale warehouse was planned as a single-span hall for shelving. The prefabricated concrete truss is 28 metres (92 feet) long.

This initially austere-looking structure is less overtly witty than Hild und K Architekten's slightly later project of a screen wall, behind which to hide recycling containers, but both show an inventive use of standard precast elements to turn prosaic functional briefs into exciting sculptural forms.

It may seem perverse to design a building that will never need painting for a paint manufacturing company, but this is precisely what the practice has done. The exterior of this part-wholesale, part-retail outlet consists of fair-faced concrete, treated with a special mineral glaze that is designed to preserve its lively surface quality.

Since paint is highly flammable, it was essential to use a fireproof material. The longitudinal walls are constructed from standard precast-concrete panels, which come in a set width, but have six different lengths and three depths. These elements are arranged to create a vibrant pattern, while jiggling the lengths of the pieces allows three different window sizes to be formed. By day, the striated exterior looks almost woven.

A thicker element is used above each window, forming a protective hood over the flush glazing. Running full height to the top of the building, thinner panels create irregularly spaced recesses, at the top of which exterior lights are fitted. At night, the brightly illuminated windows read like notes on a long stave, with more light pouring downwards from the external fittings – as though the building is being freshly painted with light at the end of every day.

Since the warehouse sits on the floodplain of the River Altmühl, it was hard to construct foundations. A pre-stressed, single-span, concrete-truss structure was more cost-effective than several smaller spans with rows of internal supports. The trusses are set 6.25 metres (20 feet 6 inches) apart. The interior is therefore a simple open volume, a container for shelving. There is, however, a row of small cellular offices against one end, constructed over a special store for the company's most flammable products, such as solvents.

The base of the building is a chunky frost apron that incorporates insulation. This band is taken up and led asymmetrically around each of the main delivery doors, where a tougher edge is required. The architects describe the finish as a 'strangely irregular surface' – the result of not hand-finishing the panels, but leaving them 'rough as shaken' – in the state in which they left the vibrating table.

Goods are delivered via a low-level road to the 'light-washed' side of the building. Customers come to the other side, which was largely cast in situ, using broad, rough tongue-and-groove shuttering – in contrast to the smooth steel shuttering used for the prefabricated elements. This highly articulated panel is framed by a narrow band of glazing and two, slim recessed doorways, one at each end. There is a precast-concrete projecting cornice. By using a mix of precast and in situ concrete, the architects have given themselves a varied palette to create a sophisticated composition, focused on light and texture, rather than on colour.

The sides of the building use broad, rough, tongue-and-groove concrete shuttering.

Hild und K's subsequent 'Gold Containers' project in Landshut spells out the word SAMMELN, which means 'collect' in German, with a separate precast slab for each letter. The same perimeter formwork was used each time, and the separate letters achieved by rearranging the same two, small rectangular pieces of formwork. Up-ended and painted gold, they were erected between two standard-concrete prefabricated elements – a bus stop and a transformer station. The project was the focus of a special recycling campaign.

Hild und K Architekten was formed by Hamburg-born Andreas Hild and Tillmann Kaltwasser. Their interest in precast concrete and willingness to give the most prosaic of building types intense design scrutiny continues with a project for a sleek multi-storey car park – bands of undulating precast concrete across its façade create looping shadows internally and a sense of shimmering movement externally.

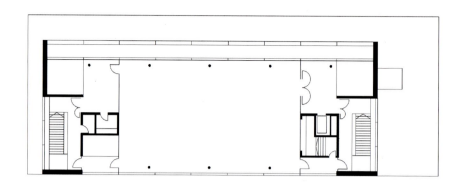

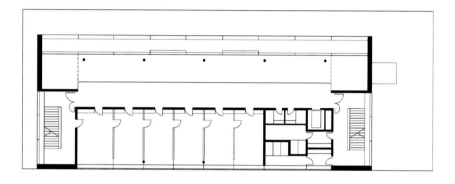

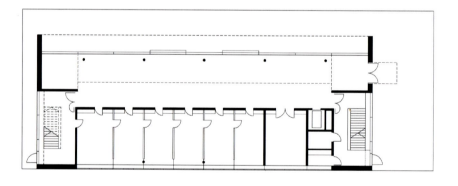

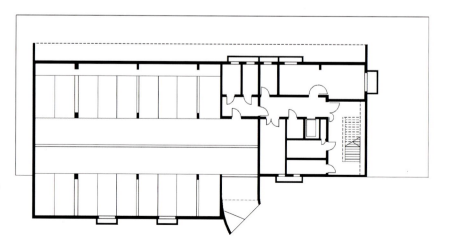

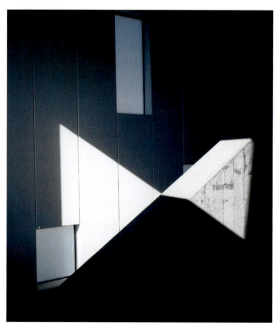

Left
The interior spaces are articulated by light and texture.

Right
From bottom: basement, ground-, first- and second-floor plans.

The building is constructed from prefabricated concrete panels of set widths but varying lengths and depths. These variations are orchestrated to form three window shapes as well as an undulating façade.

The back of the building was cast in situ and is freestanding under the roof truss. An office section has been placed between the axes, and the gap between this and the truss above it has been filled by a band of glass bricks.

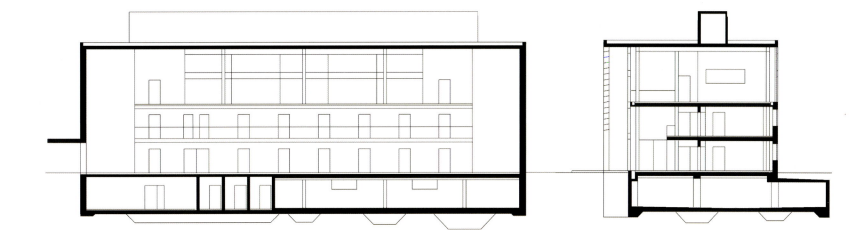

Above
From left to right: Long and short sections.

Right
In the 1996 'Gold Containers' project in Landshut, precast slabs were erected to form the word SAMMELN.

Far right
A close-up photograph of the paint warehouse reveals the subtle detail in the concrete used on the sides of the building.

The Laban Centre

London, UK, 2003
Herzog & de Meuron

The curving façade of this dance centre is a softly coloured double wall of polycarbonate sheeting, but inside is a complex arrangement of studios, performances spaces and teaching areas. It is both a community for staff and students, and a public venue. The use of concrete for the circulation ramps and staircases (as well as for the structural frame) is a practical solution, since these internal elements are subject to heavy wear, but concrete also contributes to the sense of a semi-external space and encourages students and visitors to congregate and mingle.

The concrete is a dense, glossy black – described by architect Michael Casey as 'like liquorice'. It is almost as if the murky, polluted world of the former industrial site has risen up and become solidified and contained. The black is, in fact, only a pigmented polyurethane coating, underneath which is standard grey concrete, but the surface has been bush-hammered, so that the black appears to run right through.

The plastic shininess of the concrete is the total antithesis of the blurry lime-turquoise and magenta washes of the skin, both in its colour and its apparently monolithic nature. Only the inner skin of the polycarbonate is pigmented (colour is added prior to the extrusion process), and a third layer of translucent glazing behind completes the sandwich. This forms a highly reflective, almost mirrored perimeter – wonderful for body-conscious dancers, whose indistinct shadows are visible from outside after dark. The curve of the skin is a response to the form of the steeple and cylindrical end-elevation of Thomas Archer's St Paul's Church (1712–30), arguably one of the few architecturally distinguished buildings in this part of south-east London.

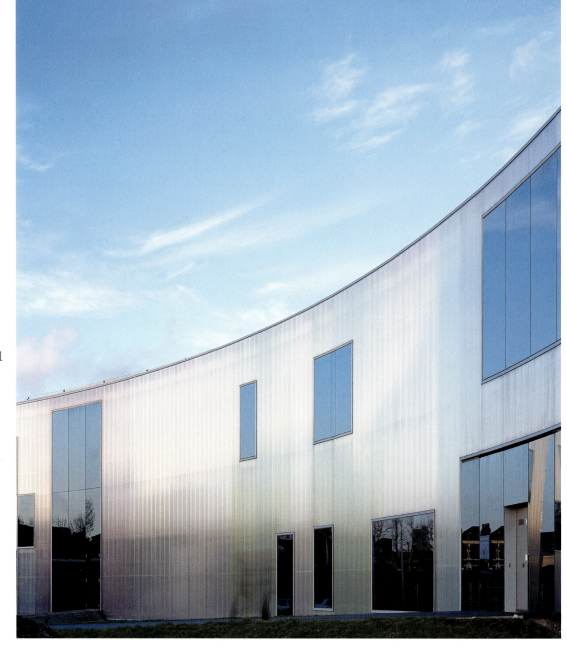

A concave double layer of softly coloured polycarbonate forms the front elevation.

Right
From bottom: plans of the ground and mezzanine levels.
1. dance studio, 2. circulation space, 3. stage, 4. auditorium, 5. courtyard, 6. library, 7. cafeteria, 8. lecture theatre, 9. therapy area, 10. staff area

Below
During the day, the skin of the centre is opaque, but at night shadowy forms can be seen moving behind the translucent walls.

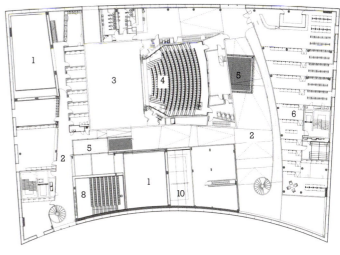

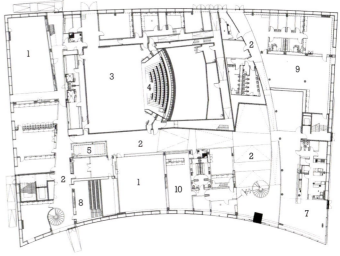

On entry, another gentle curve becomes apparent, cutting through the building in a scissored-ramp formation – a narrow, enclosed downward ramp and a much wider upward one. The former leads past the café (double-height at the front of the building) to more private therapy areas. The latter forms both the public access to the main performance space and the route to the primary cross corridor and to teaching and studio rooms. It leads to the library at the back of the building, which then gradually steps up, back across the depth of the building, with ends of rows of desks and bookstacks visible through a glazed screen wall. The research and academic study element of the building's programme is therefore clearly visible. This is important because the institution's founder was Rudolf Laban, an émigré from Nazi Germany, who developed 'Labanotation', a system of notation that records choreography, and who emphasized an academic approach to dance. His theories still dominate.

Finding one's way to the main performance area in this almost labyrinthine building is surprisingly straightforward. Artist Michael Craig-Martin, who collaborated with the architect on the use of colour throughout the building, has produced a computer-generated mural to delineate its shell. His black line drawings of everyday objects representing the five senses (for example, sunglasses and earphones) are an immediate visual draw from the entrance to the theatre. The downwardly projecting canted form of the end of the mossy courtyard, which pierces the upper floor, both provides a gathering space and allows light to penetrate. It appears to be propped up by a single, slender, bright-pink stilt, which is, in fact, a down pipe.

The corkscrew staircase is a quick route up to the top layer of the building and emerges as a circular concrete island at the broad end of a more private, tapering, magenta-coloured, street-like space, which has a view back to St Paul's Church. The stair can easily be shut off when a large audience is arriving or departing. Other circulation spaces are differentiated with similarly intense versions of the cladding pigments, with doors and lockers in jarring contrast. The dark-painted shadow gaps are like the black outlines in Craig-Martin's mural.

The Laban Centre has been compared to Rem Koolhaas's Kunsthal in Rotterdam, where galleries and lecture hall similarly consist of counterpoised slopes, arranged around a wedged-shaped ramp cutting through a basic box-like envelope. The use of materials recalls Bétrix and Consolascio's sports hall (2001) in Zug, Switzerland, which has a coloured-glass-panelled façade and black-pigmented concrete for internal service spaces.

Herzog and de Meuron studied in Zurich with Aldo Rossi. Their only other British project to date, Tate Modern, also has a sloped entrance ramp, but there it is the outer brick skin that is solid and an internal wall that is translucent. The collaboration with Craig-Martin is part of their work with artists, which in the past has included Thomas Ruff. Herzog & de Meuron's experience with concrete is varied and extensive, and includes, most famously, Ruff's images printed on the blocks of the Technical School in Eberswalde, Germany (see page 23). Casey says he admires concrete because it can provide 'structure, finish and space-making' and promises more innovative uses of the material to come.

Above
The interiors are surprising in their use of an unusual 'black' concrete. This is, in fact, ordinary grey concrete treated with a very darkly pigmented polyurethane.

Right
The exterior walls are lined in translucent glazing. The middle layer of polycarbonate has had a pigment added to it before the extrusion process, while the outer coating is clear. This extra-shiny, subtly hued shell acts as a foil to the monolithic 'black' concrete of the communal spaces.

Far right
The colour tints in the polycarbonate are taken up in the internal hues of the wedge-shaped corridors.

Mathematics, Statistics and Computer Science Building University of Canterbury

Christchurch, New Zealand, 1998
Architectus (with Cook Hitchcock Sargisson and Royal Associates)

Architectus was founded in 1987 in Auckland, New Zealand, and in 1994 won a competition to draw up a master plan for a new Mathematics, Statistics and Computer Science building and a science library at the University of Canterbury in Christchurch.

The completed MSCS building has two elements. Three seven-storey towers house postgraduates and staff. These are linked to a four-storey wing, where undergraduate teaching takes place. The skewed blade walls between each of the tower offices give the building its most dramatic face. It is as if each block has been dragged off alignment with the main grid of the university to face north, giving the impression that a solid building has been sliced up and rearranged, with the deep balconies suggesting fragments of internal spaces forcibly exposed. Squat piloti and stout brackets at the base add to this impression and create the appearance of a building that can pivot and rotate, like a windmill swinging to catch the breeze.

The architects have explained that concrete was an obvious choice of material, rather than something lightweight, since much of the university's existing architecture, and, indeed, the city of Christchurch itself, is constructed in concrete. The design of the MSCS building has been compared both to local buildings, such as Warren and Mahoney's university Students' Union, which has concrete beams that extend beyond their supporting piers, and to the work of Louis Kahn, especially the Salk Institute in La Jolla, California. The comparison to Kahn has been made, in part, because there is a direct lineage – the design leader for Architectus was Patrick Clifford, who had worked in London for Turkish architect Ilhan Zeybekoglu, who, in turn, had been taught by Kahn.

The brief for the project specifically asked for north-facing offices (so that staff would be able to enjoy both sunshine and views across the flat plain to the southern Alps). It was suggested that these could be organized in a 'clustered arrangement' with 'an associated "common area" for staff uses and student-waiting', as an alternative to a more traditional corridor arrangement. The solution that was eventually adopted has groups of ten rooms, each accessible from a shared double-height space. In total, there are 90 offices, arranged around nine double-height areas – so the basic configuration is stacked three high in each tower. As well as encouraging social interaction between staff and students, these double-height spaces (which include a staircase) have made good informal tutorial locations and are horizontally linked at each level by walkways.

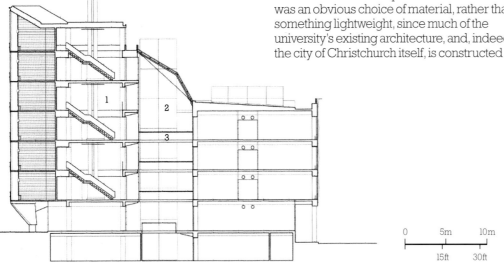

Above and left
Three seven-storey tower blocks, linked by skewed blade walls, house staff and postgraduate research facilities. They are connected by a circulation zone to a four-storey teaching wing.

Opposite
Short section.
1. double-height common space, 2. atrium, 3. bridge

The fin walls of the academic offices use precast Thermomass concrete panels, so that three functions – structure, insulation and finish – are served in a single, monolithic element. The panels consist of a layer of expanded foam insulation between two layers of concrete, the former thicker than the latter – 150 millimetres (6 inches) versus 70 millimetres (2 ³/₄ inches) – which maximizes the wall's ability to moderate temperature extremes. The floors, also constructed from precast units, have a sine-wave form to their underside, creating an air-movement duct within the floor depth; this increases the surface area of the ceiling and allows the concrete structure to have an increased passive heating or cooling effect.

The timbered screening system on the balconies adds a colourful articulation to the otherwise monochromatic walls.

Concrete was used to blend in with the rest of the university and with the city of Christchurch itself. The walls of this classroom wing include a surprising amount of glazing, which creates a sense of 'illumination'.

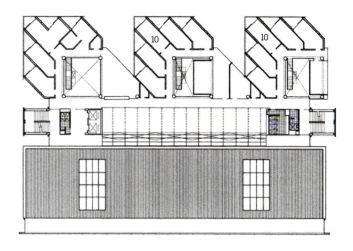

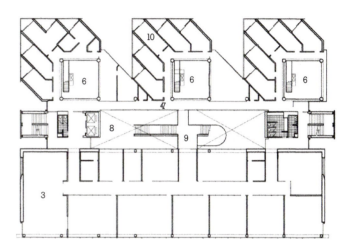

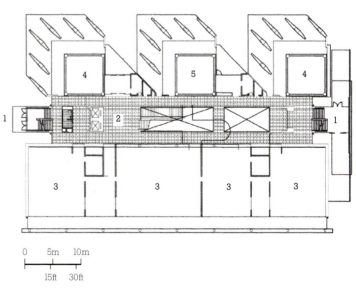

Top
Ninety academic offices are stacked in ten suites around double-height spaces (three in each tower). Breakout areas, such as the one shown here, are used for informal study and research.

Right
Barely visible from the exterior, the central atrium is unexpectedly dramatic. It is the major social space within the complex and contains the main staircase. Walkways link the teaching and academic areas at every level.

Far right
From bottom: ground-, fourth- and fifth-floor plans.
1. entrance, 2. concourse, 3. computer lab, 4. tutorial room, 5. work room, 6. double-height communal space, 7. walkway, 8. atrium, 9. bridge, 10. office

119 Work

LOOK UP Office Headquarters

Gelsenkirchen, Germany, 1998
Anin Jeromin Fitilidis & Partner

Like quartz within a stone, a glass box is wrapped in concrete. Designed for a young international advertising agency, the offices have three floors – two fully glazed creative zones and a concrete ground floor for production.

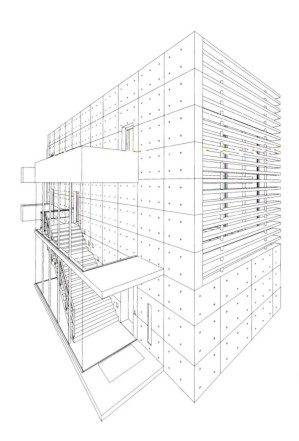

Anin Jeromin Fitilidis & Partner explain the defining principle behind their design of this headquarters building as maximizing the contrast between the heavy, monolithic concrete walls and the lightness of the glass façades. It is a very small structure, but one with a great deal of presence – just what the advertising company who commissioned it was seeking.

The concrete walls use a construction method not previously tried in Germany. There are two layers of concrete, both cast in situ, using yellow pine formwork. The inner load-bearing skin, cast first, has a thickness of 17 centimetres (6½ inches); it is separated from the outer 10 centimetre (4 inch) skin by 8 centimetres (3 inches) of insulation. The outer skin is so slender that it would buckle unless supported, so it is fixed back to the inner one by cast-in-place masonry anchors. In addition to the glass façades, floors were chosen to contrast with the concrete surfaces – white epoxy on the ground floor and Jurassic sandstone in the offices. This contrast is emphasized on the balconies, where a concrete strip 10 centimetres (4 inches) wide edges the sandstone.

The building is a simple three-storey plan, with the production department on the ground floor and the two floors above referred to as the 'creativity zone'. The entrance to the offices is at the foot of the main stair, which fills a projecting rectangular volume and takes visitors past the production studio and up to the double-height reception area. The projection has three glass walls, with the glass set directly into grooves in the concrete, so no framing is required. The fourth side is the main concrete wall, first seen from outside, but now experienced close up. The design offices are on the first and second floors in the northern half of the building, with loads carried on steel columns at 6 metre (19½ foot) centres. Internal subdividing walls are made of frameless glass, apart from the solid cores, which house the kitchen and toilets. Each office includes access to a small projecting concrete balcony, like a pop-out pulpit. Above the main stair is a much larger balcony, which opens off the conference room and also acts as a fire-escape refuge.

At the building's south end is a wall of concrete louvres, resembling a vast industrial air grill, suggesting intense production inside. This is the only part of the building to use precast-concrete elements. The building as a whole reads as a set of interrelated planes and boxes. From the south-west, the structure looks like a box, but at night the staircase is lit up, taking on the appearance of a freestanding smaller box in front of a stage-like concrete backdrop; from the north-west corner, the concrete looks like an punctured screen in front of a floating glass box. The west façade has two uninterrupted floors of larch-framed glazing (all the ventilation is via openings in the concrete sections and in the roof) over-sailing a concrete plinth. For a small building, there is a lot going on.

The LOOK UP offices were the second building on a new industrial estate created on reclaimed land in Gelsenkirchen, a small industrial town near Essen, in western Germany. The architects hope that their project has set a high standard for subsequent developments, and justifiably claim that they have achieved a 'pure and significant' design solution to a fairly standard brief and an unpromising location. They are a young firm, but have already built a successful precast-concrete building – an administrative office in Krefeld for the coffee-machine company bonOFFICE. The structure, which had to be completed in eight months, buries storage facilities underground in a structure of precast riveted components, which also act as a grass-covered 'socket' for the superstructure.

Concrete balconies protrude from the glass cube, offering access to the open air and a secondary escape route.

Since the aim was to emphasize the immateriality of the office spaces, opening windows (which would need heavy frames) could not be used. Apertures in the concrete façade and on the roof provide ventilation.

Above
Detail of the glass-enclosed staircase.

Below
Clockwise from bottom right: gound-, first- and second-floor plans. 1. entrance, 2. toilet, 3. production, 4. deliveries, 5. reception, 6. office, 7. kitchen, 8. conference room

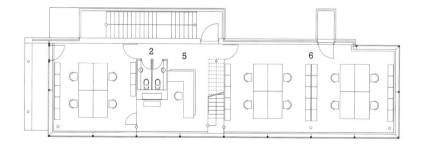

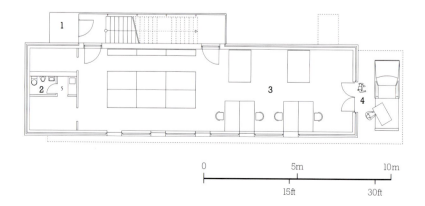

The concrete leaf panels on the southern side of the building are formed from precast components. The main stairwell is enclosed on three sides by a glass façade.

The west elevation has a brise-soleil of cantilevered concrete blades.

123 Work

Lecture Hall 3, University of Alicante

Alicante, Spain, 2001
Javier Garcia-Solera

This lecture hall at the University of Alicante in Spain was designed and constructed as fast as possible to provide urgently needed additional accommodation for the institution. It is the result of only a month and a half's work in the office and six months on site. There was no scope for the overall size of the cramped campus to be extended, so a decision was made to halt the building of a block of parallel warehouses that was going up at the edge of the site. The location is not glamorous – indeed, the architects describe it as 'highly hostile'. It lies outside the ring road that surrounds the pedestrianized area of the campus and is flanked by car parks. For reasons of cost and time, the foundations of the planned warehouses had to be used, imposing a further constraint.

The existing foundations' load-bearing strength meant that only a single-storey structure was possible. To overcome the limitations of the 5 x 10 metre (16$^{1}/_{2}$ x 33 foot) grid, which had been intended solely for utilitarian storage purposes, a structure of concrete walls and slabs was designed that could fly in any direction from the supporting foundations. The brief required the building to contain several lectures halls of a variety of sizes, some offices and a small shop. The challenge for the architects was to how to fit these onto the prescribed floor plan, while at the same time achieving an elegant design.

The solution was to construct seven buildings with identical floor plans. The front two vary in section, but the remaining five are identical. A series of lightweight metal bridges link the blocks, which all look onto inner courtyards between the buildings. In some instances, a complete slice of a block has been omitted to provide a more generous open area for relaxation and enjoyment. Although the courtyards are narrow in form, they are planted with trees, which penetrate through the bridges, lending the project as a whole the air of a section of wooded park. In contrast to the full glazing on the long elevations, the short ends of each block are formed of solid, horizontally banded concrete. Like a row of sturdy bookends, they function as a tough outer shield against the car parks that come right up to the site.

Cost restraints meant that existing foundations for planned warehouses had to be adapted. These had low loadbearing strength, restricting the edifice to a single storey.

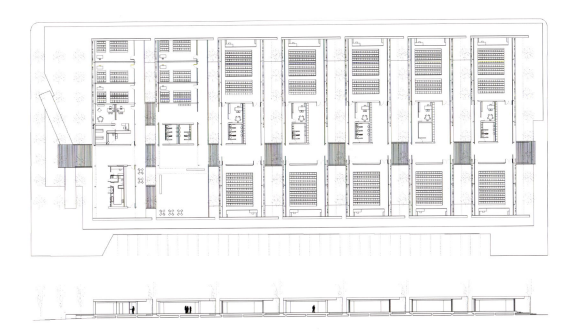

Left
From bottom: section and plan.

Below left
To maximize the size of the inner courtyards, and create areas for recreation and informal meetings, whole sections of some of the blocks have been cut away.

Below right
The blocks, which have identical floor plans, are linked by planted longitudinal inner courtyards.

Garcia-Solera chose in situ concrete for several reasons. He admires what he calls 'the sincerity' of the material, the fact that it does not have an applied surface or covering, but he also sees it as the material best suited to creating the sense of a natural environment, in this case the wooded park. While some architects use concrete to express continuity between the mass of the ground and their building, this structure seems to float, with the trees securing it to the earth. Although Garcia-Solera insists that what he likes most about concrete is 'the fact that you can resolve everything – structure, floor, ceiling and façades – with the same material', in this instance he has used concrete for the walls and slabs only. To aid speed of construction, the building is framed with metal columns, and there is a metal roof system.

Below
Concrete was chosen not only because it can be mass-produced at low cost and erected quickly, but also because of its 'sincerity'. It presents a natural-looking foil to the trees in the inner courtyards.

Top left
The long elevations are fully glazed.

Left
In accordance with a predetermined floor plan, the building had to accommodate lecture halls, offices and a shop. Seven separate blocks were built from concrete cast in situ.

Top right
Located on the outskirts of the campus, the site is surrounded by car parks, which come close to the building itself. To make it more appealing, Garcia-Solera has planted trees, which have yet to mature.

Right
The courtyards allow light to penetrate into the middle of the blocks without the need to open up the façades.

Haus der Architektur

Munich, Germany, 2002
Drescher + Kubina

The north façade was cast in situ and articulated by two bands of glazing on the first and second floors, and by floor-to-ceiling windows in the lecture room on the third floor.

The Haus der Architektur provides a new home for the Bavarian Chamber of Architects, which had outgrown its base in a 1924 villa. Drescher + Kubina's pristine building sits alongside the villa in a parkland site of 6,000 square metres (64,500 square feet), providing a venue for public programmes, as well as services for the 1,700 architect members of its client organization.

While the villa is a symmetrical composition facing the road, the new building runs back from it at a right angle. It is a slim block made of glass and in situ concrete, with a simple internal division of space on the main floors – circulation to the south and habitable rooms to the north. The south façade, looking towards the villa, is fully glazed and recessed in a panoramic concrete frame.

The foyer runs along this elevation – a double-height volume with a cantilevered first-floor gallery giving access to a single row of small offices. The series of slim concrete columns does not align with the external glazing mullions, but, in combination with the regular spacing of door openings, creates the impression of a separate internal rhythm. The doorframes are narrow steel sections, and the doors themselves single sheets of toughened glass (including those that link the individual offices, so that the whole enfilade arrangement can be seen from within each one). The openings from the foyer read as dark, equal-sized rectangles. The place has an otherworldliness that is enhanced by the absence of a visible linking stair and by the glowing band of light – the only artificial lighting – that comes from fluorescent fittings in a narrow recess between walls and ceiling. The second floor consists of a large lecture hall, which also functions as a reception space, and which is glazed on both sides, with views out at treetop level.

Concrete was selected in part for its thermal qualities – for environmental reasons, the architects did not want to use mechanical cooling. Brises-soleil cast wonderful patterns on the austere interior walls and the floors are made of semi-reflective poured asphalt.

Drescher + Kubina cite environmental considerations as their main reason for choosing in situ concrete. They wanted the building to be naturally ventilated, and not to require mechanical cooling. Concrete provides a high thermal mass, which helps to regulate temperature – especially important in a structure with so much glazing. But the architects have also exploited concrete's aesthetic qualities. On the façades the day-work joints are clearly visible, and on the north and end elevations they align with glazing mullions that sit flush with the concrete surface. The projecting entrance porch reads as if a flap of wall has simply been lifted up to give rudimentary shelter. From inside, the end elevations deliberately contradict the basic internal layout – one sees stairs to the north and solid wall to the south. The concrete stairs, enclosed internally, look like two taut diagonals, with smooth concrete soffits and barely visible balustrades.

The overall crispness of form, the precision of the glazing and the sharpness of the corners all act to emphasize the contrast between the old villa and the new language of Drescher + Kubina's project.

The smooth concrete stairs, their balustrades barely visible, seem to hang in mid-air.

Left
Outgrown by the Bavarian Chamber of Architects, the 1924 villa (right) was replaced by a new building (left) that houses services and provides a venue for public events and other functions.

Above and left
The south elevation is fully glazed. The top floor accommodates a lecture theatre, which has windows to the north as well, creating light and 'open' space among the treetops.

Armani Headquarters and Theatre

Milan, Italy, 2002
Tadao Ando Architect and Associates

Fashion designer Giorgio Armani commissioned Tadao Ando to convert an industrial building in the suburbs of Milan into his world headquarters, complete with its own theatre for staging fashion shows. This large, low brick structure was formerly a Nestlé chocolate factory. 'Our main aim,' says Tadao Ando, 'was the creation of "flexible" space that enables cooperation and fusion with the disciplines of art and music.' Construction in concrete is generally perceived as being at odds with long-term adaptability, but Ando has created a space that can be easily reconfigured without departing from his signature material.

From the exterior, there is little clue to the interior transformation that has taken place. Conservation rules prevented alterations to the outside. There is just a modest sign and some inset panels of translucent glass. The entrance consists of a sliding glass panel, from where a corridor 100 metres (330 feet) long slopes gently upwards, penetrating through the building towards the theatre. What Ando describes as a 'colonnaded approach' (a passageway with a central spine of concrete columns) leads past two showrooms to a tilted, arc-shaped concrete wall that encloses the theatre-foyer space. While the square section columns of the passageway are freestanding monoliths and clearly not structural, the circular cross-section columns in the foyer penetrate the white plaster ceiling, and their separation is emphasized by recessed lighting in the void. Add to this the way in which the curved wall leans (made all the more obvious by the triple opening in it), and it seems as if the concrete elements are as movable as the internally lit glass reception tables, which can be instantaneously wheeled away. By contrast, the outer skin of the original building has permanence and solidity. The interstitial spaces between it and the theatre are especially powerful, including the space above the auditorium, where the cove-lit ceiling vault is cut away to show the original steel-framed butterfly roof and clerestory.

To the side of the theatre is a gallery, separated from the adjacent showrooms by an internal pool. The gallery doubles as a dining room or reception hall, depending on the event planned, and features a long, low window that encourages both seated or standing guests to glance out across the reflective surface of the water.

Although the project is beautifully finished, there were problems with construction, and Ando has expressed frustration at the lack of control he had when working on a project so far from Japan. He found the level of construction skills in Milan unexpectedly low, and some of the concrete had to be recast. 'Several times, when problems piled up at more than one site, I have come close to abandoning the whole idea of doing any more overseas work,' he says, explaining that his office regards foreign projects as 'onerous'. However, he is, to use his own words, still keen to 'jump at offers of new jobs', since his 'desire to create architecture is simply too powerful'. This highly commercial brief has proved that Ando's skills can suit a dynamic, as well as a contemplative, environment.

Opposite
The entrance is by way of a narrow, colonnaded passageway 100 metres (330 feet) long, which belies the grandeur of the foyer in which it culminates.

Below
The original building was a brick-constructed chocolate factory. Ando was briefed to turn this industrial site into a cultural centre by adding new, independent spaces.

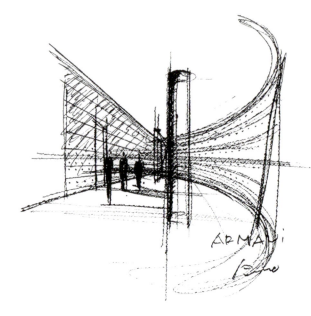

Right
Sketch of the curved foyer.

Below and opposite
A massive, slanting concrete wall defines the foyer. Glowing reception desks, recessed lighting and a trio of oblique cutaway openings add to the other-worldly luminescence of the area.

Right
Braced by polished steel rods, the gallery's cove-lit vaulted ceiling is dramatically cut away to reveal the original steel-framed butterfly roof and clerestory.

Above
The gallery/dining hall extends along one side of an internal court with a reflecting pool (not illustrated). Visitors are encouraged to look out at the pool through a band of low windows.

Opposite top
Sketch of the theatre with the hallway and curved foyer to the left.

Opposite
Plan showing the theatre (A) and the three possible variations in seating arrangements (B, C and D).
1. foyer, 2. banqueting space, 3. backstage, 4. storage, 5. catering, 6. water court, 7. showroom, 8. court, 9. office

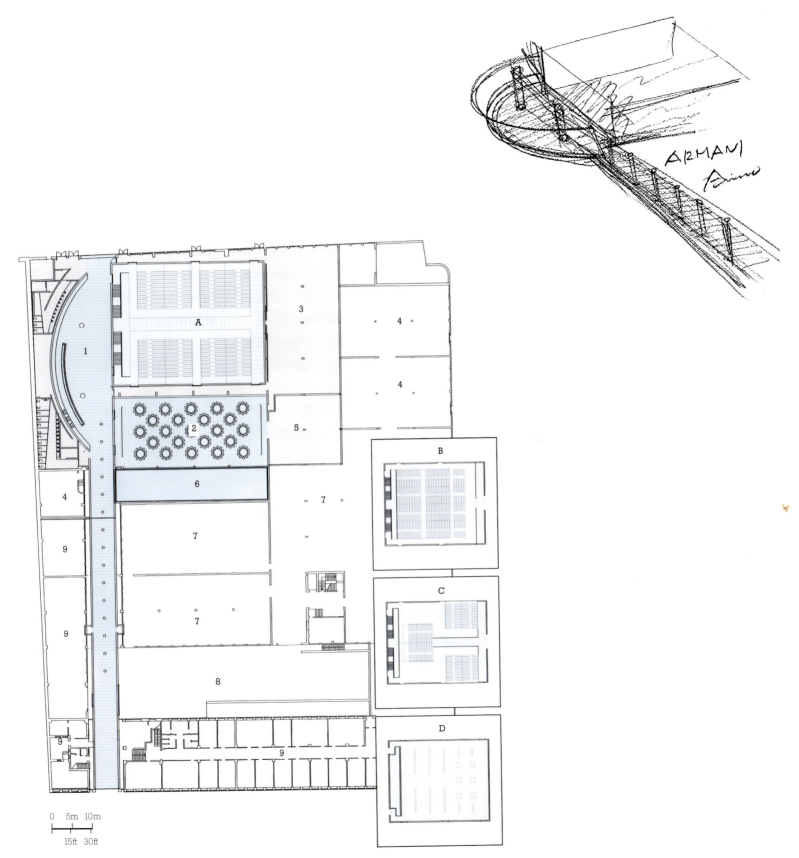

Chapter 3
Play

Since the 1960s the use of concrete for new museums has become relatively commonplace. It seems that it is the monumentality of concrete and its sense of permanence that makes this the case. The perception of concrete as an austere material with a neutral colour, and as the quintessential material of modernism, has also made it an especially popular choice for museums displaying modern art in particular. Perhaps the memory of process evoked by the texture and surface of concrete is even seen as subliminally appropriate, and the use of a 'difficult' material for the context of challenging works (both aesthetically and symbolically) a comfortable fit. When Frank Lloyd Wright's Guggenheim Museum opened in New York in 1959, the building received much criticism for the way in which the enforced downward circulation dominated the art on view. But admirers emphasized the formal genius of the cantilevered concrete floor that allowed a single, continuous spiral space. At Marcel Breuer's Whitney Museum of American Art (1966) in New York, the stepped inverted ziggurat forms of the façade were created using in situ-cast concrete, which was then faced in granite. Inside, the exhibition spaces were kept as flexible as possible with precast, open-grid, suspended concrete ceilings. Tsien and Williams, the architects of the nearby American Folk Art Museum (see page 170), cite the Whitney's concrete entrance staircase as one of their influences.

The myriad finishes and effects made possible by concrete are well represented in the examples featured here. Concrete is not just suitable for slick, urban gallery spaces. At the Fishing Museum in Karmøy, Norway (page 148), the surface was covered in yogurt to promote the growth of a particular type of local lichen, linking this distinctly contemporary structure with the surrounding landscape. The robust precast concrete sections of Page and Park's Museum of Scottish Country Life (see page 154) reflect the local industrial vernacular in a blunt contrast to the twee glamorization of many 'countryside' visitor attractions.

Special finishes and mixtures have also been used to acknowledge historical context or to celebrate the contents of museum structures. At the Oskar Reinhart Collection, Winterthur, Switzerland (see page 162), the concrete mixture used for this extension to an existing structure of 1915 incorporates ground-up materials also used in the original building. This not only links the two buildings materially, but also means that the surface of the new extension will quickly age and form a patina more sympathetic to its neighbour. The polished concrete used to face the Kunstmuseum in Vaduz, Liechtenstein (see page 178) was treated and finished as if it were a costly stone, fitting given the treasures contained within.

By contrast, the big advantage that concrete brings to the sports buildings featured in this chapter is that of toughness and durability – the rawness of the outside world brought pragmatically indoors, combined with the memory of the iconic sports buildings of the mid-twentieth century, such as Pier Luigi Nervi's Palazzo dello Sport in Rome (1958) and Lindegren and Jäntti's Helsinki Olympic Tower (1952). Concrete's functionality is ideally suited to the two municipal swimming-pool projects in Spain (see pages 140 and 166), while at Rémy Marciano's Marseilles gymnasium (page 144) the gritty urban aesthetic of the patchwork concrete blocks is complemented by the elegant, glazed light boxes on top. But, in some instances, this material's practicality is combined with a lyrical quality, the sensuous use of concrete in many cases inspired by Peter Zumthor's Thermal Spa at Vals, Switzerland – a much publicized building of 1996 – where concrete and natural stone are combined to create a sense of calm, austere beauty.

Tussols-Basil Bathing Pavilion

Olot, Girona, Spain, 1998
RCR Arquitectes

Ramon Vilalta, Carmen Pigem and Rafael Aranda grew up in the small Catalan town of Olot before studying architecture in Barcelona. On graduating in 1989, they returned to Olot to set up a practice together. Vilalta explains, 'We know our place. We need our peace to work and think.' Each partner has declined teaching and lecturing opportunities to concentrate on building, and the partnership has managed to find support and clients for a series of uncompromisingly modern, frequently minimalist buildings in a conservative and traditional location.

The bathing pavilion is perhaps the starkest of their designs and has the most beautiful setting. It is made of oxidized iron and stainless steel, but its coloured concrete plinth, so low that it is almost flush with the ground, is also an important part of the composition. Although from a distance the structure reads as a straight bar, it is, in fact, a very gentle crescent with a monopitch roof, echoing the slope of the bank and the soft curves of the gently flowing river – across the flat reflective surface of which the structure is best seen. This mesmeric, highly sculptural building has a prosaic function. It was commissioned by the local town council to provide basic facilities for park activities. Each of the three wedge-shaped stainless-steel boxes houses a separate shower, WC and changing room, with a flush steel door for each box, so that the three elements read as solid forms almost prizing apart the slim steel bars of roof and base. At the opposite end of the pavilion, there is a small bar, encased in a oxidized-iron box – a bunker-like haven in foul weather, and a hub to serve larger numbers of customers on good days.

Top
Although, at first glance, the pavilion appears to be straight, it is, in fact, slightly curved to reflect the meandering course of the nearby river.

Bottom
When closed, the flush-fitting doors give the changing room a sense of solidity, but they open to reveal a generous space inside.

Three stainless-steel boxes – containing toilets, a shower and changing rooms – stand between an oxidized-metal roof and a coloured-concrete base. To the left is a small, oxidized-iron drinks counter.

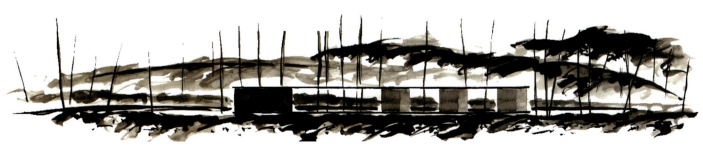

The concrete is constructed in paving slabs 8 millimetres (⅓ inch) thick, containing quartz particles and black colouring materials. The result is a highly polished and reflective finish.

Like the oxidized-metal soffit, the concrete flooring is darkly reflective. It is made of large paving slabs 8 millimetres (1/3 inch) thick, cast with quartz particles and black colouring material. These span the full width of the pavilion, resting on a tongue-and-groove insulating base. The edge of this sandwich is finished with a metal section, giving a crispness and linking it to a generous terrace of the same construction and footprint. It is as if the structure had shifted sideways, but remains tightly constrained, the terrace being the shadow of where the building once stood.

From the terrace, the views of the park are framed by the voids between the elements, and the palette of building materials blends with the colours and textures of the landscape. Aranda says that all three partners want to make 'architecture of value, well-set in the landscape, and with formality and restraint. Our parameters are order, clarity, clear composition. Horizontality, volumes and spaces are very strong themes with us.' The practice is now working on a larger scale, with commissions for law courts in Tarragona and the aquatics centre for the Universal Forum of Cultures in Barcelona.

'Horizontality, volumes and spaces' are the architects' key themes. Born and bred in Olot, the partners have returned to their native town to design a series of uncompromisingly modern and often minimalist buildings in a traditionally conservative area.

Below and below right
Section and plan.

The pavilion is in harmony with its setting. The browns, greys and black of the materials used in its construction complement the colours of the winter landscape, while in spring and summer the polished surfaces reflect the fresh greens of the countryside.

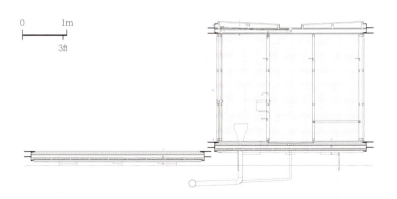

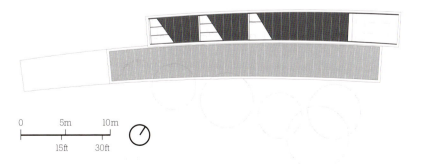

143 Play

Ruffi Gymnasium

Marseilles, France, 2001
Rémy Marciano

Top
A cruciform window in the end wall of the changing room frames the church of St Martin, which is situated north-west of the site.

Above
Light boxes over the gymnasium bring a daylight quality to the cavernous space below. To prevent glare between the clerestories and the opaque concrete walls, the upper parts are clad in reflective stainless steel.

Rémy Marciano's Ruffi Gymnasium is part of his scheme for the redevelopment of a whole city block as a sports complex, with outdoor sports pitches and gardens for *pétanque* (the Provençal version of boules). The gymnasium's solid base contrasts with its superstructure. The patchwork of differently toned concrete panels provides a deliberately tough aesthetic, whereas the three interconnecting light boxes above look as if they are carefully balanced and might even move. They overshoot the walls, and at night, when the building is lit up inside, light washes down the concrete.

The site for the building was a run-down part of the Marseilles waterfront. A gigantic regeneration project of a 300 hectare (740 acre) area began in 1995, with a combination of public and private investment. Underneath the site runs a new freight-train tunnel, and to the north-west is the church of St Martin. The complex history of the location inspired the architect, Rémy Marciano. 'In Marseilles, the history of beliefs is often mingled with the world of sport,' he says, and it is the energy he finds inherent in this essentialist mix that has permeated the project.

The view of the west door of the church is framed by the glazed doors at the end of the corridor that links the changing rooms to the gym itself. This is in fact an entrance, and the narrow outdoor space leading to it, between the two blocks of the building, is also on an axis with the church and flanked by a single cruciform window punched through the end wall of the changing block. The building's form refers to the ubiquitous concrete sheds of the area's more recent industrial past, and it has been described as 'already looking like a derelict factory' – a comment no doubt intended to be derogatory, but one which can in this context be taken as a compliment. Marciano also sees the influence of more domestic sheds or chalet structures.

The gym stands at the site's top corner. Entry into the complex is in the middle of the block, which Marciano feels parallels the main entrance to the church. The colour differentiation on the concrete panels is achieved by using various types of varnish, and the structure is a steel frame, with a roof of exposed steel girders. The light boxes cover only the gym itself, and the pitch of the roofs is set by the requirements of the aluminium roofing material. The sides and overhanging bases of each are made not of glass, but of polycarbonate sheet.

Inside, in order to minimize the potential problems of glare that might be caused by the juxtaposition of the glazed top portions of the walls with the solid wall beneath, the upper part of these walls, with their sloping or jagged tops, are sheathed in reflective stainless steel.

Marciano set up his practice in his home town in 1996, and has already completed several housing schemes, a high school and a bus drivers' staff room, all in Marsailles. The latter is located in a park and has an outer skin of metal sheet, perforated with a leaf pattern – another patterned exterior. He says his aim is to design buildings that encapsulate 'the life of the people, their memories and the land itself', and his projects combine a strong geometry with a sense of underlying narrative that is almost domestic. Thus, he has described the gymnasium as 'a mineral plinth on which float boxes of light', but in using the French word *socle*, which can be used to describe the base of a lamp as well as a plinth, he is suggesting something simultaneously both grand and homely.

Above
The colour in the concrete is achieved by using different types of varnish.

Right
Plan of the gymnasium. The roof light boxes are indicated by the dotted lines.

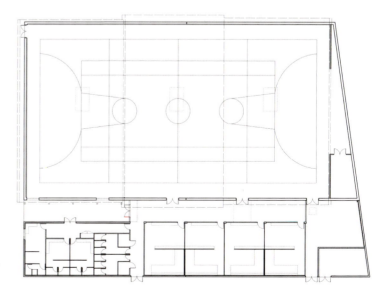

145 Play

Above
Three giant light boxes sit on top of concrete blocks constructed in panels of varying shapes and colours. Protruding from the roof, they create a wash of light over the walls at night.

Below
Long section.

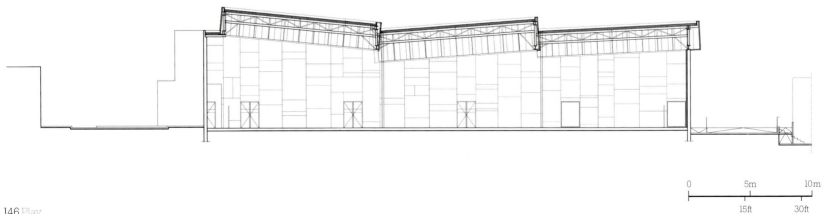

146 Play

Above
The sides and overhanging bases of the light boxes are built from polycarbonate sheet.

Right
Marciano's architecture is strongly geometric and well suited to its setting. The sports complex responds to the warehouse vernacular of semi-industrial Ruffi.

Fishing Museum

Karmøy, Norway, 1998
Snøhetta

Made from a green-tinted concrete, covered by an epoxy coating, the floor reflects the light that pours through the large panels of the glazed end façade.

The most unusual aspect of the use of concrete in this project was the desire to achieve a naturally aged appearance as soon as possible. It rains a lot on this remote part of the Norwegian coast and the architects like the moss and lichen that grows on the rocks as a result. Unfortunately, however, these lichens do not readily grow on concrete, so experiments were done to see what would encourage them. Various fertilizers were studied to see if they would address the problem – either by being added to the concrete mix or applied to the surface after drying. Yet it transpired that they were all too acidic and degraded the concrete. The solution, in fact, was found to be yogurt. A coating of the stuff was applied to the building and left for several weeks until the spores had settled. It seems to be working.

The elongated, box-like form of the museum stands above a small saltwater inlet. In effect, it is an enclosed passageway, 45 metres (148 feet) long and 7 metres (23 feet) wide, pointing towards the fjord and running parallel to an old gravel track. Its primary structure is in situ concrete, with individual panels measuring about 1.5 square metres (16 square feet).

Snøhetta principal Kjetil Thorsen and project architect Lisbeth Funk grew up on the island of Karmøy, a day's drive north-west of Oslo, where the practice is now based. It is an area of traditional structures, but Snøhetta describe their project as as 'a more neutral, sculptural form, delicately placed in the landscape'. They made a positive decision not to adopt local forms or techniques. Neither does their building have a traditional relationship to the terrain. The fully glazed end wall looks as if it is sliding clear of its envelope, about to launch off into the water 20 metres (65 feet) below. As Funk puts it, 'The building lies firmly on the ground, but looks as if you could take it away.' It is a landmark structure, heftier than a shed, but not dug into the ground, so that it maintains a sense of detachment.

The museum is entered at the landward end, and visitors are drawn towards the fjord. The green-tinted concrete floor is treated with an epoxy that makes it reflect the sky, so it looks like an extension of the sea flowing into the building. A small section of the ground floor houses ancillary services, but most of the building is given over to a single exhibition space, a wood-clad volume with a metal roof 6 metres (20 feet) high. A plywood ramp rises, via a landing that gives a raised view of the fjord, to a mezzanine, which is two-thirds of the way up the building and lined with floor-to-ceiling windows on each side. From here, there are lateral views out over the sheep meadow.

Externally, one of the large side windows is flanked by a framed wall, clad with a panel of woven juniper branches, a local form of thatch. This was hand-made by friends of the museum, mostly pensioners in their seventies, and it took them 450 hours to do. While structural concrete is hard to adapt, this section could be removed easily if a second concrete box adjoining this one gets the go-ahead.

Left
The east-facing front entrance is at ground level.

Below
Section showing the ground-level entrance ramp on the right and the overhanging west end on the left.

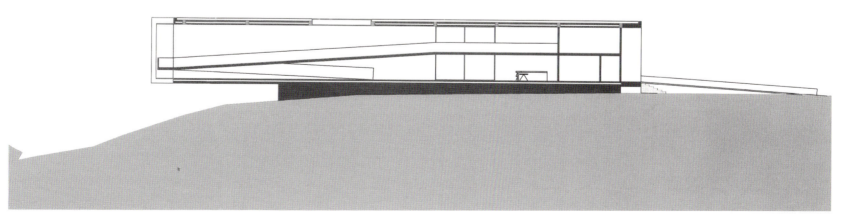

The fully glazed end elevation is cantilevered out over the sloping site.

151 Play

Above
The architects added a coating of yogurt to the surface of the concrete to encourage lichen spores to develop. Lichen is a prominent feature of the area's smooth grey-green rocks.

Below
Ground-level plan.

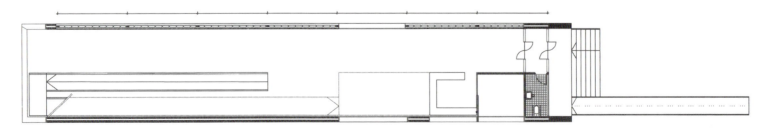

152 Play

Above
Part of the north elevation is softened by a cladding of woven juniper branches, traditionally used for local thatching.

Below
Upper-level plan. The ramp is on the left and the mezzanine level on the right.

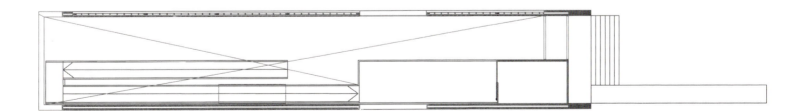

153 Play

Museum of Scottish Country Life

East Kilbride, Scotland, 2001
Page and Park

Above
The entrance elevation, with its drawbridge ramp, adopts a timbered agricultural vernacular and looks towards the historic farm of Wester Kittochside.

Left
The axonometric diagram shows just how complex the arrangement of buildings and interior spaces is. The entrance is on the bottom right.

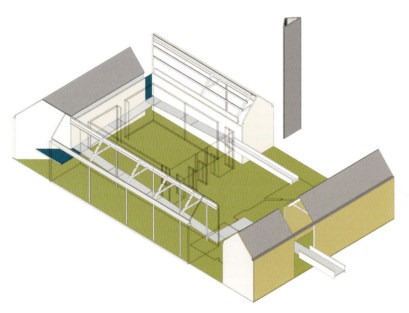

The Museum of Scottish Country Life is designed as a spatial and psychological bridge between two worlds: the urban fringe of the new town of East Kilbride, south of Glasgow, and the traditional farming landscape that, in part, made way for it. The building uses concrete, a modern industrial material, to frame a structure that is part traditional barn and part industrial shed.

Responding to a brief that called for 'a modern industrial vernacular for the twenty-first century', Page and Park's building appears, at first, to be a single-storey timber-clad barn. The sense of drama, a preparation for complex storytelling to come, is enhanced by the drawbridge-like entrance. Once inside, it is at once clear that the building is much bigger than it initially seems – the space drops away to a large basement courtyard, and beyond, visible through side windows, is a landscape that, as becomes apparent, is an exhibit in itself.

Wester Kittochside farm, the site of the museum, was given to the National Trust for Scotland in 1992. It was unusual in that the last owners had not modernized their home, the outbuildings or the landscape. It is a classical farmhouse, with most of the buildings around the farmyard built before 1784 and a larger byre added in the mid-nineteenth century. In the twentieth century the economically driven change to intensive arable production, requiring both bigger buildings for machinery and larger fields, meant that most farms demolished these traditional 'steadings' and took out hedges and walls – but Wester Kittochside continued to graze cattle and had no need to change. This does not mean that the landscape is 'natural'. In fact, Wester Kittochside is a rare example of an 'improvement farm', a product of the Agricultural Revolution, which, although slower paced, was every bit as dramatic as the Industrial Revolution. At that time, square hedged fields replaced open ones, and there were few trees, apart from the shelterbelt around the buildings.

The elevation facing East Kilbride has exceptionally small, high-set windows. Concrete was used to echo post-1945 agricultural buildings as well as for its thermal qualities.

A dramatic balcony marks the transition from the entrance level to the concrete courtyard below.

155 Play

By positioning the new building at a distance from the old steading, it was possible for the architects to keep the farmhouse and outbuildings essentially in their 1950s state. What is clever about the new structure is that, while leading visitors on a spiral route down through the exhibits to the departure point for a walk or tractor ride to the old buildings, it constantly undermines any romantic sense that an urban visitor might have of the countryside. This is, in part, due to the use of concrete.

Precast-concrete sections were chosen for the basic frame because the architects felt that they were robust, and because they wanted the structure to have integrity. Concrete is also used for the roof, which is framed out superficially, just like a traditional A-frame barn roof. The pitch is an exact 45 degrees, which, as project architect Karen Nugent points out, is not typical; it gives the building a slight abstracted appearance.

As well as satisfying the aesthetic requirements of the project, concrete was also a highly practical solution. Using precast elements meant that the in situ construction period was relatively short, and the complex geometry of the hip roofs had all been finalized off-site. The threaded sockets for the lifting bolts were left on each concrete element, filled with a small nut that can be removed easily if the curators wish to have a fixing point from which to hang a new exhibit. The high thermal mass of the concrete also helps to keep the building cool in summer and warm in winter.

Page and Park have also used exposed concrete on other recent Scottish projects, including a students' union building in Paisley and a visitor centre for a newly created national park. The latter project, the Drumkinnon Tower on Loch Lomond, has a cinema space over a foyer, supported by a 'concrete tree' cast in situ. Like the barn roof at the museum, this is both a structurally efficient solution and something that is deliberately meant to recall another form. It is what the architects describe as a 'recognizable, naturalistic and symbolic expression of the place'. In both instances, using concrete, rather than timber, makes an important point – the new building is a modern structure for modern use.

Above
The large interior courtyard enjoys impressive views out to the countryside, thanks to the full-height glazed terrace façade.

Below
Plan of the upper, entrance level. The entrance ramp is on the right.

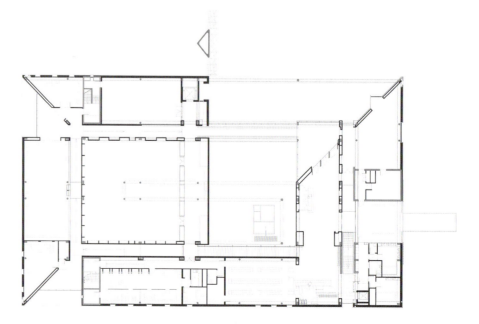

Page & Park's Drumkinnon Tower on Loch Lomond similarly alludes to the close relationship between nature and industry. The roof is supported by a concrete 'tree' cast in situ.

Given the modesty of the entrance façade the museum is deceptively large, housing a triple-height courtyard exhibition space in the centre.

Innside Hotel

Düsseldorf, Germany, 2001
Schneider + Schumacher

The hotel is a horizontal concrete rectangle (left), which sits behind the glass Cubus office block (foreground).

Two buildings in Düsseldorf by Schneider + Schumacher make up a hotel and office complex. Cubus is a 40 x 40 x 40 metre (125 x 125 x 125 foot) office block, which stands in front of the horizontal-slab form of the Innside Hotel. The hotel's volume is defined by a concrete wall 80 metres (250 feet) long and 20 metres (65 feet) high that runs along its entire length and shields the rooms from outside noise; 57 centimetres (22 inches) thick, the wall was cast in situ using a light-coloured concrete. It is a solid foil to the reflective prism of Cubus.

On the inner face of the concrete wall, the conical holes left by the anchor bolts used to hold the formwork during casting have been plugged with glass rods; these form a pattern that animates a surface that remains fully visible from the narrow six-storey atrium space. The hotel bedrooms are reached from galleries overlooking this space, which allows close-up scrutiny of the wall. Lateral restraint to the floor slabs is provided by stainless-steel bars bridging the 2.4 metre (8 foot) space. These create a kind of sinuous filigree, suggesting that the wall has been pulled back from the rest of the building to let in light and air. A skylight above a glazed end wall means that dramatic shadows are cast on the wall's surface. Sunlight catches the glass rods, and what is effectively a vast abstract mural constantly changes throughout the day.

The atrium is reached via the hotel entrance, which is situated in a single-storey link building between the two main volumes. The link contains the hotel reception, restaurant and gym, but the only access to the rooms is via a narrow opening in the concrete wall, as if the realm beyond were secret and private. This makes the wall itself feel even more like a castle wall, a protective barrier. It is the only in situ element in the complex; the internal walls and floor/ceiling slabs are precast.

Both Schneider and Schumacher were taught by Peter Cook at the Staedelschule in Frankfurt. Cook predicted that their analytical talents, together with a 'killer instinct' – which meant that they 'sharpened their objectives by experience, rather than compromising their vision' – would ensure their success. Michael Schumacher worked briefly for Norman Foster, and high-tech influences can be seen in the practice's work.

Another project from 2001 shows a more sombre use of concrete. The Sachsenhausen concentration camp, on the outskirts of Berlin, was used after the war until 1950 as a place of detention by the Soviet secret police – a period interpreted at the visitor centre built there by Schneider + Schumacher. The architects felt that there was 'no question of creating a dominant architectural structure that celebrates its own aesthetic in an area so encumbered with the burden of history', but wanted 'to encourage contemplation without being overwhelming'. The result is an austere concrete box, set 1 metre (3 feet) below ground level.

The visitor centre has, of course, a totally different character from the Innside Hotel – dark and more introspective – but both buildings reflect Schneider and Schumacher's conviction that concrete is an admirable material because it is 'powerful, honest, direct and malleable'.

Above
The solid concrete façade forms a protective barrier between guests inside and the city outside. Light enters the main interior space through a glazed strip which runs up the side wall.

Below left
Section through the hotel (left) and the office building (right). The two structures are linked by a single-storey entrance.

Below right
Section through the office with the front elevation of the hotel behind.

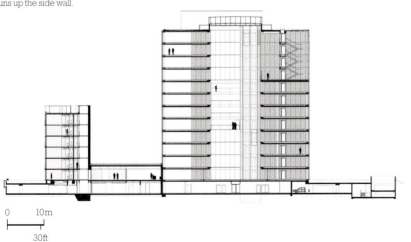

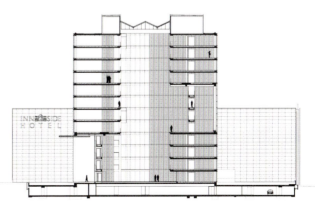

159 Play

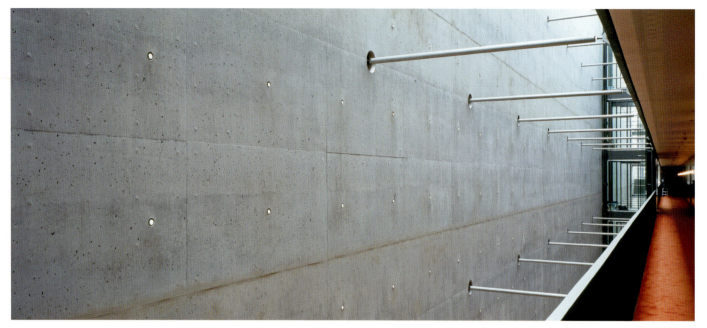

Above
The holes left by the anchor bolts during casting have been plugged with glass, which catches the sunlight and animates the surface of the interior wall.

Below
From left: ground- and roof-level plans of the hotel (the narrow rectangle to the left). The glazed atrium is to the right of the plan, with the guest rooms to the left.

Opposite
Light entering through the skylight and glazed end-wall strip creates an ever-changing pattern on the atrium wall.

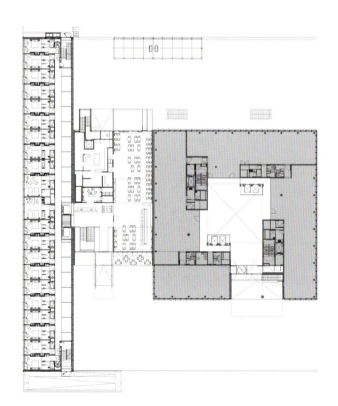
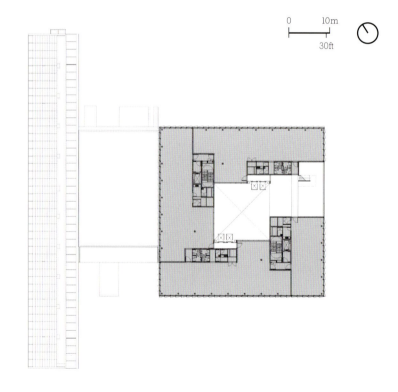

160 Play

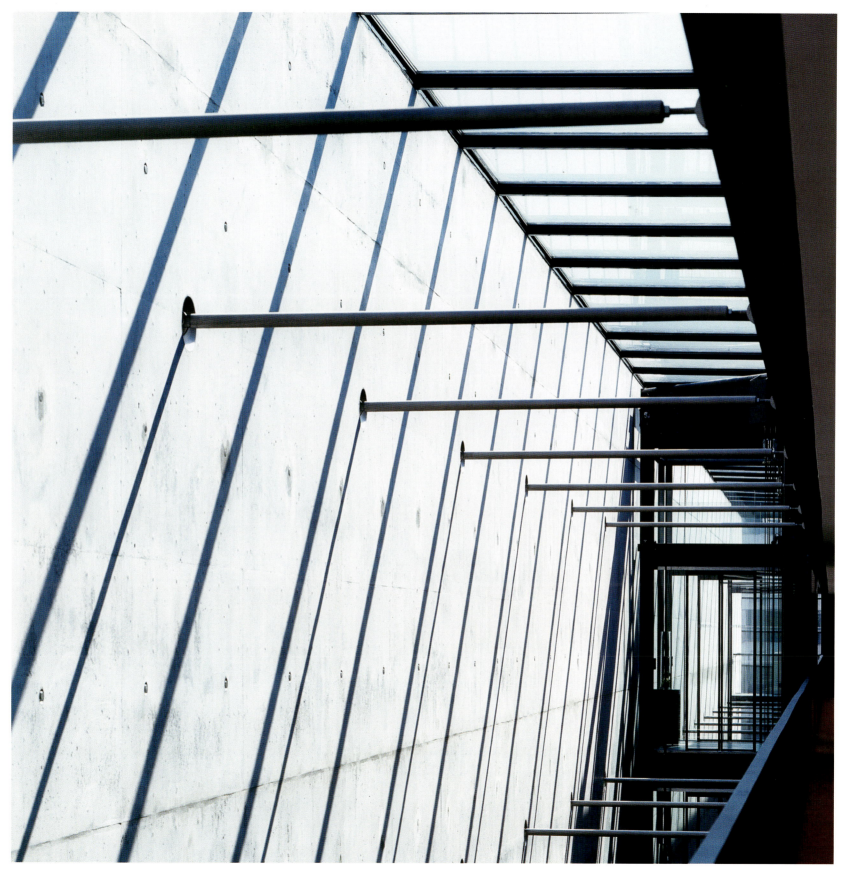

Oskar Reinhart Collection 'Am Römerholz'

Winterthur, Switzerland, 1998
Gigon/Guyer

The extension cubes, including the overhead lighting structures, are clad in concrete. The original 1915 villa is on the right.

Opposite
Elevation showing the villa (left) and the new extension (right).

It is most unusual for a young practice with no track record to receive a prestigious museum or gallery commission – but, remarkably, Gigon/Guyer's first jobs included three major museums, all won in competition and all making discreet but critical use of concrete as part of a varied palette of smooth, precise materials.

The Oscar Reinhart Collection is both a renovation and an extension to an existing museum. The core structure was built as a villa in 1915 by Geneva architect Maurice Turrettini, in French Renaissance style for a private client. It was sold less than ten years later to Oskar Reinhart, who invited Turrettini back to add a gallery to house his art collection. On Reinhart's death, both house and collection passed to the Swiss state, and the building opened to the public in 1970 after extensive alterations.

The most prominent part of Gigon/Guyer's project are the three new exhibition rooms wrapped tightly around the 1925 gallery. The new perimeter is seemingly defined by drawing intersecting lines out from the existing structure. Large prefabricated concrete elements form the cladding of both the walls and the set-back skylight lanterns. Essentially, each gallery reads as a stacked set of box volumes, whose heights relate to parapet levels on the existing building. It is the tension between the use of simple forms and the structure's complex and contextual geometry, together with the parallel contrast between the initial perception of the extension as being made of planes of a simple material and the close-up revelation of a richness of surface, that is characteristic of Gigon/Guyer's work. It has been dubbed 'variegated minimal'.

Opposite
The sophisticated interiors rely on a discreet combination of concrete and other smooth, precise materials, and are lit from above by set-back skylight lanterns.

Below right
The new extension is at the top left of the plan.

Below
Jurassic limestone and copper (materials occurring in the original buildings) were ground down and added to the concrete as aggregate. The walls of the extension will therefore quickly aquire a patina.

The building's rich surface derives mainly from the unusual concrete mix that was used. Two materials employed in the construction of the original villa were added in powdered form: the Jurassic limestone of the masonry walls, and copper, the original roofing material. The idea is that the extension will undergo an accelerated ageing process and patinate fast. The detailing of the new copper roofs, which allows run-off water to streak the walls with copper ions, will add to the effect.

The firm used a similar technique for their signal box in Zurich, this time incorporating an iron-oxide pigment in the concrete mix. The structure varies in colour from yellow and orange to deep purple, and was inspired by the red iron dust deposited along a railway by train brakes, which changes over time as the iron rusts. Annette Gigon insists that the practice has no 'material preferences', however, and other works have used sandblasted chromed-steel panels as large shingles, and glass. Mike Guyer says, ' "Form follows function" as dogma, as an inevitable, consistently employed principle, possesses no meaning for us,' but the separate volumes of each gallery (one for paintings and the other two for prints and drawings) can be clearly read. Nevertheless, there is a sense of deliberate blurring of this legibility, of an interest in a larger scale of composition.

Annette Gigon and Mike Guyer met at the Swiss Federal Institute of Technology in Zurich, from which they both graduated in 1984. Annette Gigon went on to work for Herzog & de Meuron in Basel, and Mike Guyer for Rem Koolhaas OMA in Rotterdam. Both set up their own individual practices, before joining forces in 1989. In 1993 (when they had completed only two buildings), they were invited to show their work in Lucerne, and chose to display samples of components and materials, like recipe ingredients neatly lined up for a demonstration – emphasizing just how important choice of material is for this practice.

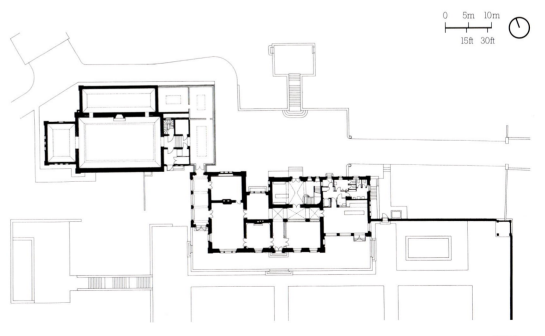

La Coruña Swimming Pool

La Coruña, Spain, 1999
Estudio Cano Lasso

In response to its unprepossessing site on the outskirts of Ordenes, the building is inward-looking. The pool faces the cafeteria over one of the internal courtyards.

Rather than being a one-off design for a specific location, this competition-winning scheme for a swimming pool for La Coruña local authority takes a modular approach, which can be adapted to suit different sites in the area. Estudio Cano Lasso's base prototype packs together all the functions of the building – but this is really no more than a theoretical proposition. The idea is that the base diagram should be manipulated to expand the overall footprint and to introduce open spaces between different activities.

Describing the process as 'displacing or shifting its parts in different directions', the architects explain that the vacated spaces 'relate and function as transition areas between the interior and the exterior'. The quality of the introduced spaces is key to the success of each version of the scheme – and, as the architects put it, 'They possess different degrees of permeability, like a diaphragm, depending on the conditions imposed by each plot: geometry, topography, orientation, views, landscapes, urban links, etc.'

So far, two pool buildings have been constructed. The one featured here is in Ordenes, on a steeply sloping site on the outskirts of La Coruña. This is an attractive area, fast being encroached on by poorly regulated development. For this reason, the pool building is largely inward-looking. It has a more compact plan than its sister building at nearby Santa Comba, and the architects are very pleased by the way the long concrete walls 'disappear into the hillside' and 'act as guides, along which the parts of the basic module begin to slide, totally fragmenting the initial geometry'. The sense of sliding is purely conceptual, but it is appropriate that the process of rearrangement, the idea that a basic set of elements can be made to respond to specific circumstances, is perceptible in the finished product.

Above
The entrance is located between
two of the main concrete walls.

Right
Long section through the pool.

167 Play

The entrance is situated between two of the main concrete walls, making the importance of concrete in this structure immediately apparent. The actual pool is clad both inside and out with phenolic wood panels, which are resistant to humidity, but it is the rhythm of the concrete piers that dominates. A courtyard separates the pool from the café, while two others form enclosed open spaces for the changing rooms and saunas.

The rationalist strategy employed by the local authority of La Coruña, which formed part of its 'Sports Plan 2000' – an ambitious programme of new facilities – has helped to keep costs down, but without imposing a uniform design solution. The swimming pool is a relatively modest project compared to others with which Estudio Cano Lasso is involved. These include a prestigious scheme to house the Royal Collections in Madrid, and the SACE Laboratories at the University of Murcia, which are clad with white, brick-sized concrete tiles and have roofs covered with white crushed concrete.

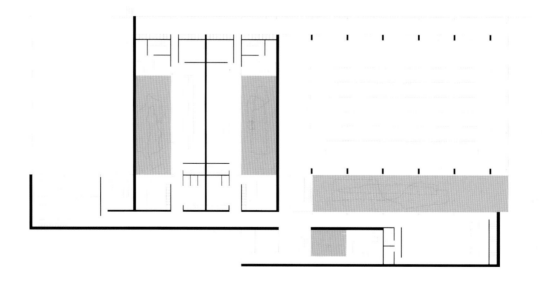

Top right
The rhythm of the concrete piers dominates the interior and gives a pattern to the view outside.

Right
The plain concrete wall at nearby Santa Comba pool acts as a guide, around which the other elements of the module slide into place.

Opposite
Plan of the Ordenes pool complex, with the pool on the top right and the café at bottom. Changing facilities are housed in the building to the left.

American Folk Art Museum

New York, USA, 2001
Tod Williams Billie Tsien & Associates

A pitted, bush-hammered concrete light well over the central stair is adorned with metal weathervanes.

Hailed as New York's greatest new building in decades, the American Folk Art Museum has a cast-bronze façade and a dramatic interior, with galleries wrapped around a central in situ concrete staircase. The site is surrounded on three sides by land belonging to the Museum of Modern Art, and, once MoMA's reconstruction by Yoshio Tanaguchi is complete, the larger institution will surround it. As architect Billie Tsien puts it, 'We would like to think that we are the jewel in the belly-button of MoMA, but I don't think they think that.' It appears that MoMA would have preferred to acquire and incorporate the 20.5 x 12 metre (100 x 40 foot) piece of land, hardly greater than a domestic lot, but the American Folk Art Museum wanted to stay put in this prime midtown location.

The top four floors are for the display of folk art, objects from temporary exhibitions as well as the permanent collection. These include paintings, textiles, boxes and baskets, toys and tools. A display of weathervanes, mounted on the bush-hammered concrete wall of what the architects call 'the ceremonial staircase', casts dramatic shadows on the highly textured surface, and draws attention to the beauty and strength of the material. It is as if a tough outdoor surface had been brought indoors to provide the perfect context for these battered, rust-pitted exhibits. One gets much closer to the weathervanes than one normally would, and the open texture of the concrete feels appropriately blown up in scale.

The ceremonial staircase rises from the first floor to the top of the building. It is centrally placed and parallel with the side walls of the site. It is the literal and metaphorical heart of the building, and a large roof light above it brings daylight into the core of the display areas via a sequence of narrow, parallel voids. Tsien explains, 'Todd and I have always loved the Whitney stair and the idea of making the stair into a great journey.' But while the concrete stair at Marcel Breuer's nearby Whitney Museum (arguably the last great New York building before theirs) is largely an enclosed structure, this stair is much more open. In fact, the galleries themselves are little more than generous stair landings; the horizontal voids and vertical openings in the staircase structure allow both lateral and diagonal views from one area to another.

In addition to the Whitney, another New York museum is brought to mind – like Frank Lloyd Wright's Guggenheim Museum, the American Folk Art Museum is designed to be visited from the top down. While the Guggenheim has a single major route, the position of the stair here, and its juxtaposition with the alternative 'ornamental stair' at the back corner of the building, allow visitors to meander and cut back on themselves, as if in a giant game of snakes and ladders. It is not immediately obvious where to go. 'We'd like you to be able to recall it, but not be able to recall exactly where it is,' says Tsien. A blue-green resin screen, composed of riveted, translucent, shallow-trough sections marks the centre point of each floor.

Where the side wall of the building has not been clad with display panels, it too is bush-hammered concrete, and like, the stair walls, is divided into a regular, large-scale grid by casting joints. The ceremonial steps, and some areas of the floor, are made of polished concrete, and the use of a large blue-black aggregate gives a terrazzo-like finish.

Above
In the great hall, glass panels and a translucent, riveted resin screen, marking the centre of the building, open up the spaces around the monolithic concrete walls, stairs and mezzanine block.

Left
The built-in furniture was designed by the architects.

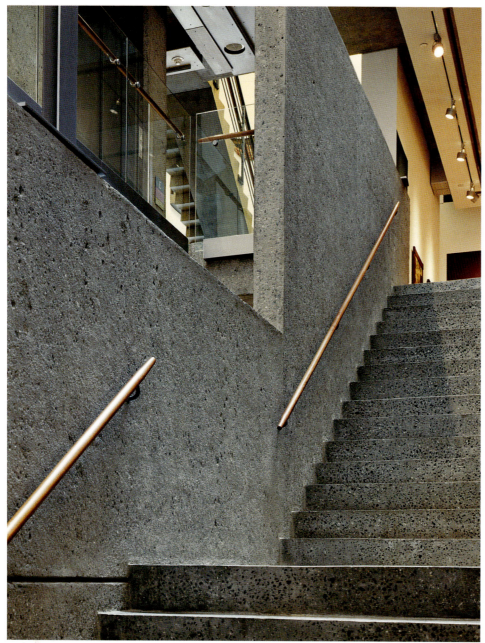

Above
A grand staircase leading from the second to the third floor uses blue-black aggregate to achieve a terrazzo-like finish.

Top right
The eight-storey museum building is clad in panels of Tombasil (a white bronze used in the manufacture of propellers and fire-hose nozzles), which has never before been used architecturally.

Right
Openings create views from gallery to gallery and from floor to floor, allowing exhibits to be seen from varying angles. The floor glimpsed below is made of salvaged Ruby Lake fir.

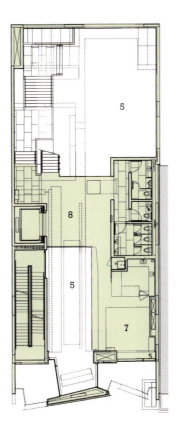
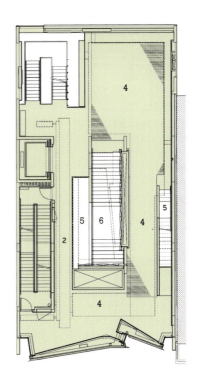

From left to right: plans of the ground floor, mezzanine level and third floor. 1. entrance foyer, 2. shop, 3. Great Hall, 4. gallery, 5. void, 6. ceremonial stair, 7. café, 8. mezzanine bridge

In the upper display areas, the use of salvaged Ruby Lake fir floorboards, up to 5 metres (16½ feet) long, and with an exceptionally tight grain, brings a richness and warmth to the overall palette. This, combined with the rooms' small dimensions, makes the spaces seem domestic in scale – which is appropriate, since most of the exhibits were originally made for modest homes, and to be handled and used. As there is no 'ceremonial stair' from ground to first floor, the ground-floor gallery, referred to as the Great Hall, is much larger. The change works well for the display of bigger objects. Throughout the building, cherrywood handrails and furniture designed by the architects and made by a Japanese-American cabinet-maker provide a tactile continuity.

The mezzanine-level coffee bar overlooks the street, and the ground floor is arranged so that the small shop can open separately to the museum. There are two levels of basement, which house an auditorium, lecture hall, library and offices, and a tightly planned fire stair and elevator are both placed against the west wall. The building's façade is primarily opaque, but is angled to catch shafts of light entering 53rd Street. Tsien describes the structure as 'an abstraction of a mask and open hand', and wanted to use a material that was 'reflective to catch light, yet warm in tone in order to address the personal and often warm tone of the folk art'. Concrete was considered but rejected because it would have been 'more absorbent than reflective' and because it was 'impractical to cast in midtown Manhattan'. Aluminium was a possibility, but the ideal was 'a material that felt as if it was made by hand'. The white bronze finally selected is called Tombasil and is used for fire-hose nozzles and propeller fittings. It is 57 per cent copper, and the sections were made by pouring molten metal onto both steel and concrete. 'A steel surface produces a flatter finish, showing the liquid flow of the metal, and a concrete surface produces a cratered and coarse finish.'

Pulitzer Foundation for the Arts

St Louis, Missouri, USA, 2001
Tadao Ando Architect & Associates

The entrance to the building is hidden behind a high, monolithic wall of concrete, cast in situ.

Built as a museum to house the Pulitzer family's collection, and to act as a base for its charitable foundation, Ando's Pulitzer Foundation for the Arts is both a site for contemplation and a focus for regeneration of a city-centre area that has been devastated by a long-term exodus to the suburbs. The new Museum of Contemporary Art, designed by Brad Cloepfil adjoins it.

A main aim of the Pulitzer Foundation is to foster an understanding and appreciation of the relationship between modern art and architecture, so the commissioning of a new home was very carefully considered. In the ten-year period of development, initial plans to renovate an existing building (which had been a car-repair shop) evolved into a new-build project, after the client visited Japan and saw Ando's works there. Artists Ellsworth Kelly and Richard Serra were commissioned to produce works in dialogue with Ando's project.

In contrast with many recent, comparable museum projects, the Pulitzer Foundation has a simple form and is designed on a modest scale. It is, in fact, much smaller than a number of the buildings that surround it, including a substantial Masonic temple. Ando describes his building as 'just two simple rectangles'. These two elongated elements, each 7.5 metres (24 feet) wide, are placed parallel to one another, with a rectangular pool of equal width sandwiched between them. One block has been built 3 metres (10 feet) higher than the other, and is as tall as it is wide. Towards the street, the roof of this element oversails the lower block, forming an enclosed glass pavilion and an open terrace. The concrete cantilever rests on a single internal column.

It is the interplay of levels, the relationship between the interior space, the water outside and the quality of light that give the building its strength. Ando explains on the Foundation's website, 'As you enter this simple figure or box, you discover a space that is complex and rich. Once inside, you learn things that could not be foreseen from outside … I hope it might make you realize that life holds all kinds of possibilities and wonders, if only we make the effort to discover them.'

The spareness of detailing allows attention to focus on the purity of the building's proportions, rather than on minutiae. It is its fundamental complexity that Ando wants visitors to appreciate. Floors run smoothly from inside to out – there are

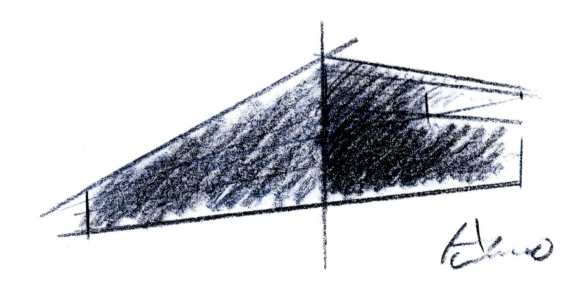

Left
Sketch of the entrance façade.

Top
The Foundation has been a focus for urban regeneration.

Above
Once inside the entrance area, the building's geometric composition of masses and planes becomes even more apparent.

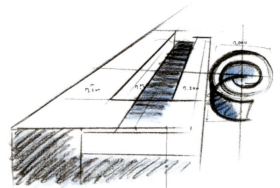

Left
Aerial-view sketch showing the central pool.

Below
Upon entering the east wing, visitors are encouraged to cross to their left, which takes them into a double-height space with a wall of windows onto the terrace.

Bottom
Long section.

no skirtings or architraves. The stair is a pure geometric form, with the glass handrail set in a simple groove. The simplicity of the internal surfaces – planes of concrete or plaster – is reflected in the exterior landscaping, with its uninterrupted plane of water, and the roof of the lower block, which is thickly planted with pygmy bamboo.

At first sight, the building looks almost domestic. Its entrance is hidden behind a high, monolithic wall. The reception area is in the low east wing, and visitors turn around to cross to the main galleries in the west wing. The principal gallery is 52 metres (170 feet) long; from the halfway point, full-width stairs descend to create a double-height, top-lit volume. It is here that Ellsworth Kelly's *Blue Black* hangs. Beyond is a cube-shaped gallery, 7.5 metres (22 1/2 feet) on each axis, with a smaller gallery placed to one side. Ando recalls that, when he was initially discussing the project with Joseph Pulitzer, Pulitzer described how standing in front of an Ellsworth Kelly made him feel that he was standing in front of the Parthenon. The architect felt that it was this sense of 'simple perfection' (his words) that his client was seeking.

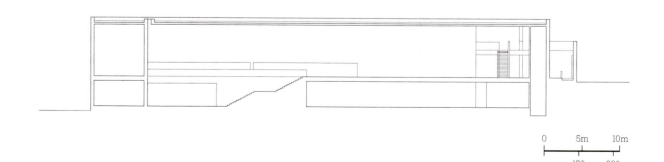

176 Play

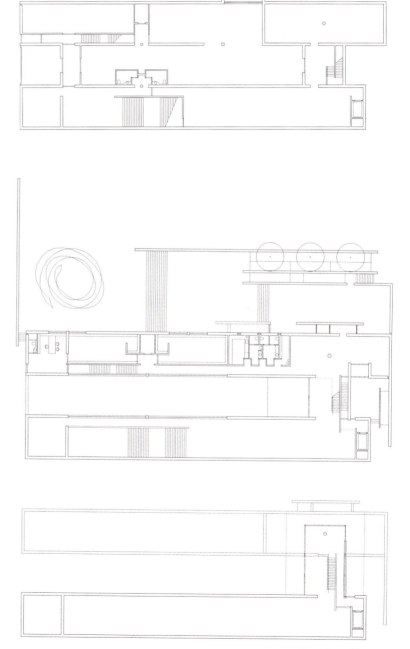

Top
The constantly changing effects of light and shadow enliven the concrete walls. Ellsworth Kelly's *Blue Black* is given pride of place on the south wall.

Above
The space created between the blocks is the same width as the wings and contains a shimmering pool, which is illuminated at night by light from the interiors.

Right
From bottom: plans of the basement, ground and first floors. The central rectangle is the pool.

0   5m   10m
15ft   30ft

177 Play

Kunstmuseum

Vaduz, Liechtenstein, 2000
Morger Degelo Kerez

Above
The wall surfaces were rubbed down and polished to reveal the true nature of the concrete. Rather than using sophisticated sealants, the architects wanted to let the material speak for itself.

Right
An aggregate of broken black basalt and fine-grained green, red and white Rhine gravel was combined with black-coloured cement to create a semi-reflective surface, which changes constantly in response to the weather conditions and time of day.

The Basel-based architects Morger & Delago can identify no direct parallels to the way they have used concrete in this project. They had never used polished concrete before, and set out to experiment. They describe the surface they have created as resembling a terrazzo floor. Their explanation of their method focuses on an intense scrutiny of material and process.

The architects were frustrated that 'the cement slurry that rises to the surface of a concrete wall seals off the additives that are to be found in the concrete and makes them invisible.' They decided that this problem had to be overcome: 'We were interested in the interior richness and presenting the internal structure, so we did not enhance the façade with any kind of fashionable coating, nor did we decorate it subsequently. The topmost layer of concrete was rubbed down and polished, which revealed its inner life, like that of a costly stone.' They felt that this was symbolically appropriate to the museum, reflecting its function as building that has wonderful things inside it, concealed from the outside world. The materials used in the mixture are broken black basalt, fine-grained green, red and white Rhine river gravel, and black-coloured cement. This creates a gleaming, almost shiny surface, which is constantly changing – at different times of the day and in different weather conditions it reflects its surroundings in diverse ways. The wall is loadbearing and was cast in situ in lifts 8 metres (20 feet) high.

Vaduz is the capital of Liechtenstein, and the site is at the foot of the cliff that is dominated by the white, ornamental ducal castle, set in dark-green wooded parkland. The town is undistinguished architecturally, with kitsch detailing and a suburban scale. Morger & Delago wanted to design a museum that would fit in unassumingly with the structure of the town, but that would at the same time be distinctive. The plan of the building is very simple. Visitors enter via a ground-floor café with full-height flush glazing, from where a generous, enclosed oak stair leads upwards. The height and width of this opening mark it out as more important than the smaller one, which gives access to the basement.

Below right
The impressive, monolithic block form of the museum stands out on its site at the base of a cliff, dominated by the ducal palace.

Below
The museum shop: interiors are kept simple with oiled oak floors and white plaster walls.

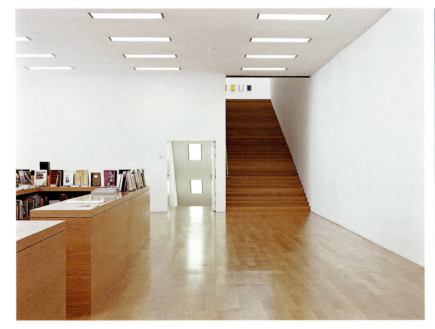

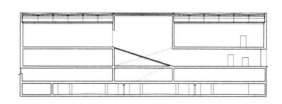
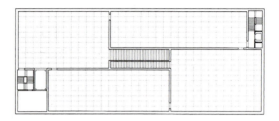
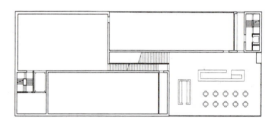
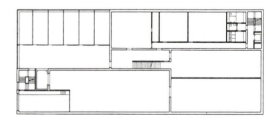

Above
From bottom: basement, ground- and first-floor plans, and long section (top).

Left
Visitors enter the museum through a ground-floor café with full-height glazing looking onto the terrace.

The galleries have oiled oak floors, simple white plastered walls, and on the first floor a luminous ceiling allowing natural light to be balanced with discreet artificial lighting. The gallery spaces are arranged in a pinwheel formation around the stair, and a second juxtaposed flight of stairs makes it possible to loop through the building in ways different from the prescribed route. In fact, the architects see circulation in this project as their 'major preoccupation', and have even described the exhibition galleries as the 'missing landings' of the uninterrupted flights and the dividing gallery walls as blades of a weathervane. Meinrad Morger and Heinrich Delago studied in Switzerland, and Delago worked for Herzog & de Mueron before the practice was formed in 1988, in Basel. The museum is typical of their work in that its exterior gives few hints of the plan that lies within. They say that 'classical modern architecture is an important reference and source of inspiration in terms of technical and aesthetical intentions, but we long ago left the ideology that the outside appearance has to express the interior.'

Far left
Detail of the polished-concrete entrance elevation.

Left
The luminous ceiling on the first floor depends on both natural and artificial lighting.

Chapter 4
Landscape

Can concrete structures enhance a landscape? In 1961, American sociologist Lewis Mumford suggested 'our national flower is the concrete cloverleaf', alluding to the rapacious alliance between concrete and the car. Although concrete may be seen by some as anathema to natural beauty, there are countless examples of concrete interventions in stunning landscapes that have been enormously successful, focusing attention on the surrounding scenery, and on the colours, textures, shapes and forms of the natural world. Early examples include Robert Maillart's bridges (see page 13) in Switzerland and the Hoover Dam in the USA. Dams and bridges have continued to use concrete in increasingly expressive, and even flamboyant, ways – look for instance at the work of Santiago Calatrava – but it is the less obvious ways in which concrete has had an impact on landscape that are more interesting.

The use of concrete for cemetery structures has its own history and imagery. Perhaps the most famous twentieth-century concrete cemetery project is Carlo Scarpa's Brion Vega cemetery at San Vito di Altivole, Italy (1969–78). Here, a concrete bridge structure hovers over the clients' sarcophagi and a concrete watercourse. The overlapping circles motif used throughout lent itself to concrete construction, but it is the richness of the texture of the surfaces that is most impressive. The cemetery of Saint-Pancrace, Roquebrune-Cap-Martin, France, is where Le Corbusier is buried. It is sited in a crevasse, looking out to sea, and was extended in 1992 by Marc Barani, who used squares of Carrara marble to seal tombs set in white concrete walls, which contrast with tapered yellow freestone walls. At Enric Miralles' Igualada Cemetery in Barcelona (1990), exposed reinforcement bars deliberately stain the surfaces of precast concrete elements, and the steel cemetery gates look like reinforcement waiting for concrete to be poured. The whole effect is designed to suggest the language 'of the construction site', a sense of 'incompleteness awaiting decay' – the idea of the cemetery as a point of transition, rather than a final resting place.

Concrete has been used for sculptural interventions in many settings. Donald Judd (an artist enormously sensitive to the effect of changing natural light on his work) placed his concrete boxes outside the range of sheds he acquired when he purchased a former air-force base at Marfa, Texas, as a centre for his work. Concrete monuments have also successfully given identity to urban locations – Luis Barragán's Satellite Towers (1957) are coloured prisms of concrete, with horizontal shutter marks clearly expressed. They stand in the centre of a motorway, marking the entrance to one of Mexico City's satellite towns.

The examples that follow show concrete set in a variety of landscape situations, where it is used to create new settings. The piazza of the new Los Angeles Cathedral (see page 224) draws on a tradition of cathedrals, which, rather than standing alone, generate a feeling of enclosed and public space around them – in this, the architect Rafael Moneo is following in the steps not just of great medieval and Renaissance builders, but of twentieth-century examples, too. The vast, concrete crystalline forms of Gottfried Böhm's Church of the Pilgrimage at Neviges, Germany (1964), deserve to be better known, and the organic shapes of Rudolf Steiner's Goetheanum at Dornach, Switzerland (1925–28), similarly use concrete to create a world apart. At London's South Bank arts complex (see page 6) it is the seamless use of concrete for walkways and stairs, as well as for interior and exterior surfaces of individual buildings, which creates a series of spaces between the buildings with a unified character. Denys Lasdun's pyramid structures at the University of East Anglia, Norwich, England, (1963–72) were seen by him as a concrete shore line, around which the soft landscape could lap, like water entering a harbour. Elsewhere in this chapter, the Oulart Hill monument in Wexford, Ireland (see page 218) uses landscape intervention to commemorate a historical event, while the Sculptural Overlook complex in Washington State (see page 192) seeks to enhance visitors' appreciation of the surrounding landscape.

Chapel and Residential Buildings

Valleacerón, Ciudad Real, Spain, 2001
Estudio Sancho-Madridejos

Above
Natural light pierces the building through trapezoidal openings in the south-east elevation, giving life to the massive, sombre interior. Religious iconography is minimal.

Left and top
The chapel is built of golden concrete, which captures every nuance of sunlight.

The chapel is one of a group of buildings designed by Barcelona architects Sol Madridejos and Juan Carlos Osinaga for a private client on a rural estate in Valleacerón. Set at the top of a slight incline, it can be seen from the entrance to the property, over 2 kilometres (1 1/4 miles) away. To reach the palatial residential buildings, visitors drive up to and around the chapel. It is therefore a gatehouse, as well as an eye-catcher and a place to stop and admire the landscape and the architectural composition.

The extraordinary form of the chapel arose from the study of how a single piece of paper could be folded and sliced to make a three-dimensional object. These initial explorations were developed in a series of models. The architects describe the building as a 'naked design' – despite its complex shape, it is a structure pared down to a skin and nothing more. It makes no concessions to everyday life, and has no artificial lighting. A simple cross on one wall marks it as a chapel; there is no conventional altar or imagery.

The chapel was constructed in a golden concrete, which the architects chose because 'it captures all the nuances demanded of the volume.' It is as if the chapel exists to give a heightened awareness of light and air, a sensual appreciation of the passing of days and seasons.

While the residential buildings together form a tight compound, and are built into the slope of the land, the chapel is perched on an elevated site, looking almost fragile. It has an air of lightness and ease, which is truly remarkable in a concrete structure, and which the architects attribute to the way in which light has, in effect, been corralled into acting as second building material. Light, for them, is the antithesis of concrete – it is 'mobile, unstable' and sometimes 'vanishing'.

Below right
Section through the north elevation.

Below
In contrast to the chapel, the villa has a straightforward rectangular design, with glazed walls giving views of the surrounding countryside.

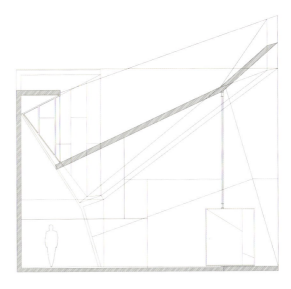

185 Landscape

Above
The design developed from simply box-folding and slicing a piece of paper to create a three-dimensional shape. Models were used to work up the building to its present form.

Right
Elevations of the group of buildings. The chapel is to the right and the residential buildings in the centre.

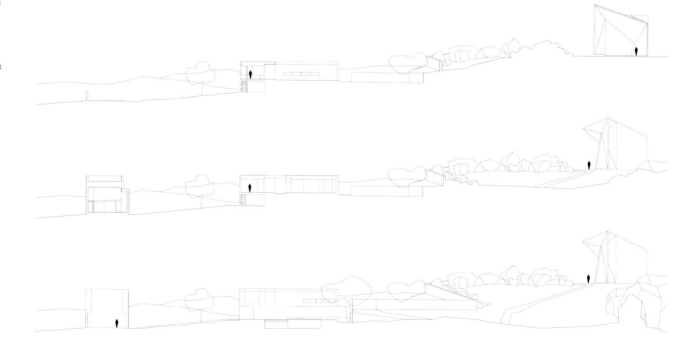

186 Landscape

Right
Site plan. The chapel is to the far right and the residential buildings in the centre.

Below
Set on an elevated site 2 kilometres (1¼ miles) from the villa, the chapel acts as a gatehouse, as well as a place of worship.

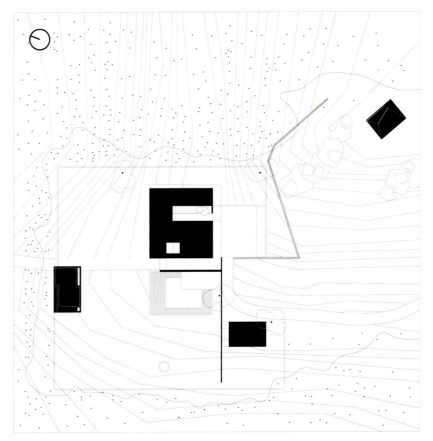

187 Landscape

Barcelona Botanic Garden

Barcelona, Spain, 1999
Carlos Ferrater, Bet Figueras and José Luís Canosa

Above
In this project, concrete is sliced, angled and propped up, rather than moulded into organic forms. Major paths are wide and flat, so as to be wheelchair accessible.

Right
A triangular concrete lattice-work, with retaining walls of Cor-ten steel, zigzags through the site on the western reaches of the Montjuïc hills.

Opposite
Site plan. Entrance and visitor facilities are at the north, while the concrete terraces zigzag their way southwards down the site.

While many traditional botanic gardens arrange plants in square grids, this project uses a triangular concrete lattice, which is distorted to fit the slope of the site. Cor-ten steel sheets are used for retaining walls, but the entrance, drainage channels and paths are concrete. The Cor-ten sheets – 3 millimetres ($1/10$ inch) thick, and generally placed at 8 degrees to the vertical – are complemented by elegant, zigzag-bent, stainless-steel chairs, designed by the architect Carlos Ferrater and distributed throughout the site. The juxtaposition of the steel elements with the slab-like concrete emphasizes the monolithic nature of the latter. As used here, concrete is a sharply angled material to be sliced, propped up or laid in position, rather than a curvaceously moulded or softly fluid one.

The original competition for a new botanic garden in Barcelona was won in 1989 by the landscape architect Bet Figueras. The initial idea was that it should be ready for the 1992 Olympic Games. It occupies 1.2 hectares (3 acres) of the upper-west reaches of Montjuïc, the green, rocky headland that overlooks, but lies within, the city. Montjuïc is dominated by a castle and was transformed into a cultural district for the 1929 International Exhibition. More recently, it was chosen as the location for Josep Lluis Sert's Fundació Miró (1975). Arata Isozaki's Olympic Arena and the refaced 1929 stadium are close by, and the site's elevated position offers views of Foster and Partners' 800 metre (2,600 foot) high communications tower and the city below, and beyond. But in 1989 the site was essentially a rubbish tip, and the deadline proved unrealistic. The previous botanic garden (created in 1929) lay neglected in a former sandstone quarry; it had been declared unsafe and Atlas cedars had grown to shade it. The short-term solution was to build an escalator for visitors to the Games, which passed over it.

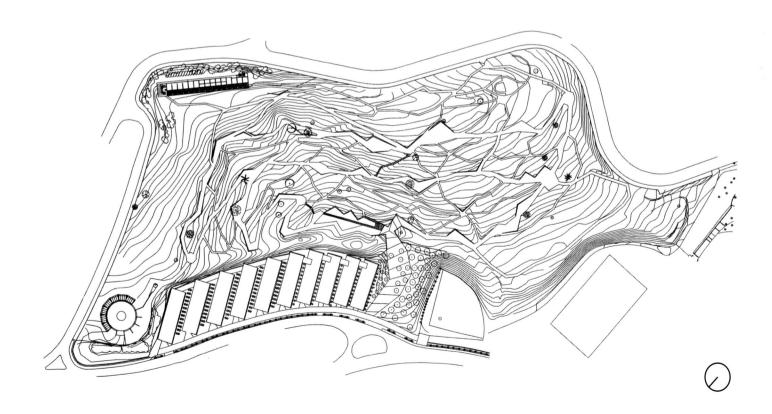

The bent stainless-steel chairs in the foreground, designed by Carlos Ferrater, complement the angularity of the concrete pathways and entrance building.

The team who finally implemented the project included botanist Joan Pedrola, horticulturalist Arthur Bossys and architects Carlos Ferrater 0and José Luís Canosa. Figueras refers to Carlos Ferrater as 'the soul of the project'. 'He was very, very good, he was tough,' she says. Ferrater explains the genesis of the project in a surprising way. 'We imagined some sort of fishnet stocking going over the land and how it would reflect the different kinds of slope,' he says, pointing out that where the land is flatter the 'mesh' of planting bed is more open, while on steeper sections of the site it is tighter.

The plants are not arranged by botanical family but divided into 72 'plant communities' – groups of plants found in places with Mediterranean climates – that is, places with hot, dry summers and cool, damp winters. These include South Africa, Australia, Chile and California, as well as the Mediterranean itself and the Iberian Peninsula, the Balearic Islands and the Canary Islands.

The entrance court is a large circular space, surrounded by a ring of radiating stub walls, which are either freestanding or form the sidewalls of the ticketing booth and maintenance buildings. Beyond, a boardwalk leads across an angular pool and on towards the rising slopes. Major paths are 3 metres (10 feet) wide and slope gently enough to be wheelchair accessible, while minor ones are narrower, steeper and, in some cases, stepped. Figueras insists that the abstract geometry was not based on a traditional precedent: 'Long after we designed this, I found a photograph of some agricultural drystone-wall terraces in a Majorca landscape, and the way they were organizing the land was the same thing we were doing here. So it was a natural strategy ... It is very rewarding to see that you have done something logical, that you haven't just been whimsical, that you have done something that is needed in this type of landscape. Because they are steep, you need to protect the soil from erosion, to contain the soil; and also, in the end, you need this sort of cultural order to the land. So this was good, that the wise generations did it before us.'

The project is environmentally sensitive, with pole-mounted solar panels powering irrigation. At present, water is being drawn from the main city supply, but the system can be adapted to use water piped uphill from the city's problematically high water table.

Carlos Ferrater has used concrete in many other projects, most notably the Cataluña Congress Centre in Barcelona, which comprised steel formwork and white concrete, and exploits the play of light and shadow against the whiteness of the smooth, flat planes.

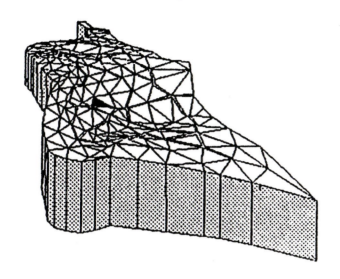

Left
Ferrater envisaged the project as encased in a 'fishnet stocking'. The size of the holes marking out different areas of the slope varies according to how the terrain affects the shape of the 'stocking'.

Below
The colour of the concrete slab terraces appears to change with the weather and time of day.

191 Landscape

Sculptural Overlook, Maryhill Museum of Art

Goldendale, Washington, USA, 1999
Allied Works Architecture

The first of five 'Sitings' projects planned for the grounds of the museum, the Overlook stands on a bluff above the Columbia river gorge.

193 Landscape

Above
The form boards were made from presealed MDF panels, which were tongue-and-groove, fitted together and resealed. The concrete was poured in one day and the resultant surface is completely smooth, with no sign of joints.

Opposite
Site plan.

'I am interested in architecture as sculpture in form and space,' says Brad Cloepfil of Allied Works Architecture, Portland, Oregon. 'That is not to say that I am interested in self-referential structures, but in the ways in which these structures can make something fundamental, a silence.'

The Maryhill Museum of Art's Sculptural Overlook project frames the landscape and encourages museum visitors to focus and refocus on different panoramas, to choose a viewpoint and yet be aware that their choice is, in essence, arbitrary – that it is one of an infinite number of possibilities. It demonstrates, in short, that the landscape is uncontainable. It also provides rudimentary shelter and enclosure, reminding us of the basic functions of architecture – but, by avoiding specifics, it invites interpretation at the most basic level. Is that a bench or a table? Are we inside or outside? At its most explicit in the Overlook, the mixture of emotional and intellectual confrontation is constant in Cloepfil's work: 'As an architect I recognize the fundamental need for rooms, but I believe we need rooms which are not closed, that are nervous. In my buildings, you never know where things stop or start. This evokes a sense of both terror and calm. It is the sense that something is not quite right, that you can't quite trust in the nature of things, that makes you aware of where you are.' An illustration of this can be found in the firm's conversion of a cold store in Portland, Oregon, into the headquarters for advertising agency Wieden + Kennedy. In this project the space is partially framed and

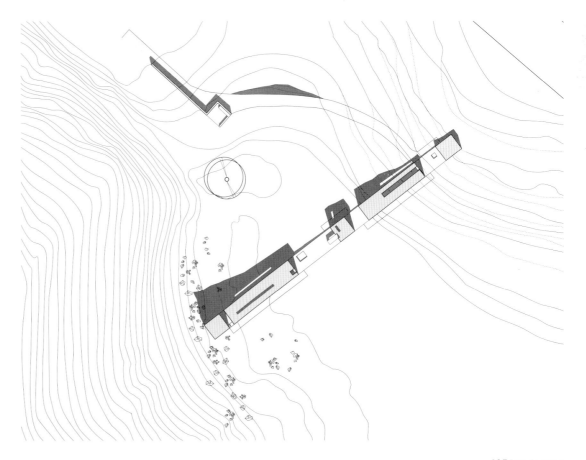

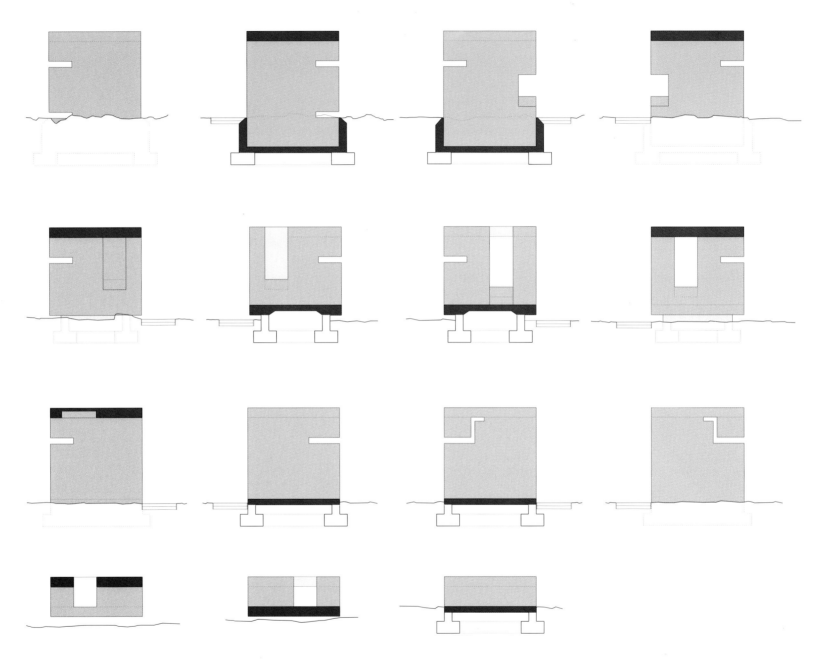

Sections through the various slabs and walls of the structure.

The modules have been carefully placed to maximize the effects of light and shade, which become additional materials, adding a painterly effect to this piece of land art.

subdivided by concrete beams and lintels, and has laminated timber elements and heavy, reclaimed pieces of building, the latter making one wonder whether this is an old or new structure.

The Overlook is the only one of five proposed 'sitings' projects to have been built. The others remain theoretical explorations of contrasting types of terrain – the forest, agricultural land (an orchard), the suburbs and the city centre. Cloepfil is interested in the variety, and in intensifying the specificity of each experience. The Overlook was constructed in the high desert, one of the most dramatic and inhospitable of environments. It is almost like a ruin, suggesting that man has tried and failed to inhabit it.

The structure was site-cast and the two main spans were post-tensioned. The shuttering was made from MDF with a pre-applied, clear sealant, and the joints between sheets were tightly tongued and grooved and then resealed to ensure that no line would be visible. The pouring took place in a single day, so that there are no horizontal joints, and channels were inserted to make sure that the concrete totally filled the formwork. The channels were cut off after the formwork was removed.

'In the West, most of the built environment is not houses or other buildings, but railroads, silos and dams,' says Cloepfil. 'This piece is part of that world.' His subsequent building project, the new Contemporary Art Museum in St Louis, Missouri, stands next door to Tadao Ando's Pulitzer Foundation for the Arts (see page 174). Asked to compare his use of concrete on the museum with the 'special concrete' used by Ando, Cloepfil emphasizes the practical reasons for his choice of material and the comparatively low cost of his project. 'The concrete finish for the Contemporary is very common. It is carefully placed, in an effort to maintain a sense of uniformity to the surface, then sandblasted or etched to render the entire building as a monolithic whole.' It is also partially screened with steel-mesh overlay. Cloepfil has criticized the 'current excesses', in terms of cost, of many recent arts buildings, for while the Overlook required skilled craftsmanship, he has shown that concrete can be used both inexpensively and effectively.

Left
The structure comprises nine slabs and eight walls, and was designed to encourage an intimate relationship with the landscape by offering a multitude of viewpoints, modulating light and creating a dialogue between interior and exterior spaces.

Opposite
From top: plan and long section.

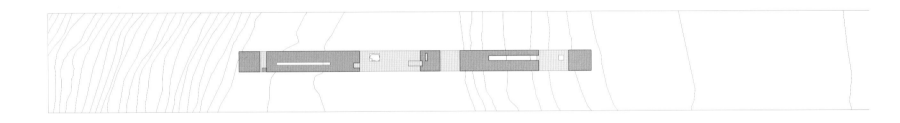
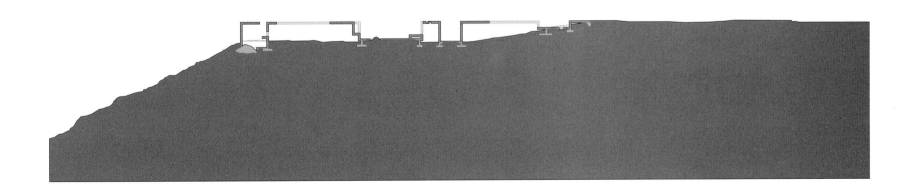

199 Landscape

Municipal Mortuary

León, Spain, 2001
BAAS

Irregularly shaped light wells, placed at oblique angles to one another, let daylight into the chapel below, while reaching symbolically towards the sky.

Barcelona-based BAAS architects chose to construct this building completely from concrete because they regard it as 'the only fitting material for a tomb' – for building what is basically a totally subterranean structure, but one which is far from utilitarian. The complex houses a funeral chapel, private chapels of rest, and administrative and service spaces, much of it beneath a vast pool, and incorporates recessed courtyards and projecting concrete light scoops.

However, rather than a tomb or a point of eternal rest, the place is one of transition and farewell. The competition assessors were concerned that the proposed main hall might feel too much like an airport departure lounge, but were assured that this space, which lies east of the building and has a glazed wall along its length, would have a very different atmosphere because of the view out onto the steep grassy bank and belt of trees beyond. The sense of being in a landscape is emphasized by the paired concrete columns inside, their V forms resembling spreading branches.

The atmosphere of rural isolation is, in fact, a clever construct; the site for the mortuary is surrounded by new multi-storey housing blocks. While privacy and quiet are important for the bereaved, the sensitivities of the neighbours needed careful handling also. Building a mortuary in the middle of a residential area can be problematic. Those who overlook it do not want a constant reminder of death, but, conversely, hiding the building away might suggest a lack of respect for the dead or undermine the importance of its function.

The success of the building lies in the tension between inside and outside, above and below. The light scoops draw daylight and the changing patterns of water-refracted sunshine into the chapel, which lies at the building's very heart. The architects have likened the scoops to 'mysterious fingers in search of light for prayer'. It is no surprise to learn that they cite Le Corbusier as an influence – the debt to the Notre-Dame-du-Haut chapel at Ronchamp is clear, especially in the way in which the scoops suggest a carving out of space, a slicing into a thick skin.

The courtyards that separate the chapels of rest have rectilinear walls, which rise up beyond the surface of the water above in a simple row, at once suggesting the work of minimalist artists and also an abstracted line of gravestones. The water laps their edges, but is contained by a firm edge, a simple barrier.

This project – a very literal burial – could have been oppressive, even frightening, for visitors, but it is not. The use of concrete, combined with water and thoughtful landscaping, has created an atmosphere that is serene and contemplative.

Bottom
There was a concern that a mortuary in the midst of residential blocks could cause offence. To overcome the problem, the architects have placed most of the project underground and covered it with a serene pool.

Below
In situ cast concrete with phenolic panels was used for the mortuary. To match the colour with the vernacular buildings of Leon, a local stone called *bonar* was added.

Although the chapel is placed well below ground, the light wells admit daylight from different angles and levels to create a bright and airy space.

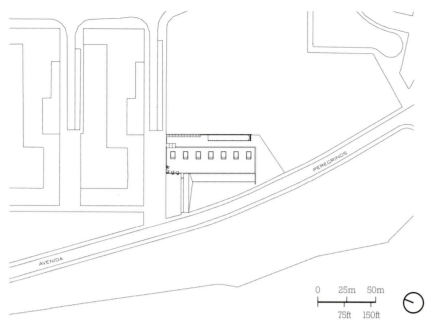

Top left
Site plan. The mortuary (centre) is very close to a residential development (left).

Left
A glazed wall running the entire length of the main hall faces onto a tree-planted grass slope. Iroko wood, soft recessed lighting and the use of domestic lamps and furnishings make this an unintimidating and welcoming area for the recently bereaved.

Top right
From bottom: plans of the below-ground and upper levels.

Bottom right
Sections through the four light wells show how they direct light into the underground space.

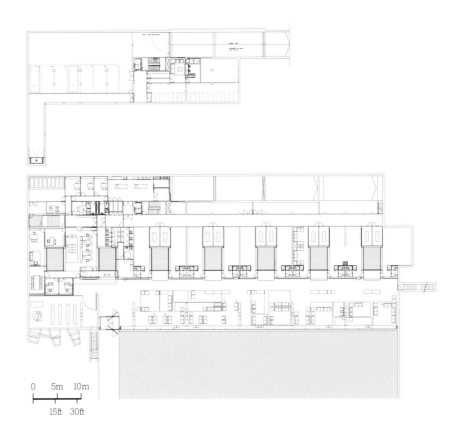

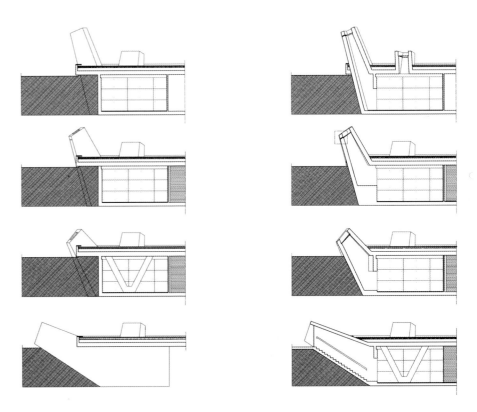

205 Landscape

La Granja Stairways

Toledo, Spain, 2000
José Antonio Martínez Lapeña &
Elías Torres Tur Arquitectos

Opposite top
The fretwork of the belvedere resembles a large bird with outstretched wings, poised to take flight over the Tajo plain below.

Opposite bottom
At night, the escalator is ablaze with light. Incised deep into the terrain, the illuminated ochre concrete cascades down the hillside like molten lava.

Below
A stepped route, one of a pair, has been built beside the escalator.

Below right
The zigzag staircase structure can be seen at the top right of this site plan.

This spectacular project is an external escalator, cut into a steep hillside that links a large car park to Toledo's historic city centre over 30 metres (100 feet) above. Both practical and poetic, it provides easy access and dramatic views. From below, it reads as a jagged zigzag, hacked into the turf, as though the land has been prized apart to accommodate it or to let a mysterious creature break the surface. It is a site of surgical incision or archaeological excavation.

The setting is dramatic. Toledo was originally a Roman town, became a Visigoth capital, then an Arab intellectual centre, and was a seat of Catholic kings until 1561. Its importance lies in its strategic position, perched above a loop in the River Tagus. From a distance, little of the concrete structure of the staircase is visible – it is just a narrow edge to the dark void of the cut – but inside the escalators are flanked by a concrete retaining wall, which in fact, wraps over them, and is set with built-in downlighters. Its green-planted, cantilevered roof protects equipment and visitors, and continues the slope of the hill, rather than being horizontal. This means that it has to be capable of supporting up to 1,200 millimetres (47 inches) of earth. The internal cross-section changes, giving differing senses of enclosure and varied widths of aperture. Breaking the overall rise into six flights allows the structure to respond to the irregularity of the site, reduces vertigo and allows sightseers to pause and admire the views of the Tajo plain and the new areas of the city. There are also two more direct, stepped routes, branching off to the left of the escalators.

Ochre-coloured, like the traditional architecture of the city, the concrete is vertically board-marked. Since the ground is unstable, it was necessary to sink the foundations to loadbearing rock, some 30 metres (100 feet) deep; to bridge the remains of the city walls, the base slab is supported on bored piles. The up escalators are reached by a short passage, which ducks under the foundations of the city wall, and at the top sits a belvedere.

From the city, the belvedere resembles a large bird, poised for take-off, but from below, its roof propped on concrete stilts, it hovers like a sheet of rock, raised up and precariously balanced. When the escalators are turned off, slatted screens are slid across on heavy-duty runners to block the entrance. The sides of the escalators and the handrails are made of stainless steel, but the hardness of the surfaces is softened by the plants and shrubs that have been put in circular

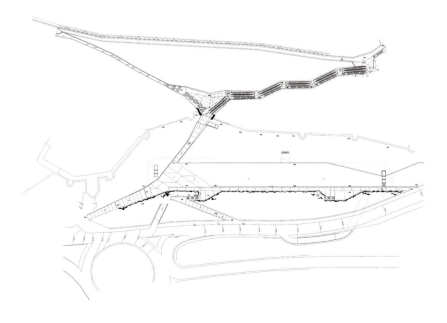

holes cut into the concrete. José Antonio Martínez Lapeña and Elías Torres Tur have been in practice for more than 20 years, but still bring a fresh approach to each project. When asked to define his basic philosophy at a recent London lecture, Torres said he was determined to 'have as much fun as possible' with design, and to be 'incorrect' – to avoid the obvious or the predictable solution.

An early project of theirs was an open-air church in Ibiza, and the firm have also established a reputation for imaginative interventions in historic buildings. They have re-landscaped the promenade beneath the city walls of Palma de Mallorca, and have gradually restored Antoni Gaudí's Parc Güell in Barcelona, as well as designing a department store, also in Barcelona, and a hospital in Tarragona.

Divided into six stages, the burnished stainless-steel escalator is flanked by retaining concrete walls, which wrap around the apparatus to protect the users and the mechanism from the elements.

The escalator links a large car park at the base of the site to Toledo's historic city centre above.

A model of the site reveals how, in response to the unstable ground, foundations had to be sunk 30 metres (100 feet) into the loadbearing rock below.

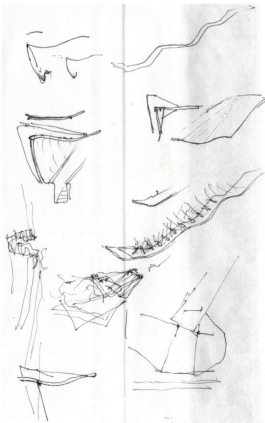

209 Landscape

Thames Barrier Park

London, UK, 2000
Patel Taylor/Groupe Signes

This collaboration between London-based architects and French landscape designers is intended both as a riverside park for immediate use and to establish a sense of scale and place for a new urban quarter that will be built next to it. As Alain Cousseran, director of Groupe Signes puts it, the park is the 'initiation' of the city that is to follow. This aspiration makes the integration of planting, park buildings and earth movement especially crucial, and concrete walls play a key part in the whole project.

The location is an area of abandoned dockyards and industrial buildings in east London. A chemical works, a dye works and an armaments factory had all contributed to contamination of the land, and the site was used for building the huge Thames Barrier – the dramatic row of stainless-steel-clad shells that stretches across the river, designed to protect the capital from extreme flooding – which dominates some views from within the park. Derelict for years, it had recently been used as a bleak location for the film *The Cement Garden*.

The principal feature of the park is the long 'green dock', which cuts diagonally across the site towards the river, and is angled so that it appears to end at the Barrier. Its steeply walled, flat-bottomed form recalls the landscape of the working docks that once defined the character of this area. Fair-faced in situ concrete is used for the walls of the dock at the point of entry and as it approaches the river. The austerity of the horizontal banding of the concrete contrasts with the lush planting of the walls in between. Tough yew hedges grow in reinforced cages of earth. The horizontal emphasis echoes the strips of fragrant planting at the base of the dock, described as a 'rainbow garden', which consists of bands of grass and narrow paths. The enclosed form and rigour of the linear planting suggests a botanic garden or a walled kitchen garden, while the undulating profile of the interspersed hedges (yew again) recalls lapping water.

At the entrance end, the concrete walls enclose a fountain courtyard, with two straight rows of single jets of water, like a pair of colonnades, rising through a granite floor. As it reaches the river, the planting gives way to another surface contrasting with the concrete – a timber decking that leads to a simple grass bank, sloping up to the Pavilion of Remembrance. This is a memorial to local people who died in military conflict, and is reached by a narrow, ramped concrete passageway. It is also a place to sit and relax overlooking the river. Over a concrete substructure, an informal grouping of 23 delicate steel columns supports a slatted timber roof structure, with a huge circular hole in it. The park's other architectural element is more robust in appearance: a concrete and timber-framed visitor centre and café, which is also oriented towards the river, but set further back, and positioned above the green dock on the grassy plateau, through which the dock cuts. Planted with copses of trees, softened with rough-cut grass and wild flowers, the area resembles a meadow. Fears of vandalism influenced the design of the building. The concrete walls around the kitchen, toilets and other amenities clearly signal their impermeability and, during the day, read as a solid volume next to an open glazed pavilion. However, at night, steel shutters are pulled down between the green-oak columns of the surrounding portico, not only protecting the building, but producing a secure storage area for tables and chairs.

Above
Timber decking contrasts with the concrete. A simple grass slope leads to the Pavilion of Remembrance, dedicated to the war dead of the area.

Opposite
The entrance is marked by a fountain courtyard, enclosed by concrete walls.

211 Landscape

The concrete and timber-framed visitor centre looks out onto the river through walls of glazing. At night the glazing is protected from vandalism by steel shutters, which are pulled down between the green-oak columns of the surrounding portico.

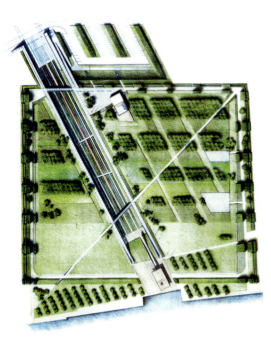

The 'green dock' is surrounded by a plateau used for recreation and public events. Rows of trees are interspersed with wild-flower meadows. The visitor centre is at the bottom centre of the plan.

Above and below
The main feature of the project is the planted valley that slices through the site, terminating at both ends in concrete walls and contained between banks of yew. The linearity of this 'green dock' is emphasized by rows of fragrant shrubs, which alternate with narrow paths.

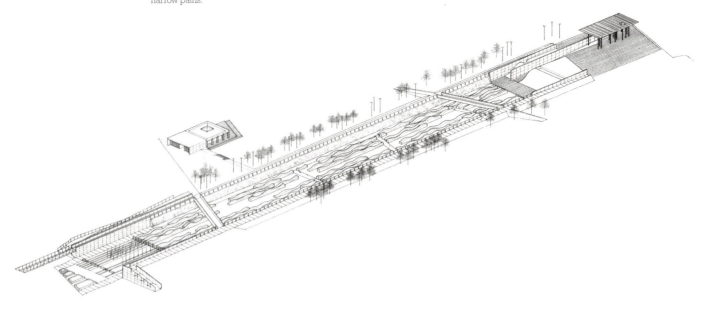

Cemetery

Borghetto Santo Spirito, Italy; phase one completed 2002
Marco Ciarlo

The structures were designed to protect visitors from the intense summer heat and from the strong winds that batter the Ligurian coast.

Below right
The gate and upper lawn are at the top right of the site plan.

Below
The linear concrete construction culminates in a wall of smooth stone. The architect chose these materials for their neutrality, chromatic value and monumentality.

Borghetto Santo Spirito is a seaside town on the Ligurian coast of Italy, between Savona and the French border. Behind the apartment blocks and shops, which bustle with activity in summer, but mostly close down when the season ends, the land rises very steeply. This new cemetery is halfway up the hillside, on land too steep for other development. Its gates are located at the top of the site, and all that is visible to someone entering is the uppermost lawn, planted with rows of olive trees and bordered by a wall of concrete panels, above which nothing can be seen but the flat plane of the Mediterranean, stretching out to the horizon.

Although there will be some earth burials, most interments will be in above-ground niches, or *loculi*, with some smaller niches for urns, and it is the structures which incorporate these that form the most dramatic part of Marco Ciarlo's project. To enter this part of the site, visitors step down the hill via a second and third terrace, each itself a small graveyard, to a linear structure set into the hill. To date, only this first stage of the project has been completed, but the municipality will gradually finance further construction stepping up the hill, as well as the roofing over of the first four blocks of *loculi*, which are currently open-air.

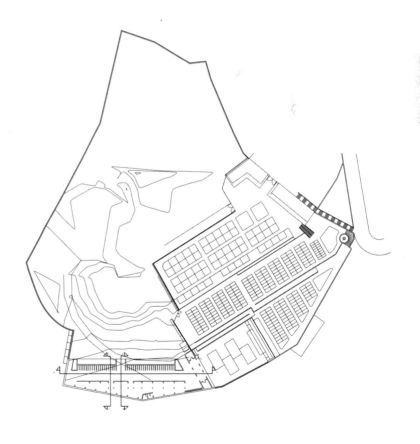

Beyond these, the structure is already enclosed. It feels totally subterranean and is designed to offer shelter from harsh winds and the intense heat of the midsummer sun. This is not a dark or sinister environment, but one that is suffused with dramatic light, and which concentrates the eye on elemental views – the uninhabited hillside, framed in wide, unglazed, picture-window openings at the far end of the colonnades or avenues, and the sky, seen though the long, narrow slots above.

The concrete structure is far from pristine. Joints between shuttering panels are roughly expressed, and this vertical surface contrasts both with the smooth stone of the square panels that seal the ends of each *loculus*, and with the concrete of the floor and of the roof soffit, which were cast against steel, rather than wood. However, even the steel-shuttered areas are not crisp but mottled and blotched, what Ciarlo describes as *cavillatura* ('freckled') – an imperfection that adds character. 'I admire the perfection of Tadao Ando's concrete,' he says, but he has not sought to emulate it. Rather, he sees the result he has achieved as 'reminiscent of the "unfinished" concepts of Michelangelo'. After rain, the surfaces are beautifully reflective, and this will be enhanced when a reflecting pool is built above the colonnades. But already, the character of the space changes dramatically with the shifting quality of light throughout the year, and from day to day, or even from hour to hour.

Ciarlo's small practice has specialized in projects for local municipalities. (It already works for an astonishing 24 such public-sector clients.) In general, this requires both a political astuteness and an ability to phase projects, keep construction costs low and details robust. What is remarkable is that he is able to deliver projects that meet these requirements, but simultaneously provide lyrical, modern spaces that have the strength to retain their power when they accumulate the clutter of life (or death). For instance, here and at another cemetery project in nearby Finale, the graves will be individually specified by relatives of the deceased, but Ciarlo has no desire to restrict the typical photo-ceramic images, vases of flowers and poetic inscriptions.

The cemetery is located on the steep slopes above Borghetto Santo Spirito. From the top of the site, all that is visible is the uppermost lawn, which offers calming views of the Mediterranean.

Above
Longitudinal cuts allow sunlight to penetrate from above. The fissures are emphasized by rows of parallel lights. Natural and artificial light complement each another.

Right
The monumental columbarium is housed in an austere concrete structure which exploits the ever-changing light conditions to dramatic effect.

Tulach a'tSolais

Oulart Hill, Wexford, Ireland, 1998
Scott Tallon Walker

The 'Mound of Light' commemorates the United Irish Rising of 1798. Two parallel walls of pristine white concrete slice through a grass mound and frame a view of Vinegar Hill, site of the defeat of the Wexford Republic and many Irish deaths.

Two parallel planes of pristine white concrete slice through a flat-topped grass mound. This is Tulach a' tSolais – the Mound of Light – a memorial constructed with funding from the Irish Millennium Commission to mark the 200th anniversary of the United Irish Rising of 1798.

Within the mound lies a rectangular concrete-lined chamber, illuminated only by a concrete slit, which is positioned to allow in maximum light on 21 June, the summer solstice and the anniversary of the Battle of Vinegar Hill. It is Vinegar Hill that the slit frames – clearly visible since the local landowner agreed to fell trees and create an extension of the east–west axis towards its summit.

The architect, Ronnie Tallon, says that concrete was chosen because 'We wanted a basic, monolithic material of strength and nobility, with which to create a modern Stonehenge.' But this is a far from 'basic' form of concrete, and the finesse of the project is very different from the rough-hewn power of Stonehenge's loosely articulated forms, which had to be laboriously dragged hundreds of miles and then raised into position. Here, the remoteness of the site determined the use of in situ, rather than precast, concrete.

Symbolizing death and resurrection, the structure had to be pure white. The supplier was paid to stop production of grey concrete and thoroughly clean the works before producing the white concrete – a procedure that occupied a whole day.

The Mound of Light recalls a burial mound, but its rectilinearity also suggests a modern defence bunker or engineering form. Tallon explains that the slit represents the Rising as a watershed between feudalism and the age of Enlightenment, and emphasizes its importance as the first attempt to establish a popular democracy in Ireland. The choice of material was also symbolic. 'White concrete gave us a clean, light colour symbolizing the pallor of death and the light of resurrection; of past events linked with the future,' says Tallon.

Because it was so important to maintain the purity of the white concrete, the supplier was paid extra to stop work on its usual grey concrete, clean the works of all traces that might contaminate the white mix and produce nothing for a whole day but the white concrete for this project. The contractor also used a high-frequency, electrically powered poker-vibrator from Germany to compact the concrete. The grid of tie boltholes is also very precise. Each shuttering panel had to measure 90 x 180 centimetres (35 $1/2$ x 70 $3/4$ inches) and have eight boltholes, perfectly positioned. The seam lines between panels had to form continuous bands, and even the upper edge of the concrete planes is neatly marked with regularly spaced boltholes.

The concrete-lined chamber, with its granite floor, is illuminated by natural light alone. The chasm was aligned east–west, so that the light would be at its strongest on 21 June, the date of the battle of Vinegar Hill.

From the side, the concrete walls read as a crisp, white coping, a bridge form, a spine or fin. Within, the threshold to the chamber is demarcated by a change in the pattern of the bush-hammered granite flooring slabs. The 'path' that takes over from the simple, mown-grass external path does not run across the chamber, but delivers visitors to its perimeter. At the heart of the mound is an artwork by sculptor Michael Warren. Two squares of ancient Irish oak (from trees which must have been standing at the time of the battle), gently float on the floor, subtly warped, as if stretching upwards and seeking the light. Tightly controlled concrete combines with natural materials, also precisely handled, to create an atmosphere of isolation and of connection to a wider landscape. It is a place for contemplation about the relationship of the modern and the traditional, concrete suggesting both a crisp mechanical newness and a sense of rooted continuity.

Seen from the side, the walls of the monument outline the mound like a backbone.

223 Landscape

Cathedral of Our Lady of the Angels

Los Angeles, California, USA, 2002
Rafael Moneo

Unmistakably set in Los Angeles, the cathedral is bordered on its northern side by the Hollywood freeway. At night, light shines through the protruding light box, silhouetting a giant cross.

Steps lead visitors from the piazza up to the 25 tonne (25 ton) bronze entrance doors, seen at the left of the picture.

Below
A campanile 48 metres (156 feet) high occupies a small north-west courtyard.

Bottom
Light-coloured, sandblasted architectural concrete was used as a reference to the golden adobe of California missions. The heavy materiality of the blocky forms evokes the Romanesque style.

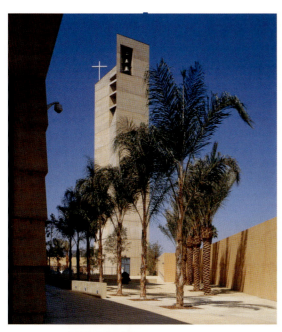

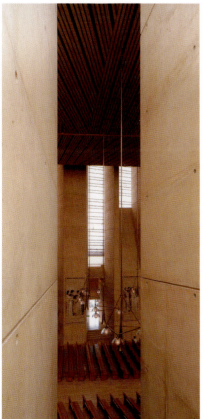

The rich, honey-coloured concrete of Rafael Moneo's Cathedral of Our Lady of the Angels is designed to last for 300 years. No mean feat, especially since it stands close to the Elysian Park fault and has to be able to withstand earthquakes of 8.5 on the Richter scale. One's first assumption is that a building of this size and colour must be of stone, and traditionally constructed, but it consists of very high-quality in situ concrete. Using solid blocks of stone would have been too expensive, but, as Moneo explains, 'Thinking of the direct use of stone in churches of the past, I was against using cladding. I wanted the material and substance of the building to be seen from the start.' Concrete enabled him to achieve this. But why was it so important to him?

Moneo drew on the ideas of John Ruskin and the Arts and Crafts concept of honest use of materials. He felt that using a material that doesn't cover up anything inferior, and a method of construction devoid of virtuoso techniques, was especially important in a cathedral, describing it as 'a way of recognizing the dignity of the building itself'. Concrete was also practical given the measures needed to combat potential earthquake damage. In addition, Moneo liked the fact that it is both an interior and an exterior material. 'Concrete can give a double-edged condition, indoors and outdoors – continuity between walls within and walls without, which enables the building to be seen and understood as a homogeneous whole.'

Without a major tower or spire, the cathedral looks nothing like the medieval cathedrals of Europe, its blocky forms and planar enclosing walls, together with its colour (created by using a pigment in the mix), recalling instead a more local precedent: the Mission churches of the American Southwest. However, Moneo sees his building as being linked to the great ecclesiastical architecture of the past, via the modernist canon. He cites Bryggman's Resurrection Chapel (1938) at Turku, Finland, Asplund's Stockholm Crematorium (1940) and Le Corbusier's Chapel of Notre-Dame-du-Haut (1950–54), Ronchamp, France, as modern buildings in which 'one senses a sacred presence'. He points out that 'each one of these examples awakens echoes of architecture we know well.' By this, he means that Turku recalls the verticality of Gothic architecture, and the atmosphere of Ronchamp that of a small Romanesque church. 'I think that the spirit of the Christian faith was made more manifest in the Middle Ages than during the Renaissance or Counter-Reformation,' he says, and it is this spirit he has set out to capture in concrete.

Moneo attributes the power of both Ronchamp and Turku to their manipulation of light. 'I understand light as the protagonist of a space that is aimed at recovering the sense of transcendence, and presenting it as a sense of the sublime.' At the Cathedral of Our Lady of the Angels, light is filtered through thinly sliced alabaster to create an effect that is both warm and mysterious. Moneo first used this material for the Fundación Miró, a gallery and study centre in Palma, Mallorca.

Because the thickness of the cathedral walls varies from 0.3 to 1.5 metres (1 to 5 feet), there was a risk that in the thick sections the mass of the wall would trap the heat generated by the chemical reaction between the cement and water to such an extent that the internal temperature would be too hot for curing and could lead to thermal cracking. To overcome this, a special cement was used. Lehigh Aalborg cement is a white cement produced in Denmark. It has a uniform colour (which was also desirable) but, more importantly, it generates a lower hydration heat than other white cements. The temperature was minimized further by starting pours at 3 o'clock in the morning in warm weather and by using chilled water, mist and refrigeration cooling to keep the materials cool on site. The mix also included pozzolan fly ash, the siliceous by-product of coal burning. This improved workability, and therefore surface quality, as the mix flowed tightly up against the formwork. It was also an economical choice, since it is readily available in southern California, and a practical one because the supplier, Boral Materials, was able to guarantee a narrow colour range of light grey to off-white. Since Moneo wanted to create spaces with non-parallel walls, to maximize the play of light on surfaces throughout the building,

Light is diffused through a monumental alabaster wall that acts as a prism, giving the interior of the vestibule a warm luminescence.

more than 800 different corner angles were needed for the formwork. Three-dimensional CAD modelling was used to produce formwork shop drawings, and the formwork was constructed from a double layer of plywood, with an aluminium and LVL backing. The textured effect on the exterior walls was created by building a pattern of 1.2 metre (4 foot) tall 'shingles', each 8 centimetres (3 inches) apart from the next, into the formwork. Work proceeded in 3.6 metres (12 foot) lifts, and the forms remained in place for two and a half days. Of the 60,400 square metres (650,000 square feet) of concrete used, only 7.5 square metres (80 square feet) failed to meet the standard required and had to be redone. Finally, the surface was sandblasted, eliminating minor imperfections.

The earthquake risk meant that the whole building is designed in such a way that it is isolated from its foundations on a series of rubber pads and sliders. This system was developed by structural engineer Nabih Youseff. A standard reinforcement bar was used, but with a minimum depth of cover of 7.5 centimetres (3 inches) rather than the standard 5 centimetres (2 inches).

Top right
The piazza is at the centre of the site plan with the cathedral building to the left.

Centre right
Plan of the cathedral.

Bottom right
Long section through the cathedral.

Below
Detail of a chapel interior.

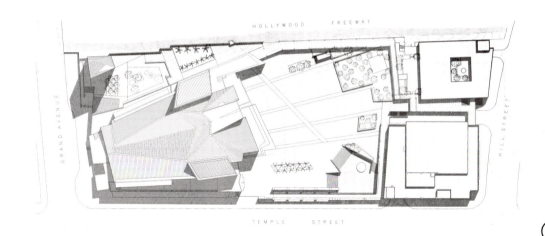

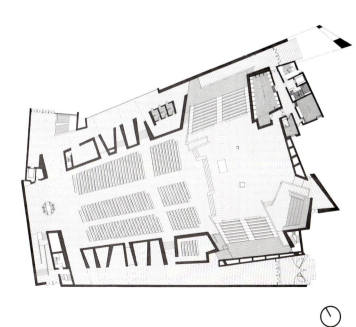

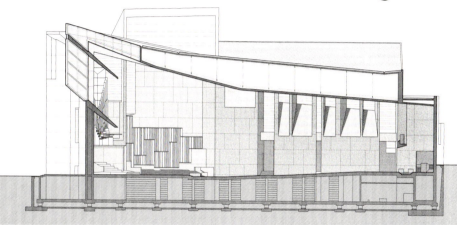

227 Landscape

Footnotes

Notes on the Preface

1 James Lasdun, 'The Master Builder', *The Guardian Review*, 29 Nov 2003, p. 6.

2 Sarah Gaventa, *Concrete Design: The Extraordinary Nature of Concrete*, Mitchell Beazley, London, 2001, p. 30.

3 Kenneth Hudson, *Building Materials*, Longman, London, 1972, pp. 58–61.

Notes on the Introduction

1 John W. Cook and Heinrich Klotz, *Conversations with Architects*, Lund Humphries, London, 1973, p. 102.

2 International Congress of Architects report in *The Architect and Contract Reporter*, July 20, 1906, pp. 42–6. Foreign representatives at the conference included Otto Wagner, JT Cuypers and Herman Muthesius. Bassegoda quotation appears on p. 46.

3 'The Architectural Treatment of Reinforced Concrete', report of a lecture given by WR Lethaby at the Northern Polytechnic Institute, Holloway, London, in *The Builder*, 7 Feb 1913, p. 175.

4 The same article reports that Mr R Graham Keevill, the organizer of the classes on ferroconcrete in conjunction with which Lethaby's lecture was presented, responded by saying that he 'opposed putting anything on to concrete at all' and that 'everyone knew it was going to revolutionize construction and architecture'; *The Builder*, 7 Feb 1913, p. 176.

5 Peter Collins worked for a number of years as an architectural assistant in the offices of Auguste Perret's pupils in France and Switzerland before going on to lecture in the history of architecture at McGill University, Montreal, where he wrote *Concrete: The Vision of a New Architecture*, Faber and Faber, London, 1959, subtitled *A Study of Auguste Perret and his Precursors*.

6 Collins, pp. 64–75.

7 This was the best known of their works and was described as having a 'strange appeal' and 'fascinating structure'; quotation appears in TP Bennett and FY Yerbury, *Architectural Design in Concrete*, 1927, p. 18.

8 AEJ Morris, *Precast Concrete in Architecture*, George Godwin Ltd, London, 1968, p. 62.

9 'The Decoration of Steel and Reinforced Concrete Structure', text of a paper read before the Glasgow Institute of Architects on March 11, 1908; quoted in *The Builders Journal and Architectural Engineer*, March 25, 1908, p. 269–73. Quotation appears on p. 271.

10 Pekka Korvenmaa, 'Aalto and Finnish Industry' in Peter Reed, ed., *Alvar Aalto: Between Humanism and Materialism*, Museum of Modern Art, New York, 1998, p. 87.

11 Carl W Condit, 'The First Reinforced-Concrete Skyscraper: the Ingalls Building in Cincinnati and its place in structural history' in *Early Reinforced Concrete*, Frank Newby, ed., Ashgate, Aldershot and Burlington, 2001, pp. 255–92.

12 Frank Lloyd Wright, 'In the Cause of Architecture VII: the Meaning of Materials' in *Concrete Architectural Record*, August 1928, p. 99–104. Quotation appears on p. 99.

13 Wright, p. 102.

14 Wright, pp. 99, 102.

15 David Gebhard, *Schindler*, William Stout, San Francisco, 1997, p. 50.

16 First published in 1923 and translated into English in 1927 by the architect Frederick Etchells.

17 Francis S Onderdonk, *The Ferro-Concrete Style: Reinforced Concrete in Modern Architecture*, Hennessey and Ingalls, Santa Monica, 1998, p. 255. Facsimile of first edition, published by Architectural Book Publishing Company, Inc., 1928.

18 Alan Colquhoun, *Modern Architecture*, Oxford History of Art, Oxford University Press, pp. 142–4.

19 Greenside was demolished in 2003. Basil Ward of the CWL partnership acknowledged the direct debt of these houses to Le Corbusier's Domino frame, but notes the British tendency towards 'eclecticism and romance', suggesting that at this period it was more the form than the radical agenda of Modernism which was being explored. In *Connell Ward Lucas*, ed. Dennis Sharp, Book Art, London, 1994, p. 22

20 John Faber, preface to revised edition of *Reinforced Concrete Simply Explained*, John Faber and David Alsop, eds, Oxford University Press, 1976.

21 Mies van der Rohe, published in *G*, September 1923, p. 1; quoted in Fritz Neumeyer, *The Artless Word*, MIT Press, Cambridge, MA, 1994, p. 243

22 By 1927 Bennett and Yerbury could propose that 'it is possible that the day of the Renaissance is passing and that a period of more original design is at hand. It may be that the advent of new developments in steel and concrete were needed to provide an impetus of sufficient importance for the designer to cast off the restrictions imposed by tradition and to produce new forms and compositions' (Bennett and Yerbury, p. 25). They conclude that 'the use of concrete lends itself to originality of treatment because of the absence of precedent of similar work in the architecture of the ages and forces the designer to think in a fresh vein' (Bennett and Yerbury, p. 6).

23 *Architectural Journal*, Nov 24, 1926, p. 617 (the editor at the time was Christian Barman). Later in the same issue Hilaire Belloc challenged the modernist assumption that the material should determine form, saying 'that we must first all set about considering our material and then wonder how we can achieve beauty without offending the sanctity of the material, seems to me altogether putting the cart before the horse', from *On the External Effect of Concrete*, pp. 621–2. Quotation appears on p. 622.

24 *Architectural Review*, November 1932, p. 179

25 *Post War Building Studies*, vol. no. 18: *The Architectural Use of Building Materials*, HMSO, 1946. Concrete and cast stone are discussed on pp. 39–50. Quotation appears on p. 40. The writer goes on to say 'in present conditions of design and technique it would be a disaster if in situ concrete were unrestrictedly used in the rebuilding of our towns and villages', p. 44.

26 See Miles Glendinning and Stefan Muthesius, *Tower Block: Modern Public Housing in England, Scotland, Wales and Northern Ireland*, Yale University Press, New Haven and London, 1994.

27 Le Corbusier, *Oeuvre Complète: vol. 5 1946–52*, Birkhauser, Basel, Boston and Berlin, 1953, p. 191.

28 Reyner Banham, *The New Brutalism*, Architectural Press, London, 1966, p. 16

29 *Architectural Design*, January 1955, p. 1.

30 'This Business of Architecture', lecture at Tulane University, New Orleans, 1955; published in *Louis I Kahn: Writings, Lectures, Interviews*, Alessandra Latour, ed., Rizzoli, New York, 1991, p. 63.

31 Stamo Papadaki, *Oscar Niemeyer*, Mayflower, New York, 1960, and London, 1961, quoted in Rupert Spade, *Oscar Niemeyer*, Thames and Hudson, New York and London, 1971, p. 10.

32 GE Kidder Smith, 'The Architects and the Modern Scene' in *Architectural Review*, March 1944, pp. 78–84.

33 'Ancient and Modern: Lloyds Bank, Shrewsbury', in *Concrete Quarterly*, no.81, April–June 1969, pp. 2–5. Quotation appears on p. 4.

34 *Concrete Quarterly*, October–December 1966, p. 30.

35 'The Weathering of Concrete' in *Concrete*, February 1971, pp. 53–7. The article is a summary of papers given by, among others, JA Partridge of Howell Killick Partridge Amis and J Rodin of Building Design Partnership, at a RIBA symposium on January 7, 1971.

36 Peter Zumthor, *Thinking Architecture*, Lars Muller, Baden, 1998, p. 58. See also Peter Davey, 'Zumthor the Shaman', *Architectural Review*, Oct 1998, pp. 68–74.

37 Santiago Calatrava, 'The Ancient Virtues of Concrete' in *Casabella*, vol. 66 706/7 Dec 2002/Jan 2003, p. 175.

38 Gaventa, p. 116.

39 Catherine Slessor, *Concrete Regionalism*, Thames and Hudson, London, 2000, p. 51.

40 Ando writing in 1986; quoted in Slessor, p. 51.

Bibliography

Bennett, David: *Exploring Concrete Architecture: Tone Texture Form*, Birkhäuser, Basel, Boston, Berlin, 2001

Bennett, David: *Innovations in Concrete*, Thomas Telford, London, 2002

Erb, Hans F: *Beton Fundamente, Formen, Figuren*, Beton-Verlag, Düsseldorf, 1960

Gage, Michael: *Guide to Concrete Blockwork*, Architectural Press, London, 1970

Gage, Michael: *Guide to Concrete Finishes*, Architectural Press, London, 1970

Heinle, Erwin and Bächer, Max: *Building in Visual Concrete*, Technical Press, London, 1971, German edition published 1966

Morris, AEJ: *Precast Concrete in Architecture*, George Godwin Ltd, London, 1968

Newby, Frank, ed.: *Studies in the History of Civil Engineeering*, vol.11: *Early Reinforced Concrete*, Ashgate, Aldershot and Burlington, 2001

Slaton, Amy E.: *Reinforced Concrete and the Modernization of American Building 1900–1930*, Johns Hopkins University Press, Baltimore and London, 2001

Sutherland, James, Humm, Dawn and Chrimes, Mike, eds,: *Historic Concrete: Background to Appraisal*, Thomas Telford, London, 2001

Index

Page numbers in *italics* refer to illustrations

Aalto, Alvar 16, 71
airport buildings *14*, 15, 18
Allied Works Architecture 183, 192–9
Alton Estate, Roehampton, London 19
American Folk Art Museum, New York 139, 170–3
Ando, Tadao 23, 71, 132–7, 174–7, 197
Anin Jeromin Fitilidis & Partner 120–3
Aranda, Rafael 140, 142
Archigram 95
Architectus 116–19
Armani Headquarters and Theatre, Milan 71, 132–7
Art Gallery, Bregenz, Austria 22
Arts and Crafts Movement 11, *15*, 225
Arup, Ove 17
Asplund, Erik Gunnar 15, 16, 225
Axel Schultes Architekten 78–81

BAAS 200–205
Bacon Street House, London 54–7
balconies 8, 62, 116, 121, 155
Banham, Reyner 19–20
Barani, Marc 183
Barcelona Botanic Garden, Barcelona 188–91
Barragán, Luis 183
Bassegoda, Joaquin 11
Bearth and Deplazes 26–9
Becher, Bernd and Hilla 71
Bennett and Yerbury 18
Bery, Max 15
Black/White Himuro House, Osaka 44
Böhm, Gottfried 183
bonOFFICE Headquarters, Krefeld, Germany 121
Boots factory, Beeston, Nottinghamshire 71
Breuer, Marcel 139, 170
bridges 8, *13*, 14–15, 22, 23, 183
Brion Vega Cemetery, San Vito di Altivole, Italy 183
Brutalism 11, 20, 22, 25
Bryggman, Erik 225
building blocks 9, 43, 87
built-in furniture 28, 41, 53, 54, 73
Burroughs Company Headquarters, Plymouth, Michigan 16

C-House, Brisbane 50–53
Cadbury-Brown, Jim 25
Caja General de Ahorros, Granada 34
Calatrava, Santiago 22–3
Campo Baeza, Alberto 30–35
Canary Wharf Underground Station, London 71, 82–5
Canosa, José Luís 188–91
Casey, Michael 112, 114
Cataluña Congress Centre, Barcelona 190
Cathedral of Our Lady of the Angels, Los Angeles, California 183, 224–7
cement 8, 12, 13
cemeteries 78, 183, 200–5, 214–17
Centenary Hall, Breslau, Germany 15
Centre for Innovative Technologies, Majorca 34
Chillida, Eduardo 78
Church of the Pilgrimage, Neviges, Germany 183
Ciarlo, Marco 214–17
City of Science, Valencia *23*
cladding 11, 14, 18, 55, 67, 101, 139
Clifford, Patrick 116
Cloepfil, Brad 175, 195, 197
Coignet, François 12
Collins, Peter 12
colour
  in the cast 142, 148, 165, 170, 185, 207, 221, 225
  on the surface 17, 44, 108, 112, 144
Colquhoun, Alan 17
computer-generated design 91, *94*, 102, 114, 226
concrete
  aesthetic qualities 8, 11, 13, 14, 20, 21–2, 31, 96
  bush-hammered 112, 170
  criticized 8, 11, 16, 17–18, 20, 22
  frames 14, 15, 19, 22, 54, 71, 107, 154
  history 9, 11, 12–22
  insulating properties 101, 118, 130, 158
  in the landscape 31, 58, 91, 139, 148, 183–227
  manufacture 8, 12
  polished 62, 139, 170, 179
  practicality 25, 62, 65, 126, 197, 225
  prefabricated 17, 18, 19, 163
  prestressed 9, 19
  reinforced 8–9, 13, 14–15, 16, 17, 183
  in situ 54, 62, 121, 126, 130, 139, 211, 219
  special mixes 27, 48, 82, 139, 148, 165, 179, 225
  suitability 11, 14, 18, 21
  versatility 8, 11, 47, 50, 93
  see also precast panels
Concrete, Washington State 14
Connell, Ward & Lucas 17
Consoni, Beat 72–7
Contemporary Art Museum, St Louis, Missouri 175, 197
Cook, Peter 158

Cook Hitchcock Sargisson and Royal Associates 116–19
courtyards 62, 78, 91, 124, 154, 168, 201, 211
Craig-Martin, Michael 114
Cubus, Düsseldorf 158

dams 14, 183
De Blas House, Sevilla la Nueva, Spain 30–35
de Meuron, Pierre *21*, 22, 112–15
Deplazes, Andrea 27, 28
Diamond Ranch High School, Diamond Bar, California 90–5
Dom-ino House, France 17, 54
Donovan, Brian 53
Donovan Hill Architects 50–3
Drescher + Kubina 128–31
Drumkinnon Tower, Loch Lomond, Scotland 156, *157*

earthquakes 45, 225, 226
Eberswalde Technical School, Germany *21*, 22
Ehime Prefectural Museum of General Science, Niihama City, Japan 86–9
Elzner & Anderson *15*, 16
Ennis House, Los Angeles, California 16
Estudio Cano Lasso 166–9
Estudio Sancho-Madridejos 184–7
Evenden, Gerard 82

Faber, John 17
factories 12, 13, 14, 15, 71, 132
Fallingwater, Bear Run, Pennsylvania 16
Federal Chancellery, Berlin 78–81
Ferrater, Carlos 188–91
Fiat Lingotto Factory, Turin *14*, 15, 71
Figueras, Bet 188–91
finishes 17, 22, 44, 107, 112, 139, 144, 148
fireplaces *47*
Fishing Museum, Karmøy, Norway 139, 148–53
floors 28, 118, 121, 173, 175–6
Foster and Partners 82–5
Freyssinet, Eugène *14*, 15
Fukui Prefectural Dinosaur Museum, Katsuyama, Japan 87
Funk, Lisbeth 148

Garcia-Solera, Javier 124–7
gardens 50, *52*, 78, 188–91, 210–13
Gaudi, Antoni 15
Gaventa, Sarah 8

231 Index

Gigon, Annette 165
Gigon/Guyer *21*, 139, 162–5
Glancey, Jonathan 25
glass 22, 31, 41, 67, 107, 121, 129, 211
Gnadinger House, St Gallen, Switzerland 73
Godwin, George 12
Goetheanum, Dornach, Switzerland 183
'Gold Containers' project, Landshut, Germany 108, *111*
Greenside, Surrey 17
Grindelberg apartments, Berlin 19
Groupe Signes 210–13
Gruen Associates 95
Guggenheim Museum, New York 139, 170
Guyer, Mike 165

Hakuou High School, Japan 44
Haslach School, Au, Switzerland 72–7
Haus der Architektur, Munich 128–31
Hennebique, François 13
Herrle, Peter 67
Hertz, David 62, 65
Herzog, Jacques *21*, 22, 112–15
high-rise buildings *15*, 16, 17, 19
Hild, Andreas 108
Hild und K Architekten 104–11
Hill, Timothy 50, 53
Hirakura, Naoko 36–7
Holl, Steven 44, 58
housing estates 8, *17*, 18–19, *21*
Howell Killick Partridge and Amis (HKPA) 19, 71
Hunstanton School, Norfolk 20

Igualada Cemetery, Barcelona 183
Ingalls Building, Cincinnati, Ohio *15*
Innside Hotel, Düsseldorf 158–61
International Style 16

Jennings, Jim 58–61
Johnson Wax building, Racine, Wisconsin 71
Jubilee Line Extension, London 82
Judd, Donald 183

Kahn, Albert 16
Kahn, Louis *10*, *18*, 20, 116
Kaltwasser, Thomas 108
Kelly, Ellsworth 175, 176
Kemeter Paint Warehouse, Eichstätt, Germany 104–11
Kojima, Kazuhiro 42–5

Koolhaas, Rem 22, 114
Koshino House, Japan *23*
Kunsthal, Rotterdam *22*, 114
Kunstmuseum, Vaduz, Liechtenstein 139, 178–81
Kurokawa, Kisho 86–9

La Coruña Swimming Pool, La Coruña, Spain 166–9
La Granja Stairways, Toledo, Spain 206–9
The Laban Centre, London 112–15
Lapeña, José Antonio Martínez 206–9
Lasdun, Denys 6–7, 8, 71, 183
Le Corbusier 8, 15, 19–20, *21*, 54, 183, 201, 225
Le Fresnoy National Studio for Contemporary Arts, Tourcoing, France 102
Lecture Hall 3, University of Alicante, Spain 124–7
Lethaby, W.R. 11
Libeskind, Daniel 25
light
   artificial 58, 96, 101, 107, 129, 132, 144, 181
   natural 82, 158, 170, 185, 201, 216, 218–23, 225–6
Lindegren and Jäntti 139
Lloyds Bank, Shrewsbury 21
London Zoo, London 17
LOOK UP Office Headquarters, Gelsenkirchen, Germany 71, 120–3
Lovell Beach House, Newport Beach, California 16
Lubetkin, Berthold 17

Madridejos, Sol 185
Maillart, Robert *13*, 14–15, 183
Marciano, Rémy 139, 144–7
Matté Trucco, Giacomo *14*, 15, 71
Mayne, Thom 91
memorials 183, 211, 218–23
Mendelsohn, Eric 15–16
Mercer, Henry 16
Mies van der Rohe, Ludwig 17–18, 71
Minnaert Building, Utrecht *22*
Miralles, Enric 183
Möbius House, Het Gooi, Netherlands 22, 38–41
Modernism 11, 15, 17, 21, 23, 139, 225
Moneo, Rafael 183, 224–7
Moretti, Luigi *19*, 20–21
Morgan, Julia 16
Morger Degelo Kerez 139, 178–81
Morphosis 90–5
Mouchel, L.G. *13*, 14, 15
MSCS Building, University of Canterbury, Christchurch, New Zealand 116–19

Municipal Mortuary, León, Spain 200–205
Museum of Scottish Country Life, East Kilbride 139, 154–7
museums 86–9, 139, 148–57, 162–5, 170–81, 192–9
MVRDV 22

National Assembly Building, Dacca *10*, 20
National Theatre, London 6–7, 8
Nervi, Pier Luigi 139
Neutelings Riedijk *22*
Niemeyer, Oscar 20
Notre-Dame, Le Raincy, France *14*, 15
Notre-Dame-du-Haut, Ronchamp, France 8, 201, 225
Nugent, Karen 156

office blocks 71, 120–3, 128–37, 158
Office for Metropolitan Architecture (OMA) 22
OIKOS 66–9
Olympic Tower, Helsinki 139
Onderdonk, Francis S. 17
Orly Airport, Paris *14*, 15
Osinaga, Juan Carlos 185
Oskar Reinhart Collection, Winterthur Switzerland *21*, 139, 162–5

Page and Park 139, 154–7
Palazzo dello Sport, Rome 139
Pantheon, Rome *12*
Paoletti, Roland 82
Parc de la Violette, Paris 102
Patel Taylor 210–13
patterns 22, 87, 107, 158
Pearman, Hugh 22
Pelli, Cesar 82
Percy Thomas and Partners 21
Perret, Auguste *14*, 15
Pessac workers' housing, France *21*
photography 17, 71
Pigem, Carmen 140
pools 31, *51*, 87, 132, 139, 166–9, 175, 201
Portland Cement 9, 13, 14, 18, 48
Post Office Savings Bank, Vienna 16
precast panels 19, 21, 41, 87, 107, 118
   see also slab construction techniques
Pueblo Ribera, California 16
Pulitzer Foundation for the Arts, St Louis, Missouri 174–7

232 Index

Rabinowitch, David 58, 61
ramps 15, 17, 22, 71, 114, 148, 154
RCR Arquitectes 140–3
religious buildings 8, *14*, 15, *16*, *19*, 183, 184–7, 224–7
Resurrection Chapel, Turku, Finland 225
Roca, Miguel Angel 96–9
roofs 27, 82, 84, 96, 140, 156, 207
Royal College of Art, London 25
Royal Liver Building, Liverpool *13*, 14
Rudolph, Paul 11
Ruff, Thomas 114
Ruffi Gymnasium, Marseilles 139, 144–7
Russell, William 54–7

Sachsenhausen Visitor Centre, Berlin 158
Saint-Pancrace, Roquebrune-Cap-Martin, France 183
Salk Institute, La Jolla, California *18*, 20, 116
Salmon, James 15
San Simeon Estate, California 16
Sant'Elia, Antonio 71
Satellite Towers, Mexico City 183
Scarpa, Carlo 183
Schindler, Rudolf 16, 25
Schneider + Schumacher 158–61
Schocken Department Store, Stuttgart 15
school buildings 20, 21, 22, 44, 71, 72–7, 90–5
School of Architecture, University of Florida, Miami 102
School of Arts, Córdoba University, Argentina 96–9
Schultes, Frank 78–81
Schumacher, Michael 158
Scott Tallon Walker 183, 218–23
Sculptural Overlook, Maryhill Museum of Art, Washington 183, 192–9
sculpture 58, 78, 156, 183, 195, 222
Serra, Richard 58, 175
Servais, Georges 46–9
shuttering 12, 19, 20, 27, 54, 84, 107, 197
slab construction techniques 15, 25, 62, 101, 124, 158, 189
Smithson, Peter and Alison 20
Snøhetta 139, 148–53
social spaces 39, 58, 91, 114, 116
South Bank complex, London 6–7, 22, 183
Space Blocks, Kamishinjo, Osaka 42–5
sports buildings 139, 140–7, 166–9
St Mary's Cathedral, Tokyo *19*
Stadelhofen Railway Station, Zurich 22–3

stairs 31, 41, 54, 67, 91, 114, 130, 170, 206–9
Stephens, Suzanne 101
Stockholm Crematorium, Stockholm 225
Stockholm Library, Stockholm *15*
Stoll, Werner 67
Studio Weil, Mallorca 25
Swissbau Pavilion, Basle *22*, 23
Sydney Opera House, Sydney 17, *20*, 21
Syndesis, Inc. 25, 62–5

Tallon, Ronnie 219, 221
Tange, Kenzo *19*, 21
Tate Modern, London 114
Tavanasa Bridge, Grisons, Switzerland *13*, 14–15
texture 17, 20, *51*, 62, 107, 216
Thames Barrier Park, London 210–13
Thermal Spa, Vals, Switzerland 139
Thomas, Aubrey *13*, 14
Thorsen, Kjetil 148
Tilt-Up Slab House, Venice, California 25, 62–5
Tokiwadai House, Itabashi-ku, Tokyo 36–7
Tone House, Tavole, Italy 22
Toppila Pulp Mill, Oulu, Finland 71
Torres Tur, Elías 206–9
Treptow Cemetery, Germany 78
Tschumi, Bernard 100–3
Tsien, Billie 139, 170–3
Tulach a'tSolais, Oulart Hill, Wexford, Ireland 183, 218–23
Tussols-Basil Bathing Pavilion, Olot, Spain 140–3

UN Studio 22, 38–41
Unité d'Habitation, Marseilles *17*, 19
Unity Temple, Oak Park, Illinois *16*
university buildings 71, 96–9, 102, 116–19, 124–7, 183
University of East Anglia, Norwich 71, 183
Utzon, Jørn 17, *20*, 21

van Berkel, Richard 41
Vilalta, Ramon 140
Villa VPRO, Hilversum, Netherlands 22
Visiting Artists' Studio, Geyserville, California 58–61
Voysey, C.F.A. 15

Wagner, Otto 16
walls 23, 27, 58, 73, 116, 158, 189, 207
Ward, William E. *12*, 13
Watergate Complex, Washington DC *19*, 21

weathering 11, 18, 21, 139, 148, 165, 191
Whiteread, Rachel 25
Whitney Museum of American Art, New York 139, 170
Wieden & Kennedy Headquarters, Portland, Oregon 195, 197
Wilkinson, William Boutland *12*, 13
Wilkinson Cottage, Newcastle-upon-Tyne *12*
William E. Ward House, Port Chester, New York *12*
Williams, Owen 71
Williams, Todd 139, 170–3
windows 26, 27, 67, 73, 87, 107, 122, 144
Wright, Frank Lloyd 16, 71, 139, 170

Yale Art Gallery, New Haven, Connecticut *18*, 20

Zenith Concert Hall and Exhibition Centre, Rouen 100–3
Zumthor, Peter 22, 139

Project Credits

American Folk Art Museum, New York, USA
Architect: Tod Williams Billie Tsien and Associates
Project Team: Matthew Baird (project architect), Philip Ryan, Jennifer Turner, Nina Hollein, Vivian Wang, Hana Kassem, Kyra Clarkson, Andy Kim, William Vincent, Leslie Hansen
Client: The American Folk Art Museum
Associate Architect: Helfand Myerberg Guggenheimer Architects
Project Team: Peter Guggenheimer, Jennifer Tulley, Jonathan Reo
Project Management: Seamus Henchy & Associates (Seamus Henchy, Chris Norfleet, Kristen Solury)
Director of Museum: Gerard C. Wertkin
Deputy Director: Riccardo Salmona
General Contractor: Pavarini Construction
Acoustical Consultant: Acoustic Dimensions
Structural Engineers: Severud Associates
Mechanical Engineers: Ambrosino, De Pinto & Schmeider
Curtainwall Consultant: Gregory Romine
Lighting Design: Renfro Design Group
Exhibition Design: Ralph Appelbaum and Associates
Graphic Design: Pentagram
Concrete Consultant: Reginald Hough

Armani Headquarters and Theatre, Milan, Italy
Architect: Tadao Ando Architect & Associates
Project Team: Tadao Ando, Kulapat Yantrasast
Client: Giorgio Armani
Associate Architect: Intertecno (structural and mechanical engineers)
General Contractors: Marcora Costrúzioni; Kenchiku Yohu Sha

Bacon Street House, London, UK
Architect and Client: William Russell
Project Team: William Russell, Sheila Muiry, Jon Mangham, Zeno Deitrich
Engineer: Price & Myers
Construction Manager: Sheila Muiry

Barcelona Botanic Gardens, Barcelona, Spain
Architect: Carlos Ferrater
Project Team: Carlos Ferrater (architect), José Luis Canosa (architect), Bet Figueras (landscape architect)
Client: City Council of Barcelona
Collaborators: Dr Montserrat, Joan Pedrola (botanist), Urban Designs of City Council (construction)
Builder: Stachys S.A.
Engineering: Taller D'Engyniyeries S.A.

Canary Wharf Underground Station, London, UK
Architect: Foster and Partners
Project Team: Norman Foster, David Nelson, Gerard Evenden, Rodney Uren, Richard Hawkins, Ross Palmer, David Crossthwaite, Armstrong Yakubu, Chris Connell, Toby Blunet, Charles Diamon, Glenis Fan, Lulie Fischer, Mike Greville, Lee Hallman, Caroline Hislop, Eddie Lamptey, Stuart Latham, Muir Livingstone, Niall Monaghan, James Risebero, Danny Shaw, Tim Shennan
Project Architects: JLE Project Architects
Project Team: Jerszy Lachowicz, Simon Wing, Deidre Lennon, Simon Timms
Client: London Underground Ltd.
Main Contractor: Ove Arup & Partners, London
Civils: Posford Duvivier, De Leau Chadwick
M&E: JLE
Structure: Ove Arup & Partners
Lighting: Claude Engle
Landscape: Land Use Consultants
Quantity Surveyor: DLE
Contractor: Tarmac Bachy jv

Cathedral of Our Lady of the Angeles, Los Angeles, USA
Architect: Rafael Moneo
Project Team: Rafael Moneo (principal), Hayden Salter, David Campbell, Alberto Nicolau, Lori Bruns, Mariano Molina, Christoph Schmid
Client: Roman Catholic Archbishop of Los Angeles, Cardinal Roger Mahoney
Executive Architect: Leo A. Daly
Project Team: Roy Follmuth (principal in charge), Nick Roberts (project manager), John Williams (senior project architect)
Engineer: Nabih Youssef and Associates (structural), Arup (m/e/p, fire)
Consultants: Francis Krahe and Associates (lighting), Reginald D. Hugh (concrete), Dennis Paoletti (acoustic consultant), Richard Vosko (liturgical art)
General Contractor: Morley Builders
Landscape Architect: Campbell & Campbell

Cemetery, Borghetto Santo Spirito, Italy
Architect: Marco Ciarlo
Project Team: Marco Ciarlo (principal in charge), F. Melano, G. Negro
Client: Comune di Borghetto Santo Spirito
Structural Engineer: Giancarlo Meloni
Builder: CO.GE.CA Cisano sul Neva
Lighting: UpO Viabizzuno
Lighting Supplier: Ambiente; Cuneo

Chapel and Residential Buildings, Valleacerón, Ciudad Real, Spain
Architect: Estudio Sancho-Madridejos
Project Team: Sol Madridejos, Juan Carlos Sancho Osinaga, Luis Renedo, Emilio Gomez-Ramos, Marta Toral, Juan Antonio Garrido, Ana Fernando Magarzo, Patricia Planell, Javier Moreno
Client: Private
Construction: Ignacio Diezma
Principal Consultant: Ignacio Aspe (structural engineer)

C-House, Brisbane, Australia
Architect: Donovan Hill Architects
Project Team: Brian Donovan, Timothy Hill, Fedor Medek, Michael Hogg
Client: Private
Structural and Civil Engineer: Mattefy Perl Nagy
Landscape: Donovan Hill Architects with Butler & Webb
Carpentry: Jim Evans
Joinery: Phil Green

De Blas House, Sevilla la Nueva, Spain
Architect: Alberto Campo Baeza
Client: Francisco de Blas
Collaborator: Raúl del Valle González
Structure Architect: Ma Concepción Pérez Guitiérrez
Clerk of Works: Francisco Melchor
Builder: Juan Sáinz

Diamond Ranch High School, Diamond Bar, California, USA
Architect: Morphosis
Project Team: Thom Mayne (Principal), John Enright (Project Architect), Cameron Crockett, David Grant, Fabian Kremkus, Janice Shimizu, Patrick J. Tighe
Assistants: Sarah Allan, Kasper Baumeister, Jay

Behr, John Bencher, Frank Brodbeck, Takashi Ehira, Magdalena Glen, Ivar Gudmunson, George Hemandez, Martin Krammer, Ming Lee, Francisco Muzo, Christopher Payne, Kinga Racon, Robyn Sambo, Andreas Schaller, Bennet Shen, Mark Sich, Craig Shimahara, Tadao Shimizu, Stephen Slaughter, Brandon Welling, Eui-Sung Yi
Executive Architects: Thomas Blurock Architects
Client: Pomona Unified School District
Consultants: Ove Arup & Partners (structural/mechanical/electrical/plumbing; Andreasen Engineers Inc. (civil engineer); Fong Hart Schneider + Partners (landscape architect); K.I.A. (kitchen consultants); Adamson Associates (cost estimator); Bernards Brothers Construction (construction managers)
Contractors: Advance Mechanical, Anning-Johnson Company, Butler Construction/Consulting; Carmel Steel; Chino Readymix; Coastal Tile; Commercial Fence & Ironworks; Control Air Conditioning; CTE, Dow Diversified; Dupont Flooring; E.C. Construction, Enko Systems; Environmental Acoustics, Franklin Reinforcing Steel; Inland Inspection & Consulting; John Jory Corp.; L.M. Waterproofing; Leighton & Associates; Link-Nilson; Louis Todd Corporation; Maya Steel; Montgomery-Kone; Myler Construction; Norris-Repke, Inc; Prieto Construction; Robert L. Reeves, Sasco; South Shores; Stainless Fixtures; Steg Manufacturing; Tomen Building Components; Western Paving

Ehime Prefectural Museum of General Science, Japan
Architect: Kisho Kurokawa Architect and Associates
Project Team: Kisho Kurokawa, Masahiro Kamei, Michael Griffis, Shinji Nakano, Yasuhiro Fujisawa, Hiroshi Tsuto, Koichi Sugino, Yuko Oda, Chika Kumada
Client: Ehime Prefectural Government
Mechanical and Electrical Engineer,
Interior Design: Kisho Kurokawa Architect and Associates
Structural Engineer: Zokei Construction
Consulting Engineers: Kenchiku Setsubi Sekkei Kenkyusho (KSSK Consulting Engineers)
Construction Supervision: Kisho Kurokawa Architect and Associates, Department of Civil Engineering of Ehime Prefecture

Main Contractors: JV of Shimizu + Sumitomo + Noma Co. (architecture); JV of Daidan+Jumatsu Co. (air-conditioning); JV of Tokuju + Akiyama Co. (sanitary consultant); JV of Naka Denko + Echi Denki Sangyo + Nishiden Co. (electrical equipment)

Family Home, Flasch, Switzerland
Architect: Bearth and Deplazes
Project Team: Valentin Bearth, Andrea Deplazes, Daniel Ladner, Claudia Drilling
Client: Claudia and Andrea Meuli
Engineer: Conzett, Bronzini, Gartmann AG

Federal Chancellery, Berlin, Germany
Architect: Axel Schultes Architekten, Frank Schultes Witt
Project Team: Axel Shultes, Charlotte Frank (principals in charge), Christoph Witt, Philipp Heydel, Monika Bauer, Martina Betzold, Andreas Büscher, Stephan Ernst, Roland Frank, Christian Franke, Marc Frederking, Holger Gantz, Paul Grundel, Christian Helfrich, Matthias Hiby, Ayse Hicsasmaz, Casper Hoesch, Frithjof Kahl, Markus Kenkmann, Arndt Kerber, Margret Kister, Hartmut Kortner, Hans Krause, Barbara Lutz, Gerhard Münster, Cornelius Nailis, Anna Pfeiffer, Martina Pongratz, Klaus Reintjes, Andreas Schuldes, Lutz Schütter, Christian Werner, Jost Westphal
Client: im Auftrag der Bundesrepublik Deutschland für die Bundesregierung Bundescaugesellschaft Berlin mbH
Architect on Site: Diete & Siepmann GmbH
Structural Engineers: GSE Ingenieur-Gesellschaft mbh
Building Services Engineer: Schmidt Reuter Partner
Landscaping: Lützowplatz 7, Garten-u. Landschaftsarchitekten
Lighting Designer: Licht-Kunst-Licht Gmbh
Façade Engineer: R+R Fuchs Ingenieurbüro für Fassadentechnik
General Contractors: ARGE Rohbau, HMB AG/Wayss & Freitag AG, Deutsche Necso GmbH, ARGE Dickenbrok & Fröhlich, Heilit and Woerner AG.
Heat and Ventilation: Stangl GmbH
Electrical Work: Elektrobau Methling GmbH
Concrete Construction: Itter GmbH
Canopy: Skyspan Europe GmbH, Hein Stahlbau GmbH
Façade Construction: R. App GmbH & Co. Leutkirch; ARGE Gebrüder Schneider, Fensterfabrik GmbH & Co. KG, Radeburger Fensterbau
Natural Stonework: Steinindustrie Vetter GmbH

Fishing Museum, Karmøy, Norway
Architects: Snøhetta
Principals: Craig Dykers, Kjetil Trædal Thorsen
Design Team: Lisbeth Funck, Ole Gustavsen, Knut Trondstad, Rainer Stange, Ranghild Momrak, Linda Evensen

Haslach School, Au, Switzerland
Architect: Beat Consoni Architekt
Collaborator: Daniel Frick
Project Management: Fankhauser Brocker Architekten
Main Contractors: Dittadi AG; Gautschi AG; Niederer AG
Structural Engineer: Zoller AG
Electrical Consultant: Project AG
Electrical Engineers: Lutz Elektroplanung; project AG
Heating and Ventilation: Enplan
Sanitary Engineer: Tomashett
Landscape Design: Bucker AG
Special Sun Blinds: SWEMO AG
Design and Technology Room: Ballmann AG

Haus der Architektur, Munich, Germany
Architect: Drescher + Kubina Architekten
Project Team: Dieter Kubina, Gerhard Klar
Client: Bayerische Architektenkammer (Bavarian Chamber of Architects)
Structure: Bernhard Behringer
Construction: Johann Schmidhuber
Glass Façade: Ingenieurbüro für Fassadentechnik, R+R Fuchs

House in Berlin, Germany
Architect: OIKOS
Project Team: Peter Herrle, Werner Stoll, Amun Bieser, Tobias Schmachtel
Client: Private
Structural Engineer: Ingenieurbüro Wilhelm und Wulle
Concrete Construction: Kolhöfer und Grundmann
Wood Construction: Hoeft und Preuss

Innside Hotel, Düsseldorf, Germany
Architect: Schneider + Schumacher Architekten BDA
Project Team: Michael Schumacher (Project Architect), Kai Otto (Project Manager), Stefan Goeddertz (office), Mark Marten (hotel), Robert Binder, Diane Böhringer, Tamara Gorgonoska, Heike Heinzelmann, Carl-Hendrik Locher, Claus Marzluf, Michael Pleßmann, Christian Simons, Gabriele Stephan, Andreas Suck
Client: KanAm-Gruppe, Munich
Construction Management: Schneider + Schumacher Architekten BDA; Planungsbüro Hedwig; DGI Bauwerk GmbH
Project Management: SHP Projektmanagement GmbH&Co.KG
Cladding Design: Schneider + Schumacher Architekten BDA
Cladding Consultant: Albrecht Memmert & Partner GbR
Structural Engineer: Ruffert + Partner
Lift Consultant: Jappsen + Stangier
Building Services Engineer: HTW
Landscape Architect: Ulla Schuch
Civil Engineer: Trümper-Overath-Heimann-Römer
Fire Engineer: Dipl.-Ing. Karlsch
Contractors: Wiemer & Trachte AG (shell and core); Josef Gartner & Co. (cladding – office); NR Metallbau GmbH (cladding – hotel); AIT GmbH (insulation); Häcker KG (screed); Rangger Aufzugsbau GmbH (lifts); Stahlbau Frenken & Erdweg GmbH (metal and glasswork); Jaeger Akustik GmbH (plasterboard); Lienenlüke + Reinsch GmbH; Westerfeld GmbH (paintwork); F.H.L. Kiriakidis Germany (stone mason); Steinrück GmbH & Co. KG (security); Metallbau Jansen GmbH & Co. KG (metalwork); Hark Treppenbau – Beteiligungs GmbH (glass balustrades); Wahlefeld Fassadenaufzugstechnik GmbH (access); Peschkes Metall- und Stahlbau GmbH (aluminium doors); Schemitzek & Herrig GmbH (signage); Jakob Leonhards Söhne GmbH & Co. (landscape gardner); Tekla-Technik, Tor + Tür GmbH & Co.KG (fire doors); Dewes GmbH (fitout); Paroll Doppelbodensysteme GmbH & Co. KG (raised flooring); Isserstedt Fliesen (tiles); Lucht (render), Remmel + Peters GmbH & Co. KG (fire-rated façade)

Kemeter Paint Warehouse, Eichstätt, Germany
Architect: Hild und K Architekten
Project Team: Andreas Hild, Tilmann Kaltwasser
Client: Farben Kemeter
Structural Engineer: Muck und Schneider

Kunstmuseum, Vaduz, Liechtenstein
Architect: Morger Degelo Kerez
Project Team: Meinrad Morger, Heiri Degelo, Christian Kerez, Nicole Woog (Project Manager), Benjamin Theiler, Heike Buchmann, Dagmar Strasse, Raeto Studer
Client: Foundation for the Erection of a Liechtenstein Art Museum
General Contractor: Karl Steiner AG
Static Equilibrium: Frey & Schwarz
Heating, Plumbing and Ventilation: Waldhauser Haustechnik
Electrical Installations: Risch AG
Safety: Hege AG
Lighting: Ove Arup & Partner
Construction Physics: Kopitsis Bauphysik
Acoustics: Martin Lienhard
Graphic Design: Robert & Durrer

Laban Centre, London, UK
Architect: Herzog & de Meuron
Project Team: Jayne Barlow, Konstanze Beelitz, Christine Binswanger, Nandita Boger, Fun Budimann, Michael Casey, Peter Cookson, Irinia Davidovivi, Rita Maria Diniz, Hernan Fierro-Castro, Alice Foxley, Harry Gugger, Jacques Herzog, Detlef Horisberger, Jean Paul Jaccaud, Nick Lyons, Stefan Marbach, Christoph Mauz, Pierre de Meuron, Christopher Pannett, Kristen Whittle
Client: Laban Centre, London
Project Management: Arup Project Management
General Contractor: Ballast Construction
Structural and Services Engineer: Whitby Bird & Partners
Services Engineer: Waldhauser Haustechnik
Consultants: Vogt Landschaftarchitekten (landscape architecure); Carr & Angier (theatre consultant); Arup Associates (acoustic engineer); Arup Communications (IT Engineer)

La Coruña Swimming Pool, La Coruña, Spain
Architect: Estudio Cano Lasso
Project Team: Diego Cano Pintos, Gonzalo Cano Pintos, Alfonso Cano Pintos, Lucía Cano Pintos, Luis Pancorbo Crespo, Mónica Jiménez Denia
Contractor: Varela Villamor
Quality Surveyor: Marian Juárez
Structural Engineer: OTEP Ingenieros
Mechanical Engineer: JG Ingenieros

La Granja Stairways, Toledo, Spain
Architect: José Antonio Martínez Lapeña & Elias Torres Tur Arquitectos
Project Team: Jose Antonio Martínez Lapeña, Elias Torres Tur with Victor Argilaga, Josep Ballestero, Nuria Bordas, Guillem Bosch, Marta Delso, Sylvia Felipe, Marisa García, Sandrine Martínez, Forrest Murphy, Thomas Noël, Alexa Nurnberger, Perier Olivier, Alicia Reiber, Marc Tomas, Iñigo Ugarte, Ferran Vizoso
Client: Municipal Government of Toledo
Structural Engineer: Gerardo Rodriguez
Main Contractor: Necso Entrecanales Cubiertas, SA
Building Contractor: Alfonso Llorente Rincón, Francisco Martínez Ogallar
Landscape Architect: Alberto Guirao
Keeper: Isidoro Alvarez

Lecture Hall 3, Alicante, Spain
Architect: Javier García-Solera Arquitecto
Project Team: Javior García-Solera Vera (principal), Deborah Domingo (architect), Marcos Gallud (technical architect), Domingo Sepulcre (structure)
Client: Alicante University
Construction: CYES
Metallic Structure: Ferromar SA
Glass: Vitral SA
Woodwork: García Alberola SL
Aluminium: Aluminio Alumafel
Aluminium Systems: Gradhermetic

LOOK UP Office Headquarters, Gelsenkirchen, Germany
Architect: Anin Jeromin Fitilidis & Partner
Project Team: Ante Anin, Stefan Jeromin, Dimitri Fitilidis, José Garcia (project management), Anne Hömberg, Mark May
Client: Monica and Wulf Arens
Structural Engineer: Agne, Wahlen, Daubenbüchel
Planner of Frameworks: Dipl. Ing. Bernd

Jeschonnek
Engineering Consultant: Prof. Dr. Ing. Bernd Glück
Air Conditioning: Solar Kon GmbH

Loft, Sandweiler, Luxemburg
Architect and Client: Georges Servais
Concrete Contractor: Delli Zotti sarl
Bamboo Flooring: Ets. Brisbois
Windows: Schreinerei Hoffmann
Cabinet and Woodwork: Schräinerei Conrardy sarl

Mathematics, Statistics and Computer Science Building, University of Canterbury, Christchurch, New Zealand
Architect: Architectus CHS Royal Associates
Project Team: Malcolm Bowes, Patrick Clifford, Michael Thomson, Stephen Bird, Mark Campbell, Rachell Cook, Philip Guy, Graham Hoddinott, Bruce McCartney, Blair McKenzie, Sean McMahon, Juliet Pope, Jane Priest, Tadek Rajwer, Giles Reid, Andrea Stevens, Shaun Thompson-Gray, Gerry Tyrell
Client: University of Canterbury
Main Contractor: Naylor Love Canterbury
Structural and Civil Engineer: Holmes Consulting Group
Electrical and Mechanical Engineer: Ove Arup & Partner
Acoustics: Marshall Day & Associates
Quantity Surveyor: Shipston Davies
Project Planning: Woods Harris Consulting
Glazing: Smith & Smith Glass
Precast Concrete: Bradford
Construction McKendry
Stonemason: Canterbury Stone

Möbius House, Het Gooi, Netherlands
Architect: UN Studio (van Berkel & Bos)
Project Team: Ben van Berkel, Caroline Bos, Aad Krom, Jen Alkema, Casper le Fèvre, Rob Hootsmans, Matthias Blass, Marc Dijkman, Remco Bruggink, Tycho Soffree, Harm Wassink, Giovanni Tedesco
Client: Private
Landscape Consultant: West 8

Municipal Mortuary, León, Spain
Architect: BAAS, Jordi Badía/Josep Val architects
Project Team: Jordi Badía Rodríguez, Josep Val Ravell, E. Valls, T. Balagué, A. Cibiach, M Catalán, J. C. Castro, F. Massana, L. Maristany, R. Berenguena, F. Belart, S. Vinuesa, B. Camarero, G. Egea, J. Martínez, L. Victori, S. Serrat, L. Careras and J. Mercadé
Client: SERFUNLE: León Funeral Services (León City Council)
Consultants: Consulting Luis Duart S.L. (mechanical and electrical engineers), Taller de Ingenieria (structural engineers).
Site Architects: Miguel Martinez; Mariano Fernández, José Manuel Pérez
General Contractor: Begar

Museum of Scottish Country Life, East Kilbride, Scotland
Architect: Page and Park Architects
Client: The National Trust for Scotland; National Museums of Scotland
Project Manager: Osprey Project Management International
Planning Supervisor: OPMI
Landscape Architect: Ian White Associates
Structural Engineer: Will Rudd Davidson
Services Engineer: Harley Haddow Partnership
Quantity Surveyor: Thomas & Adamson
Clerk of Works: Sentinel Property Management
Contractor: Skanska UK Building, MOSEL

Oskar Reinhart Collection 'Am Römerholz', Winterthur, Switzerland
Architect: Gigon/Guyer
Project Team: Annette Gigon, Mike Guyer, Peter Steiner, Andreas Sonderegger
Client: Swiss Confederation, represented by Department of Federal Buildings (AFB)
Commissioned: Federal Office of Culture (BAK)
Civil Engineering: Dr. Deuring and Oehninger AG
Landscape Architecture: Kienast, Vogt and Partner Landschaftsarchitekten
Climate Engineer: Waldhauser Haustechnik
Electrical Engineer: ELKOM Partner AG
Daylight Technology: Institut für Tageslichttechnik
Artificial Lighting: Lichtdesign Ingenieurgesellschaft
Graphic Design: Trix Wetter

Pulitzer Foundation for the Arts, St Louis, Missouri, USA
Architect: Tadao Ando Architect & Associates
Project Team: Tadao Ando (principal in charge), Masataka Yano
Client: Pulitzer Foundation for the Arts
Architect of Record: Christner, Inc.
Construction Manager: Clarkson Consulting, Inc.
General Contractors: BSI Contractors, Zera Construction Company
Mechanical Engineers: Ove Arup & Partners International
Structural Engineers: Ege-Theiss
Civil Engineer: Kuhlman Design Group, Inc.

Ruffi Gymnasium, Marseilles, France
Architect: Rémy Marciano
Client: Ville de Marseilles, Direction des Sports
Consultants: ART'M Archtiecture, SP121, Société Phocéenne D'Ingénierie
Landscape Architect: Jérôme Mazas

School of Arts, Córdoba, Argentina
Architect: Miguel Angel Roca
Client: National University of Córdoba
Structural Consultant: Rubén Gurer (engineer)
Contractor: Kohn srl.

Sculptural Overlook, Maryhill Museum of Art, Goldendale, Washington, USA
Architect: Allied Works Architecture
Project Team: Brad Cleopfil (design principal), Corey Martin (project architect)
Client: Maryhill Museum of Art
Structural Engineer: Jok Ang of Ang Engineering
Concrete Consultant: Bob Kirk of Architectural Concrete Associates

Space Blocks, Kamishinjo, Osaka, Japan
Architect: C+A - Kazuhiro Kojima; Kazuko Akamatsu
Client: Private
General Contractor: Magara Construction
Structural Engineer: K. Nakata & Associates
Mechanical Engineer: Sou Setsubi
Sanitary Systems: TOTO
Lighting: Matsushita Electric Works, Ltd

Thames Barrier Park, London, UK
Architect: Patel Taylor; Groupe Signes
Client: London Development Agency
Engineers: Arup
Quantity Surveyor: Tweeds
Contractor: May Gurney (Construction) Ltd
Main Subcontractors: Hasmeads (landscape); Konform (concrete works); Ocmis (irrigation and water feature)

Tilt-Up Slab House, Venice, California, USA
Architect: Syndesis, Inc.
Project Team: David Hertz (principal in charge), Ken Vermillion, Neil Rubenstein
Client: Alan and Elaine Hess
Consultants: Gwynne Rugh (structural engineer), Monterey Energy Group - Radiant (mechanical engineer)
General Contractor: Owner, Syndesis, Inc.

Tokiwadai House, Itabashi-ku, Tokyo, Japan
Architect: Naoko Hirakura Architect and Associates
Project Team: Naoko Hirakura, Michiko Kajiwara, Keiko Hata
Client: Private
Main Contractor: Katsura Construction Co. Ltd.
General Contractor: Mochii Komnuten
Structural Engineer: TIS & Partner
Lighting Adviser: Reiko Chikada

Tulach a' tSolais, Oulart Hill, Wexford, Ireland
Architect: Scott Tallon Walker Architects
Project Team: Ronald Tallon, Michael Warren (concept), Brian Foley (project architect)
Client: Office of Public Works
Structural Engineer: Ove Arup & Partners
Landscape Architect: Charles Funke Associates

Tussols-Basil Bathing Pavilion, Olot, Girona, Spain
Architect: RCR Arquitectes
Project Team: Ramon Vilalta, Carmen Pigem, Rafael Aranda
Client: Ayuntamiento de Olot – Parque Naturel de la Zona Volcánica de la Garrotxa
Collaborators: A. Saez (consultant), A. Blazquez/LL. Guanter (structure), RCRM. Subiràs (project direction)

Visiting Artists' Studio, Geyserville, California, USA
Architect: Jim Jennings Architecture
Team: Michael Lin, Cheri Fraser, Troy Schaum, Paul Burgin, Les Taylor, May Fung
Clients: Steven and Nancy Oliver
Interior Furniture: Gary Hutton Design
Landscape: Andrea Cochran
Lighting: Dan Dodt www.dodt-plc.com
Consulting Architect: Tim Perks
General Contractor: Oliver & Company

Zenith Concert Hall and Exhibition Centre, Rouen, France
Architect: Bernard Tschumi Architects
Project Team: Bernard Tschumi, Véronique Déscharrières, Alex Reid, Christian Devizzi, Lauranne Ponsonnet, Kevin Collins, Joel Rutten, Peter Cornell, Robert Holton, Megan Miller, Kim Starr, Roderick Villafranca
Client: District of Rouen
Structural Engineer: Technip-TPS
Façade Consultant: Hugh Dutton Associates
Acoustic Consultant: CIAL

Picture Credits

The publisher would like to thank the following sources for their kind permission to reproduce images in this book.

Arazebra Helbling + Kupferschmid (162–164); Alejo Bagué (188–191); Marcus Bleyl (19 top, 66–69); Courtesy Santiago Calatrava (22 bottom); David Cardelús (206–209); Courtesy Concrete Information Ltd. (12 bottom, 13 top, 17 top); Peter Cook/Archipress (10); Peter Cook/VIEW (182, 218–223; Sarah Duncan Photography (6–7); Michael Egloff (72–77); Ralf Feiner (26–29); Michael Freeman (16 top); Courtesy Gigon/Guyer (165); Dennis Gilbert/VIEW (82–84, 112–115); Tim Griffith (58–60); Roland Halbe/Artur (125 right, 126 left, 224–227); Michael Heinrich (114–111); Jörg Hempel (158–161); Courtesy David Hertz Architects (62–65); Timothy Hursley (90–91, 95); Werner Huthmacher (8, 78–80); Holger Knauf (120–123); Tim Linkins (50–53); Benedict Luxmore/ARCAID (85); Paul M. R. Maeyaert (14 middle); Michael Moran (170–172); Tomio Ohashi (70, 86–89); Alberto Piavone (32–33, 214–217); Eugeni Pons (140–143, 200–204); Portland Cement Company (12 centre, 15 bottom); Paul Raftery/VIEW (178–181); Ed Reeve/Recover (54–57); Courtesy RIBA (14 top); Christian Richters (22 centre, 38–41, 100–103); Miguel Angel Roca (96–99); Simone Rosenberg (128–131); Lukas Roth (18, 46–48); Philippe Ruault (138, 144–147); Sally Schoolmaster (192–199); Duncan Shaw-Brown (118); courtesy Snøhetta (148–153); Margherita Spiluttini (21 bottom); Studio La Gonda (117, 119); Hisao Suzuki (30–31, 35, 124–125 left, 126 right, 127, 184–187); Kenichi Suzuki (132–136); Shinkenchiku-sha (36–37, 42–45); Tiefbauamt Graubünden, Switzerland (13 bottom); Shannon Tofts (154–157); Manuel G. Vicente (166–169); Hans Weslemann/OMA (22 top); Richard Weston (12 top, 14 bottom, 15 top, 16 centre and bottom, 17 centre and bottom, 18, 19 bottom, 20, 21 top and centre, 23 top); James Winspear/VIEW (210–213); Makoto Yamamori (174–177); Javier Yaya/CACSA (23 bottom); Kim Zwarts (92–93)

Author's Acknowledgements

I am grateful to the following for their help, advice and encouragement in various ways: my friends and colleagues at The Twentieth Century Society; Liz Faber, Philip Cooper and Jennifer Hudson at Laurence King, whose patience through my change of job/change of status/change of address and pregnancy was much appreciated; the designers, SEA, for their dedication and perseverance; the staff of the RIBA Library, who create a great working atmosphere to compliment their fabulous resources; many of the architects whose projects are featured in the book (especially Ben van Berkel and Marco Ciarlo and his team); Elain Harwood, whose energy and knowledge are inspirational; John Bacon, whose clipping service is matched by none; Tony Richardson, who first encouraged me not to be an architect; my parents, Roy and Patricia Croft (who didn't know what they were starting when they took me to the South Bank), Shirley Spitz, and to Stuart Davies, who has seen more concrete buildings than he ever imagined possible.